Media Ethic

D1322250

Media Topics
Series editor: Valerie Alia

Titles in the series include:

Media Policy and Globalisation
by Paula Chakravartty and Katharine Sarikakis
0 7486 1848 1 (hardback)
0 7486 1849 X (paperback)

Media Rights and Intellectual Property
by Richard Haynes
0 7486 2062 1 (hardback)
0 7486 1880 5 (paperback)

Alternative and Activist Media
by Mitzi Waltz
0 7486 1957 7 (hardback)
0 7486 1958 5 (paperback)

Media and Ethnic Minorities
by Valerie Alia and Simone Bull
0 7486 2068 0 (hardback)
0 7486 2069 9 (paperback)

Women, Feminism and Media
by Sue Thornham
0 7486 2070 2 (hardback)
0 7486 2071 0 (paperback)

Media Ethics and
Social Change

Valerie Alia

Edinburgh University Press

For Mary Margaret Zahara and Rachel Anne

© Valerie Alia, 2004

Edinburgh University Press Ltd
22 George Square, Edinburgh

Typeset in Janson and Neue Helvetica
by Norman Tilley Graphics, and
printed and bound in Great Britain
by MPG Books Ltd, Bodmin

A CIP record for this book is available from the British Library

ISBN 0 7486 1773 6 (hardback)
ISBN 0 7486 1771 X (paperback)

Contents

Illustrations

Acknowledgements

As always, I thank the family: Pete Steffens – loving partner, colleague, inspirer of ethical practice in journalism, teaching and life; Daniel Restivo and David Restivo; Susan Graber; Daneet Steffens and Sivan Steffens; Peggy Jane Hope and Bill June – for seeing ethics from fascinating other sides and angles and for insight, love, music, conversation and bad puns.

Rik Walton provided photographic artistry, patience, understanding and technical wizardry for Chapter 7. Joan and Ron Walton (no relation to Rik) saw the comic possibilities of ethics and Ron (artist and designer of magical gardens) drew the delightful cartoons.

For education, inspiration and dialogue I thank my first mentor, Jenny Wells Vincent, and Patrick Boyer, Julie Bradford, Pamela Bruder-Freeman, Simone Bull, Dumitru Chitoran, Raphael Cohen-Almagor, Kathryn Hazel, Ian Hunter-Smart, Patricia Johanson, Edmund Lambeth, Ritva Levo-Henriksson, Myra Macdonald, Kathleen McCreery (who appears in the photographs on pages 106–7), Val McLane, Mark Meredith, Howard Pawley, Michael Posluns, Tyler Resch, Amir Saeed, Anthony Sampson, John Smith, Deborah Thomas (whose suggestions enriched the Filmography), Sue Thornham, Mitzi Waltz, Angus Wells, students at the University of Sunderland who 'tested' the exercises and case studies; participants on the Journalism Ethics and Communicating Across Cultures projects and colleagues in the Institute of Communication Ethics. I am grateful to the University of Sunderland for providing the sabbatical that made this book possible, to the Social Sciences and Humanities Research Council of Canada, the (US) National Science Foundation and the Canadian High Commission (UK) for funding portions of the research, and to Margaret Burns for keeping the home fires from burning the house down; and *in absentia* – to Corinne Boyer, Paul Robeson (my earliest hero), Lincoln Steffens and my parents, Julius and Bertha Graber, who introduced Steffens' writings at an early stage of my political and moral education, never knowing that one day our families would intertwine.

Finally, appreciation is due to the stalwart and multi-talented team at Edinburgh University Press – Sarah Edwards, commissioning editor and co-brainstormer; James Dale and Edward Clark on the editorial home front; and copyeditor, Peter Williams, who tracked the valuable references to Inuit.

Preface

Ethics. The study of moral principles and behavior and of the nature of the good ... also called *moral philosophy*. The term derives from the Greek word *ethos* [or *ethikos*], which implies both 'custom' and 'character'. (Rohmann, 2000: 123)

The ethicist Thomas Cooper identifies three major 'areas of worldwide concern within the field of communication ethics': for truth, responsibility and free expression (Cooper, 1989: 20–1). These concerns are framed by the current conditions of media practice – some of them shared widely across international boundaries, some of them prevalent in particular places, nations or regions. To this, I would add that, despite persistent myths of objectivity and neutrality, it is virtually impossible to consider questions of media ethics and responsibility without also considering the effects of media professionals and practices on social change.

Britain has not had a long list of books that specifically address these concerns, and few books anywhere consider ethics in the context of social change. British readers have access to a number of thoughtful studies and collections of ethically concerned journalism, such as the work of John Pilger, Yasmin Alibhai-Brown and Anthony Sampson, and of media history and politics, such as the work of Jeremy Tunstall, Asa Briggs and Peter Burke. There are excellent books on sociology of the media, notably those of Brian McNair, and studies of issues in journalism and media ethics, such as those of Richard Keeble, Chris Frost and John Kieran.

Describing Michael Moore's work as a modern-day muckraker-humorist-activist based in the United States, a British journalist recently lamented 'a [US] journalistic culture that has produced no John Pilger or Paul Foot' (Younge, 2003; 18, 19). It was a stunning error in an otherwise well-informed feature – a wildly inaccurate dismissal of virtually all of American media history. Moore's distinction is well-deserved.

But his path was paved by a long, strong, courageous and honourable progressive journalistic culture, some of it profiled on the pages of this book. The connections between investigative reporting and 'muckraking', activist or 'campaigning' journalism and humour were made long ago, in the United States as well as Britain. That 'journalistic culture' is enriched by the works of countless men and women, among them Mark Twain, Upton Sinclair, Ida Tarbell, Ida Wells Barnett, Lincoln Steffens, Josephine Herbst, John Reed, I. F. Stone, Jessica Mitford (though a transplanted Brit) and, more recently, the caustic and critical cartoonist Gary Trudeau, the humourist Dave Barry and the columnists Seymour Hirsch, Molly Ivins and Maureen Dowd – and we have barely scratched the surface.

'Muckrakers' such as Oriana Fallaci, John Pilger and Anthony Sampson continue to inspire – and the original 'muckraker', Lincoln Steffens, is being reread and rediscovered as people learn how stunningly (and lamentably) current his late nineteenth-century exposés of government corruption and corporate greed are for our own time. Although some people have suggested that a new ethical theory is needed to keep up with current developments – including the fact that media corporations are the world's largest businesses – Clifford G. Christians thinks it is not. In his view:

> The centerpiece ought to be the ethics of justice ... The global mass media are not neutral purveyors of information, but creators and shapers of culture. They are institutional agents of acculturation ... An ethics of justice where distribution is based on need offers a radical alternative to the conventional view ... The electronic superhighway cannot be envisioned except as a social necessity.

It seems appropriate to inaugurate the Media Topics Series with a discussion of ethical media practice. I hope this volume will help to demonstrate the historical and geographical continuities in the long and honourable tradition of truth-seeking and information-sharing. One further note: British readers will be aware of the importance of the 2003–4 Hutton Inquiry into the tragic death of Dr David Kelly. I strongly recommend this as a case study for anyone seeking to examine the relationship between government, media and whistleblowers, trust between interviewer and interviewee, the protection of anonymous sources and related issues. The reader may well ask, if this is such an important case, why it is not discussed in the chapters that follow. The Inquiry is just winding down as we go to press, and Lord Hutton's report has not yet been released. By the time you read this, the report will likely be public, and may provide a rich resource for research and discussion.

Introduction: why study ethics?

> Today's history is written the very moment it happens. It can be photographed, filmed, recorded ... It can be transmitted immediately through the press, radio, television. It can be interpreted, heatedly discussed. For this reason I like journalism. For this reason I fear journalism. What other profession allows you to write history at the very moment it happens and also to be its direct witness? Journalism is an extraordinary and terrible privilege. (Oriana Fallaci, 1976)

Considering this 'extraordinary and terrible privilege', Clifford G. Christians sees an urgent ethical imperative.

> Since imminent destruction is now a possibility, our scholarship in ethics needs urgency about it unlike any of our previous theorizing. Also, our principal claims must henceforth embrace the needs of the entire human race ... (Christians, 2001: 3)

Claude-Jean Bertrand, architect of the activist-motivated principle of Media Accountability Systems (M*A*S), makes a passionate plea for us to turn what has become the usual approach to media ethics upside down: 'The most important person for a newspaper is not the advertiser, the newsmaker or the shareholder: it has always been the reader'. Except in developing nations, he sees readers moving away from newspapers.

> At regular intervals, some publisher will roar that newspapers are not dying and have a great future, but the statistics indicate otherwise. Even for US newspapers, fat and hugely profitable as they are: since 1970, the US population has gone up 34% and daily circulation down 10%. (Bertrand, 2001a: 1)

Public distrust of news media and journalists is at an all-time low. A 2001 poll in France revealed that only 32 per cent of the public considered journalists to operate independently of government, and a mere 25 per cent thought them independent from business. Despite the need for what in public relations terms would be called 'damage control' and the desire to increase profits, many media organisations all but ignore the consumers of their publications and broadcasts. Staff cuts are rampant; magazine and newspaper pages and radio and television air space are devoted overwhelmingly to advertising. The implied assumption of media owners and managers is that consumers are only indirectly consumers of mass media – via their consumption of advertisers' products, services and media interventions. The reality is that a substantial number of media organisations and empires are folding, or being enfolded into other empires and organisations. Minus the readers, listeners and viewers, there is no one to access (and presumably respond to) the ads. While Bertrand's motives are strongly ethical and oriented to positive social change, he couches his observations in practical, economic-survival terms.

> ... if a newspaper's sales decline and disaster looms, which group can it depend upon for survival: advertisers, news sources, share-holders – or readers? Which group should it be listening to in order to discover what they like and dislike? Readers, obviously ... The best way to keep readers reading is to provide good service. But good service ... cannot be provided without listening to them ... (Bertrand, 2001a: 1)

Media accountability systems encompass the widest possible range of public media accountability programmes – of varying degrees of effectiveness – press councils, 'ethical audits, awareness-raising sessions', codes of ethics and statements of principles, public response forums such as letters to the editor, organised reader, listener and viewer panels. There is no panacea for the problems that beset contemporary media practice. Bertrand and others say we must start somewhere – and M*A*S provides a 'democratic, harmless, efficient' and generally inexpensive starting point (Bertrand, 2000; Bertrand, 2001b).

Many of us who were media practitioners in North America, Europe and Britain remember the 1960s, 1970s and early 1980s as a time when journalists pounded away on loud typewriters, apprenticed their way into the field without the help of university courses, and slowly worked their way up from menial tasks to positions of increasing responsibility. By comparison, journalism today is becoming more bureaucratic, academic and professional. In many cases, it is also becoming more life threatening. Today's journalists work in a climate of rapidly changing politics, policies, technologies, media management and ownership, and professional practice. My own experience as a newspaper, radio and television journalist in the United States and Canada changed radically over the years and ended up including work for daily and weekly newspapers, weekly, monthly and quarterly magazines, radio and television. These days, a journalist would likely have to add online journalism and a range of 'new media' techniques and outlets to the list.

Having abandoned full-time journalism for the academy, I find myself reflecting on the ethical questions, dilemmas, conflicts and experiences of work in those countries and in Britain, where I now work and live. Most of the central issues are experienced internationally, though to varying degrees. It is necessary to consider not only the legal implications of media practice, but the ethical ones. Although generalised media questions are considered here, touching on the broadest definition of 'media', the primary concern is with ethical practice in journalism and mass media.

In my experience of lecturing on journalism, media and cultural studies in three countries, I have noticed two overarching responses from academic and journalistic colleagues, and from students, to the call for a more open, critical and responsible practice. The first response is excitement and a keen desire to participate in the quest for solutions to ethical problems. People have said, 'How wonderful! We need to address these issues.' The second response is a resistance to unearthing, exploring and publicising the media's troubles, myths and secrets. Some would prefer to leave the waters unstirred. Some practitioners express discomfort, even anger, when doubts, imperfections and challenges are raised. Faced with an ethics course or module, some students are excited and keen to meet the challenge. Others are annoyed at 'wasting' time instead of just 'learning the ropes' (even though the ropes are wearing thin). Sadly, educators sometimes share this attitude.

Many broadcasting, journalism and media studies programmes have ethics modules, and they are sometimes core modules. In journalism studies, they tend to be isolated from what is considered to be the 'essential', practical curriculum – implying that ethical study is not an integral part of media practice. To make a difference, ethics must be imbedded in the entire programme and integrated in professional lives and workdays. For example, there can be no teaching of 'purely mechanical operations', such as television camerawork, without addressing the ethical implications of these operations – such as who is affected by the camera and how images can be manipulated.

Moreover, ethical practices must be inclusive practices. Concerns about diversity and equality seldom have the prominence they need and deserve. The hidden assumption is that the producers and consumers of news and other media belong to the 'mainstream', dominant culture and, more often than not, are men. A few years ago I obtained a grant for a two-year study of media ethics that involved a series of workshops with lecturers and scholars in journalism studies, media studies, philosophy and applied ethics, and working journalists. Our task was to pool our knowledge and experience and discover how this might inform an approach to teaching and understanding media ethics. Once under way, the process was informative and sometimes inspiring and the collaboration resulted in a collection of essays, *Deadlines and Diversity: Journalism Ethics in a Changing World* (Alia, Brennan and Hoffmaster, 1996). However, the earliest phase of the project was more revealing than inspiring. Asked to help develop a list of potential participants – with a goal of producing an inclusive, diversity-based discussion and text – one person submitted a long roster of all-white, all-male (mostly middle-aged, middle-income, Anglo-Saxon Christian) 'experts'. When challenged about the composition of this group, he said, without any sense of irony: 'We don't disagree on the *principle* of diversity; it's just a matter of degree.' Yet a full discussion of media ethics that included only men of the above description would itself be unethical. Inclusivity and diversity are not mere 'side issues', they belong at the very core of ethical inquiry. Too much work in applied or practical ethics has been not only exclusive but reactive. Those who worked on the earlier project saw it from the start as participatory and proactive. The current project follows the same principles. This is not a text for philosophers, nor is it a panic-stricken reaction to the inevitable and never-ending rash of professionally embarrassing mistakes. The intention is to explore and develop practical solutions to everyday problems encountered by media practitioners and consumers – to discover and elaborate the goals, responsibilities and values of responsible media practice and to use the resulting insights to develop approaches to doing better work. The challenge to you, the reader, is to use this book proactively and creatively so that the media and their publics will be better served.

Although far from cornering the market on actual ethical practice, the US dominates the world in media ethics texts. There are more than 100 books and several magazines and journals, as compared to a handful of books and periodicals in Britain and Canada. For about twenty years, the literature on media ethics has focused on relating pedagogy and practice to democratic theory and classical Western philosophy. The traditional approach employs the Socratic method, starting with theory and using cases to illustrate that theory. Although I have great respect for the literature and its practitioners, I find the theory-first approach too abstract, and too remote from the realities of everyday journalism to be useful in daily practice. In addition, it tends to provide templates through which to model ethical decision-making – a system which excludes or minimises the contextual realities that inform actual cases and omits analyses of power and hierarchy and related questions of gender, class, ethnicity, culture and 'race'.

This volume is intended for advanced modules and courses in press and media ethics; journalism, new media, radio and television studies; and media and cultural studies. It is hoped that the mix of theory and practical problem-solving will engage students, academics and journalists in energetic, interactive learning and in efforts to produce a more thoughtful and ethical practice. The material is based on the author's original research as well as on several centuries of ethical, social scientific and other academic theory. This inquiry into current research, theory, issues and practice in media ethics considers British news media and other media in an international context. It includes examples from current journalism, problem-solving exercises and case studies, suggestions for further reading, suggested films, and additional material for analysis and discussion. It is aimed at theoretical and practical university journalism and media studies courses and also at industry and community training programmes. One of the objectives is to challenge and dissolve the barriers between 'theory' and 'practice', and the prejudices and traditions that maintain them.

As you progress through the book, you will find yourself able to identify and solve the kinds of real-life problems encountered by print, broadcast and 'new' journalists and other media practitioners in their daily work, with the aid of a theoretical context within which to consider and discuss them. Some topics are not covered in other texts. Included at the ends of chapters are suggested workshop exercises, case studies and seminar topics developed during more than twenty years of print and broadcast journalism, academic research and teaching, along with possible essay topics. In addition, an extensive international bibliography, a list of ethics-related websites and a comprehensive, annotated list of films on media ethics-related subjects are provided at the end of the book.

Chapter 1 contains a sketch of some of the main ethical theories and their applications to everyday media practice. Chapter 2 looks at the usefulness of some of the theories found in sociology, anthropology and cultural and media studies for students and practitioners of media ethics. Chapter 3 considers the nature and range of lying, deception and truth-telling, the ideals and realities of objectivity and subjectivity, and practical questions involved in different ways of doing media work and journalism. Chapter 4 considers the ethics of accuracy and inclusion – ways in which media reflect and respect diversity of both practitioners and consumers. The chapter includes some of my own work on minority journalism in Canada, the United States and the circumpolar regions.

Chapter 5 explores the internationalisation of today's media and multimedia empires. Chapter 6 considers relationships between media practitioners, media outlets, politics and politicians. Chapter 7 looks at the ethics of imagery – still photography, moving imagery in television and film, Internet programming, digital and other manipulation of images and manipulation of people by photographers and cameras. Chapter 8 considers the all-important issue of interviewer–subject relationships and trust – a potential minefield every journalist must negotiate because interviews lie at the very heart of journalism. Chapter 9 surveys some of the issues confronting specialist journalists – conflicts of interest in reviewing arts and entertainment; big business and sports journalism; 'junkets' and travel journalism; problems in covering science, the environment, medicine and health. Here I draw on my own extensive experience as a reviewer of music, dance and drama for newspapers, magazines, radio and television. Chapter 10 examines the ways in which technological change can make journalism more ethical, or less – depending on the nature of the technology and the ways in which it is developed and employed. There is a discussion of emerging techniques and ethical problems, including expanding surveillance and privacy issues in our multimedia world. Included are examples from my own research into ways in which indigenous people are using changing technologies to develop culturally relevant programming. Finally, Chapter 11 considers whether formal codes and statements of principles are useful in identifying acceptable practice, helping media practitioners to do more ethical work, and enforcing restrictions on unethical practice. Included is a survey of media codes and principles, worldwide. In the appendices at the back of the book you will find an array of materials, including an annotated filmography, a list of Internet resources and samples and summaries of a number of UK, US, Canadian and international media guidelines and codes of practice, followed by a comprehensive bibliography.

The book can be read sequentially, but it is also possible to select what is most interesting, meaningful or provocative and explore at will, turning to material from the other sections as it becomes relevant.

And now, I invite you to join me in an open-ended, perpetually unfinished, ongoing search for a reality-based media practice of integrity and conscience.

Exercises

Questions for discussion

1. What are the values that guide you in your daily life? What values should guide media practitioners? Are there any differences?
2. Have you encountered any ethical problems in your own work, or in your observations of others' work?
3. How were they solved at the time? Who was involved in the decision-making? Would you do things differently next time? What possible solutions can others suggest?

1 Life, the universe and ethics I: everyday problems and ethical theories

> ... no more philosophy for me. There was no ethics in it. ... I had been reading [philosophers who] thought they had it all settled. They did not have anything settled ... they could not agree upon what was knowledge, [or] what was good and what evil, nor why. The philosophers were all prophets, their philosophies beliefs, their logic a justification of their – religions. And as for their ethics, it was without foundation. The only reasons they had to give for not lying or stealing were not so reasonable as the stupidest English gentleman's: 'It isn't done'. (Steffens, 1931: 139)

Thus recalling his departure from university, the great 'muckraker' and first investigative journalist Lincoln Steffens expressed his exasperation with philosophers' uselessness for the task of developing methods for everyday, ethical practice. He was later to develop his own ethical standards – influenced, no doubt, by some of the very philosophers he had found inadequate – informed by his growing understanding of the requirements of responsible journalism.

A philosophy lecturer I know once quipped: 'You know what we say in Philosophy: men do logic; women do ethics' (Over, 2000).

As a woman 'doing ethics' (though resorting now and then to logic) I may well fit the stereotype. Since some of the major ethicists and some of the most ethically concerned media practitioners have been men, his little joke is based more on fictional clichés about 'men's' and 'women's' domains than on fact. That said, some scholars have suggested women may have different voices (for example, see Gilligan, 1982, 1986; Gilligan, Ward and Taylor, 1988; Haan *et al.*, 1983) and priorities that bring new concerns and questions to everyday ethical practice. For example:

> ... socially constructed institutions and theories have contributed to the public invisibility of women, and hence the inaudibility of female voices in the philosophical forum. (Code, Mullett and Overall, 1988: 4)

'Men do logic, women do ethics'. The woman here is concentrating on an ethics of the 'press'. (Ron Walton)

Iris Murdoch has proposed that the task in moral life is to 'move away from the self'. The kind of awareness that Murdoch describes as central to moral life is to be found by shifting our attention away from the self to an external and objective reality. (Mullett, 1988: 110)

Morals are matters of trade or profession and form the ethics they are supposed to be formed by. (L. Steffens, 1931: 180)

As the Canadian philosopher, Earl Winkler, puts it:

Context is extremely important. To understand the logic of moral judgments, we must first understand and explain variations in the light of moral reasons in different domains and contexts. For example, if a drug dealer is shot, it is less bad for a former military paramedic to refuse to help him on the spot than for a doctor to refuse to treat the same patient in an emergency room…the doctor's professional responsibility determines his or her requirement to help. (1996: 13)

In his War Song, *There is no middle ground*, the Nishnawbe (Ojibway) spiritual teacher and poet Arthur Solomon wrote:

There are many people who have seen the way things are,
　　And have asked almost in despair,
　　　　But what can I do?
　　And the only answer has been,
　　　You have to do something about *You*
　　Only you can decide whether you will be a part of
　　　　This destruction or whether you will set your
　　　　　Heart and mind against it.
You may not be able to change where you work or how
　　You earn your living.
　　　　But you are totally responsible for the direction that
　　　　　You give your own life.
We are only visitors here in this part of Creation…
If we choose to act, we must act intelligently
　　And with common sense.
It means we will do everything in our power to understand
　　The questions that we choose to involve ourselves with.
But whatever we are, we must be action people …
　　　　　　　　　　　　(Solomon, 1991: 67)

Thus Art Solomon challenges us to commit ourselves to the practice of applied ethics – the application of those philosophical meanderings that so frustrated Lincoln Steffens to the contextualised requirements of daily work. Media ethicists are 'action' people. Sometimes this means simply doing the best we can, under the circumstances of the moment, while causing a minimum of harm to ourselves and others. Sometimes, ethical practice is a matter of life and death, as we will see later in this chapter, in the case study of 'Eva the Evergreen Lady'.

Chapter 11 will consider ethical codes in detail. For the moment, let us briefly consider one of them. The Code of Ethics of the Washington Post is based on principles of fairness and justice. It says that no story is fair if it omits facts of major importance, includes irrelevant information at the expense of significant facts, or misleads or deceives the reader. It also values 'freedom, humaneness, stewardship, responsibility and regard for the rights of others' and instructs journalists to 'do no direct harm', to strive to prevent harm and to render needed assistance. The Eva case forces us to ask: how are we to decide what is 'needed assistance'?

There is widespread disagreement among media practitioners and ethicists about what constitutes appropriate and inappropriate distance between journalists and subjects, media and story. 'We're not here to help, we're here to report', says one of several journalists in the film *Welcome to Sarajevo* (Winterbottom, 1997). But the hero of the film, a British television journalist modelled on the real-life Michael Nicholson, ends up helping to smuggle a convoy of children out of the embattled city, adopting and bringing one of the children home to live with his family.

In 2002 and 2003 Polly Toynbee went under cover to research and write a first-hand account of poverty in Britain, a project for which she was praised and criticised in equal measure. Her detractors said she had presumed to 'know' the experience of people living in poverty from brief forays into their world from the safety of her comfortable middle-class life, and sacrificed journalistic credibility and truth by concealing her identity when doing so was not essential to the story. Instead of speaking on other people's behalf, she could have conducted honest interviews and invited them to tell their own stories. Her appreciators said her approach produced a level of empathy and veracity not possible with an 'upfront' approach and conventional interviews. There is truth to both perspectives.

Here, we are considering just such moral issues and decisions that daily challenge the principles and practices of individual journalists, editors, directors and media organisations. The growing dominance of business interests affects every aspect of media practice. Consider this view of their impact on journalism:

> … our newspapers do not represent public interests, but private interests; they do not represent humanity, but property…

...The methods by which the 'Empire of Business' maintains its control over Journalism are four: First, ownership of the papers; second, ownership of the owners; third, advertising subsidies; and fourth, direct bribery. By these methods there exists ... a control of news and of current comment more absolute than any monopoly in any other industry. [source identified below]

When do you think that was written? The 1990s or early twenty-first century would be a very good guess – certainly, this depiction of the news industry is relevant for our time.

Journalism and ethical traditions

Despite its currency, that statement was written very early in the previous century by the American 'muckraker', Upton Sinclair, in his book *The Brass Check* (Sinclair, 1920: 125, 241). Generally speaking, the problems observed by earlier generations are still with us today, although sometimes the modes of production and degree of impact have changed. As we will see in Chapter 7, the manipulation of photographic images has raised similar questions since the invention of the camera; what has changed is the sophistication with which images can be (sometimes invisibly) altered. Even the arrival of 'new media' has not so much changed the ethical questions as increased their difficulty.

While ethical questions may remain relatively constant over time, the underlying principles must be considered and reconsidered internationally and transculturally. Some concepts cross cultural boundaries; others do not. Even most basic moral rules vary according to particular circumstance. For example, the rule 'Thou shalt not kill', expressed in many religious and secular texts around the world, is applied differently in different contexts. Many societies allow killing. Some people criticise the different language applied to state-sanctioned killing by one's own government and killing by less powerful groups or countries. However, although killing is sometimes accepted in specified circumstances, it is seldom valued for its own sake. Most cultures are full of contradictions. We permit killing in official warfare but call it 'terrorism' when it is not sanctioned by the state – and call it 'murder' (and grounds for imprisonment or execution) when it is done at home against a private citizen.

Hamid Mowlana emphasises that 'the boundaries of the study called "ethics" vary from culture to culture'. He defines practical ethics as 'any rational procedure by which we determine what an individual human being as a person and as a member of a community ought to do as a "right" action by voluntary means'. Each person is both an individual and a member of a community. 'From an Islamic perspective, the study and conduct of politics cannot be separated from the methods of ethics' (Mowlana, 1989: 138).

He explains that in today's Islamic societies, ethical thinking and practices have two essential foundations:

> (1) normative religious ethics as explained in the primary source of Islam, the Quran, and the traditions (*al sunna*) of the Prophet and the Imams, and (2) normative secular ethics, ranging from the Greek tradition of popular Platonism, to the Persian tradition of giving advice to sultans and wazirs about government and politics, to ... more contemporary ethical frameworks ... (Mowlana, 1989: 140)

One of the pillars of Islamic ethics is the theory of *tawhid*, which stresses 'unity, coherence, and harmony among all parts of the universe' and subordinates all human behaviour and decisions to Allah's sovereign power. The principles of *tawhid* challenge or destroy 'thought structures based on dualism, racialism, tribalism, and familial superiority'. The function of 'communication order in Islamic society' is to 'break idols' and dependence on outsiders and to help to preserve and maintain 'the unity of the Islamic community' (Mowlana, 1989: 141–2, 144).

Though grounded in the Western philosophical traditions that have dominated my own experience and education, I have sought to educate myself and broaden this exploration of media theory and practices to encompass a range of principles and traditions. Here is a satirical view of the Western tradition, of which Lincoln Steffens might have approved:

> The Greek philosophers began by asking fundamental questions about the nature of life, the universe, and thought itself. They soon discovered that the answers to these questions were not forthcoming, nor likely to be. But in time they made a greater discovery: that merely posing the questions – in a suitably convoluted manner – sounded ... impressive. And a philosopher who sounded impressive got veneration, large fees, and comfortable consulting positions. (Weller, 1987: 3)

After Socrates came Plato, 'who wrote philosophical discourses in a form called the dialogue, even though one guy does all the talking'. Then came Aristotle, who is considered the 'father of modern science' and – at least, in the Western world, is known as 'the first to base his description of the world...on what he actually observed around him. Today, this idea seems obvious. It strikes us as strange that nobody had every thought of it before. And even stranger that nobody has ever thought of it since' (Weller, 1987: 3).

The word 'ethics' is derived from the Greek *ethikos*, which refers to activities dealing with human nature (McLeish, 1993: 248). Tom Weller's irreverent comments apply directly to media ethics – and to the fact that many 'serious' philosophers consider what we do 'situational' and insufficiently grounded in theory. But many of us think ethical theory has little use unless it is grounded in the daily experience of working media practitioners. There has always been debate about moral responsibility in journalism. In the United States, there was renewed noise about ethics in the 1960s and 1970s and again in the 1980s, with the discrediting of Janet Cooke's Pulitzer Prize-winning piece for the *Washington Post*, 'Jimmy's World'. Cooke's report on an eight-year old drug addict told many truths about contemporary American urban life, but Jimmy himself was a composite character of Janet Cooke's invention.

Not long after Janet Cooke lost her job and prize, Michael Daly, a *New York Daily News* columnist, said he invented the name of a British soldier in his report about a killing in Belfast, Northern Ireland. And a *New York Times* freelance confessed he had written a story datelined 'Cambodia' from his home in Spain – and stolen some of it from an André Malraux novel. Not all ethical questions are so straightforward.

In *Committed Journalism*, Edmund Lambeth writes that news is guided by 'conventions' that serve commercial interests as much as the public, and there is no such thing as purely objective reporting, because subjectivity is inherent in the editorial process that selects and emphasises some details over others' (Lambeth, 1986: 5). In Chapter 2 we will look more closely at what I call the Rashomon Effect: that no one account of a story can convey the whole story, and therefore it is impossible for any one journalist to gather all of the facts or experience all of an event.

Lambeth argues that the news media seldom fulfil their 'watchdog role' adequately, and are often 'passive chroniclers of the status quo … manipulated by those in power'. He calls media independence 'a myth' because each country's social and political system places limitations on its media. Reporters and editors are controlled by owners, publishers, peer pressure, social values, laws, customs and so forth (Lambeth, 1986: 5). We often hear that the 'West' has a 'free press' and much of the rest of the world does not. But consider the situation in Italy, where Sylvio Berlusconi serves at once as government leader, multimedia megabaron, censor and controller of public information. And consider as well the gentleness with which much of the US press treated President George W. Bush's morally and legally questionable 2000 election and subsequent manipulation of conflict with Iraq, following the events of September 11, 2001. It is hard to take the moral high ground when your own country, region or media behaves in a questionable or reprehensible manner. As we will discuss more fully in Chapter 4, an ethical media practice abandons that kind of chauvinism for a more inclusive, multi-cultural and international world view.

Just as we can develop muscles by exercising our bodies, we can develop ethical problem-solving skills by exercising our minds. Those skills include:

1. learning to recognise moral problems, questions and issues;
2. learning to critically assess different arguments and a range of relevant facts;
3. educating yourself to be aware of different, alternative responses to an issue or event;
4. learning to tolerate and respect differences of experience and perspective;
5. effectively integrating your professional life and personal convictions.

Moral theories

In Western tradition, philosophical thought is generally divided into four main types of moral theories. They focus on: (1) good consequences for all; (2) duties; (3) human rights; and (4) virtue. Let us consider each of these in turn:

1. *Utilitarian* ethicists say that good and bad consequences are the only relevant moral considerations for determining ethical principles and behaviour.
2. *Duty* ethicists say that actions are more important than consequences. We must ask whether our actions violate principles of duty and must perform prescribed duties regardless of whether their consequences are good or bad.
3. *Rights* ethicists say that moral rights determine what actions are appropriate. They agree with duty ethicists that good consequences are not the only moral consideration, but they say that we act ethically when we respect people's basic human rights, not because those rights are created by duties.
4. *Virtue* ethicists say that right actions manifest virtues (good traits and behaviours) and wrong actions manifest vices (bad traits and behaviours).

Let us expand a bit on these basic principles.

Utilitarianism, founded by the English philosophers Jeremy Bentham (1748–1832) and John Stuart Mill (1806–1873), is divided into act utilitarianism and rule utilitarianism. Act utilitarianism emphasises the 'greatest good for the greatest number', while rule utilitarianism holds that moral rules or codes come first. Mill considered happiness the main goal; Bentham said that rules must come first, even if they do not lead to happiness.

Duty ethics is most closely associated with the German philosopher Immanuel Kant (1724–1804). He said that good consequences were less important than moral duties, and specified duties must guide all of our actions. For Kant, duties must meet three conditions. The first condition is good will – the intention to do one's duty. The second is commitment to moral behaviour; you must do good because there are unconditional requirements, or *categorical imperatives*. The third condition is that categorical imperatives are required of everyone: duties are universal. Kant said that 'truth' derives from higher reasoning and not from experience. He said we must obey universal moral laws based on universal values.

Human rights ethics, represented by the British philosopher John Locke (1632–1704), was later influenced by the French and American revolutions. It emphasises the right of each individual to life, liberty and the property generated by her or his labour.

Virtue and responsibility ethics, founded by Aristotle (384–322 BC), emphasises responsibility and accountability and divides virtues into two categories: intellectual virtues are acquired habits that lead to rational activities, while moral virtues use the *golden mean* to mediate between extremes. For Aristotle, ignorance is an insufficient excuse for irresponsibility; people are held accountable if they may have known the possible consequences of their acts. This concept is an important aspect of the ethics in the film *Absence of Malice* (Pollack, 1981). Aristotle's idea of justice includes what would later become utilitarianism, with its values of maximising public good or happiness, fairness and equity in distributing goods, reciprocity and equality.

Other values, principles and theories

The American ethicist Lawrence Kohlberg was influenced by the French child psychologist Jean Piaget. In 1958, Kohlberg set out what he considered to be the stages of moral growth in the life of an individual:

1. *Stage 1: Obedience to authority.* The famous study by Stanley Milgram (1975), titled *Obedience to Authority*, showed average American adults (as opposed to those defined as anti-social or with a predilection for violent behaviour) as locked into Kohlberg's Stage 1.
2. *Stage 2: Doing right.* This is based on the pursuit of one's own interests within the limits of a system of reciprocity, with rules set up to govern conflicts.

3. *Stage 3: Empathy*. This involves increasing awareness of others, while still looking to authority figures for guidance.
4. *Stage 4: Conscience*. Obligations are met and rules followed for the good of a functioning society, not just to gain approval of authority figures.
5. *Stage 5: Moral reasoning*. This involves awareness of the differences between law and morality.
6. *Stage 6: Ethical principles*. Acts are based on ethical principles and people are seen as ends, not means.

Kohlberg's ethics emphasises motives. Therefore, he would not consider an accidental killing immoral because there is no hostile motivation, and a murder committed by a child is not immoral because children are assumed not to be morally responsible. The legal systems of many countries are grappling with this latter issue as the number of child murderers rises and legal boundaries between childhood and adulthood are shifted and reappraised. Kohlberg's work has been criticised as sexist, ethnocentric and artificially universalised because his understanding of moral development is based solely on studies of males in the United States.

In the late 1990s, the ethicist Thomas W. Cooper took his studies of US and Canadian media and communication in a new direction. Striving to challenge our ethnocentric understanding of ethical principles and behaviours, he set out to be a respectful participant observer in other people's communities. One of the communities he lived in is Rock Point Reservation in northeastern Arizona, a Navajo (Diné) Native American community. The ethical rules which Diné apply to communication include 'Avoid excess' and 'When in doubt, remain silent ...' People are taught that respectful thoughts and words are essential and they should not speak negatively of others. Lying is unacceptable (Cooper, 1989: 150–6).

The early (pre-Islam) Persian (Iranian) prophet Zarathustra, known also as Zoroaster (588–541 BCE), taught that the universe was based on twin spirits – the truth and the lie. He said that women and men could not escape from making moral choices, 'and by virtue of their choice and conduct they identify themselves with one of the two spirits in the universe, light or darkness, truth or lie, order or chaos, good or evil' (McLeish, 1993: 788).

I suspect that most people operate from a position somewhere midway between these two spirits. If we place good and evil at two ends of a continuum, we could then place individuals, their choices and actions or particular decisions and activities at points along the continuum (see Figure 1.1). We can then examine each decision (e.g. whether to publish a controversial news story) in terms of its relative position between 'good' and 'evil', weighing the values and priorities that we have chosen to guide our decisions and actions.

Good	Neutral	Evil
* * * * * * * * * * * *		

Figure 1.1 'Twin spirits' continuum

When the *The Sun* and *The Daily Mail* printed a series of anti-immigration/asylum seeker headlines in 2003, it could be seen as simply presenting one position about the acceptance of refugees and other immigrants in Britain – if not at the 'good' end of the continuum, somewhere between 'neutral' and 'good'. Consider the effects of *The Sun*'s editorial decision to print the headline:

IMMIGRATION MADNESS
1 IN 4 ASYLUM SEEKERS ENDS UP IN BRITAIN

(*The Sun*, 22 April 2003: 1) in the light of increasing violence against asylum seekers, and the *inaccuracy* of the headline. In fact, a nine-year study revealed the UK ranked eleventh in the EU in per capita refugee admissions (Brooks, 2003: 5). Or consider the large, black, front-page *Daily Express* headline,

LUXURY LIFE OF ASYLUM SEEKERS

(*Daily Express*, 17 December 2002: 1). The reader is likely to have an opinion formed, or reinforced, that all asylum seekers have an easy life in posh surroundings – long before the accurate information may reach them. Contrary to that image (and myths about the National Health Service), 80 per cent of asylum seekers and refugees said 'they cannot afford to maintain good health in Britain' (Brooks, 2003: 9).

In these cases, the editors' decisions to publish large-scale, alarmist front-page headlines would fall close to the 'evil' end of the scale. At issue here, in deciding where to place the decision and headline, are the moral principles and values that guide the decision-makers and media critics. I value human life and safety, intercultural tolerance and diversity, journalistic accuracy and fairness more than simply selling newspapers by arresting readers' attention and catering to some people's fears. I think that newspapers and other media can help to defuse intercultural tensions, and am outraged when editors like those on the Sun use their papers to inflame tensions instead. I think that such decisions can sometimes incite or inspire violence, when instead they could inspire tolerance and peace.

Because these are my opinions and values, my assessment of 'good' and 'evil' intentions and outcomes is different from that of someone for whom profits and sales are top priority. That said, I agree with Claude-Jean Bertrand's comments cited in the Introduction that service to media consumers is closely linked to media profitability and survival (Bertrand, 2001a), and I think it is possible to sell newspapers, and radio and television, to the public without misinforming the public and endangering public safety. The exercise at the end of this chapter raises some complex points about media responsibility, public information, personal health, safety and privacy. The television journalists involved are not self-serving careerists; they are deeply concerned about ethics and responsibility. Yet their chain of decision-making – based on concern for the welfare of the woman whose story they had decided to tell in what they thought was the public interest – was harshly criticised for violating the subject's human rights. Put yourself in the journalists' shoes. What would you do?

Exercises

1.1 Case study: 'Eva the Evergreen Lady'

Before you come to class, carefully read Pierre Mignault's discussion of this case in which he was directly involved as one of the key television journalists researching and presenting the story (Mignault, 1996: 8–11).

INSTRUCTIONS
Divide the class into five groups. Each group will examine the case of Eva from one of the following five ethical perspectives:

1. Utilitarianism
2. Duty ethics
3. Rights ethics
4. Virtue ethics
5. Diné principles of communication

Each group receives at least one copy of the relevant information sheet (see below) and meets for 30 minutes. You are to review the principles and outline how you would solve this case using *the particular ethical perspective which has been assigned to your group*.

The class then reconvenes and each group presents its solution, followed by general discussion of the issues, problems, decisions and solutions.

Case study group 1: Utilitarianism

*Using the principles of **utilitarianism**, define the main problems and propose a solution. You may focus on act utilitarianism, rule utilitarianism, or a combination of both.*

Utilitarianism: Good and bad consequences are what count. As developed by Jeremy Bentham, act utilitarianism emphasises greatest good for the greatest number. John Stuart Mill and others developed rule utilitarianism, focusing on individual actions and their contribution to happiness. Decide what actions and principles you will use to guide your decision, and apply them to your proposed solution.

Case study group 2: Duty ethics

*Using the principles of **duty ethics**, define the main problems and propose a solution.*

Duty ethics: Focus on actions rather than consequences. There are universal duties (what Immanual Kant called 'categorical imperatives') which are binding on everyone; good will – the intention to do one's duty – is a guiding principle; you must do good because of your commitment to moral behaviour. You must decide whether the actions support or violate principles of duty (e.g. 'avoid deceiving others', 'be fair'). Decide what guiding principles you will use, and apply them to your proposed solution.

Case study group 3: Rights ethics

*Using the principles of **rights ethics**, define the main problems and propose a solution.*

Rights ethics: We have duties to other people because other people have rights that ought to be respected (not just because it's our duty). Actions are wrong when they violate moral rights. As John Locke said, each person has the right to life, liberty and property; other people have duties not to interfere with one's life (this is also part of a person's human rights). Decide whose rights and what actions are involved and what principles you will use, and apply them to your proposed solution.

Case study group 4: Responsibility and virtue ethics

*Using the principles of **virtue ethics**, define the main problems and propose a solution.*

Responsibility and **virtue ethics:** As Aristotle said, we have a responsibility to perform morally right acts. Moral virtues reflect the tendency to find the Golden Mean between extremes of too much (excess) and too little (deficiency). For example, courage can be seen as the middle ground between foolhardiness and cowardice. Decide what moral virtues will affect your decision, and how you will find the appropriate middle ground between extremes (the Golden Mean), and apply this to your proposed solution.

Case study group 5: Diné ethics

Using the Diné principles cited in Thomas W. Cooper's work (Cooper, 1989: 150), define the main principles and propose a solution.

Diné ethics: Discuss the case in relation to the following principles: communicate with respect for the other individual; avoid excess; when in doubt, remain silent. Decide what principles will inform your decision, and apply them to your proposed solution.

Further reading

Hulteng, John (1985) *The Messenger's Motives*, 2nd edn. Englewood Cliffs, NJ: Prentice Hall, Chapters 2 and 3.

Mignault, Pierre (1996) 'A case study: Eva the Evergreen Lady', in Valerie Alia, Brian Brennan and Barry Hoffmaster (eds), *Deadlines and Diversity*. Halifax: Fernwood, pp. 8–11.

Press Complaints Commission, *Code of Practice* – see Appendix D.

Suggested viewing

For details see the annotated filmography in Appendix B at the end of the book.

Mad City
The Front Page
Front Page Story
Keeper of the Flame

2 Life, the universe and ethics II: social scientific theories and ethical practice

I do not feel myself to be ... a cold recorder of what I see and hear. On every professional experience I leave shreds of my heart and soul ... I participate in what I see or hear as though the matter concerned me personally and were one on which I ought to take a stand (in fact I always take one, based on a specific moral choice). (Fallaci, 1976: 9)

... ethnographic work reveals that morality must be understood contextually, and once that broader, more realistic perspective is adopted, it provides a sobering appreciation of the prospects for moral reform. (Hoffmaster, 1992: 1425)

Journalism is ethical to the extent that it tells as much truth as possible. It avoids ethnocentric bias that skews truth telling, and includes a range of observation that provides a context for the 'factual' information reported about people and events. Good journalism and good social science have many of the same characteristics, and – though journalists and social scientists don't always like hearing this about each other – similar research methods often serve both disciplines.

Too few journalists are prepared for the realities they encounter in the field. Whether they work at home or abroad, in cities or in remote regions, they seldom get the kind of basic training given as a matter of course to diplomats, sociologists, anthropologists, politicians and businesspeople. The result is a level of ethnocentrism long held unacceptable in other fields. Journalists persist in presenting unfamiliar people and events as cross-cultural kitsch. The best journalists are instinctive ethnographers. But we don't have to rely solely on instinct. By placing ethnographic methodology at the core of journalism studies, we can improve the quality and integrity of journalistic work. 'News simultaneously records and is a product of social reality ...' (Tuchman, 1978: 189). Events such as Watergate or the My Lai massacre were

'personal troubles' for those involved ... news accounts indicated what was happening ... in the everyday world [and] were clearly active participants in the socio-political processes. The military tried to bury the story of My Lai; the President's associates tried to bury the stories about Watergate. The media were part and parcel of the drama of structuring and releasing information that would become the basis for the shaping of knowledge. (Tuchman, 1978: 189–90)

Accuracy requires understanding of the socio-political and cultural contexts. Sometimes it also requires more than one voice. Consider the following example based on an actual event. Not long after experiencing a series of bomb threats, the local office of a Canadian political party held a holiday celebration. The people who arrived at noon witnessed Royal Canadian Mounted Police and a protest demonstration. Those who arrived *five minutes later* saw a quiet celebration with people sipping tea, nibbling cookies and chatting. If one reporter arrived at 12:00 and another at 12:05, who would have the 'real' story? I call this the Rashomon Principle:[1] 'truth' is really *truths* and is always based on multiple realities. In the case of the celebration, it would take *both* reporters to tell the story. Sometimes it takes the combined voices of insiders and outsiders.

Over the years, I have worked on several projects that encouraged journalists of different cultural backgrounds to work together. Members of minority communities said the media were disrespectful, made stereotypes of their people and issues, and seldom reported on them first-hand. Journalists said they were afraid to go into unfamiliar communities to research stories first-hand. Their fear often came from stereotypes perpetuated by the news media. I was repeatedly warned not to go into indigenous communities. Yet my experiences in these communities were generally positive, and crucial to the integrity and accuracy of my work. Media practitioners must do more than just show up in diverse communities. They must be prepared to abandon the rules of conventional training. The journalistic tradition of aggressive information gathering is not only ethnocentric and gender-centric, it's not always the best way to get the story. Quieter, less abrasive and less intrusive approaches – 'hanging around', meeting people, listening – improves trust and access to information.

The 'Rashomon Principle' is made explicit in *The Independent*'s coverage of the final phase of the Hutton Inquiry. In place of a front-page story is a cross-referenced grid of interested and involved parties and the effects of their decisions, with the headline: 'One death, five versions. Now it is for Lord Hutton to judge' (*The Independent*, 2003: 1).

Like Kurosawa, the sociologist Erving Goffman sees reality as a complex of 'multiple social realities', life as theatre and action as 'performance'. People behave informally 'backstage' (in private) and more formally 'front-stage' (in public). Unseen in the kitchen, restaurant workers may call customers names and spit in their food and then serve it, smiling politely, in the dining room. The responsible journalist understands 'front-' and 'back-stage' behaviour and develops descriptive and investigative skills, an ethnographer's eye for context and openness to new approaches. To interpret events, we must learn to 'read' non-verbal language as well as words (Goffman, 1959: 128–9).

The psychiatrist and educator Robert Coles found the conventional wisdom he had learned at university did not work with real people – the 'correct' methods failed to help his patients. He found a mentor who said, 'The people who come to see us bring us their stories. They hope they tell them well enough so that we understand the truth of their lives [and] know how to interpret [them] correctly. We have to remember that what we hear is *their story*' (Coles, 1989: 7). Coles began to *listen* to the stories, letting the storyteller's agenda take over, getting 'bogged in a mass of circumstantial detail' (Coles, 1989: 13). In journalism, as in psychiatry, we are taught to maintain order (control the interview), to avoid the subject's agenda and 'superfluous' detail. But following those rules can mean missing the story. The philosopher Barry Hoffmaster thinks such restrictions remove the context.

> To borrow an example from [sociologist Stephen] Toulmin … the question, 'Is a flying boat a ship or an airplane?' is, in the abstract, hopelessly sterile. When a context is supplied – ought the captain of a flying boat to have an airline pilot's licence, a master mariner's certificate, or both? – the issue comes into focus … (Hoffmaster, 1992: 1427)

In comparing journalism and ethnography, I use *ethnography* in its broadest sense, to refer to the work of describing a setting, situation or culture. In 1993 T. D. Allman went to the former Yugoslavia with other journalists, to learn about 'ethnic cleansing'.

> 'I need some footage of life among the ruins,' says Tom Aspell, an NBC correspondent, so we go searching. The only signs of life are occasional clumps of men – some armed, some not – sitting out in the sunshine, in front of bombed-out buildings, drinking.
>
> Then we see an elderly couple working in their garden. May we visit them?
>
> She rushes to make coffee, while he shows us the garden – tomatoes, pumpkins, plums. After serving the coffee, the old woman sits down in front of Tom's camera and is asked to describe what happened here.

Immediately, she starts crying. She tells us that she and her neighbors spent nine weeks huddling in her basement ... Sometimes, when one of them went for water, she didn't make it back ...

This couple, whose house and life were destroyed by Serb artillery, happen to be Serbs themselves. (Allman, 1993: 114)

To get the story others missed, Allman interviews this couple, a professor and several presidents, most of them not officially recognised (e.g. Albanian President Ibrahim Rugova, a literary theoretician whose first love is Edgar Allan Poe).

Tony Hillerman started as a journalist and went on to write detective fiction. His novel *The Fly on the Wall*, a portrait of the Washington journalism community, shows the place of ethnography in investigative journalism.

Whitey Robbins had just asked the usual question about Roark's political plans and Roark was giving his usual noncommittal answer ...

'Governor,' Cotton said, 'were you surprised by the move in the house ...?'

'I was surprised.' *His smile denied the statement* [italics mine]. (Hillerman, 1971: 56)

The journalist must watch for such contradictions between people's words and gestures. Often, we can best show the broad picture through small details. The American journalist I. F. Stone found stories others missed using only material which was in the public domain – by knowing where to look and how to read:

I sought in political reporting what Galsworthy in another context called 'the significant trifle' – the bit of dialogue, the overlooked fact, the buried observation that illuminated the realities of the situation. (Stone, 1970: xiv)

Stone saw himself as an independent 'guerrilla warrior'

swooping down in surprise attack on a stuffy bureaucracy where it least expected independent inquiry. The reporter assigned to specific beats ... soon finds himself a captive ... a reporter covering the whole capital on his own ... is immune from these pressures ... The bureaucracies put out so much that they cannot help letting the truth slip from time to time. The town is open. One can always ask questions, as one can see from one of my 'coups' – forcing the Atomic Energy Commission to admit that its first underground test was detected not 200 miles away – as it claimed – but 2600 miles away. (Stone, 1970: iv–v)

Doing one's job means more than stacking 'facts' in an inverted pyramid. It means loving language and its precise uses, paying attention to detail, seeing connections and clarifying them for others. It means learning to 'read' verbal and non-verbal cues in different, often unfamiliar settings and a willingness to question assumptions. The ethnographer-journalist is humble, meticulously descriptive, incisive, investigative and critical. For James Spradley, ethnography starts with an attitude of almost complete ignorance and is 'based on the principle of *learning from people*, rather than *studying people*' (Spradley, 1980: 3). His famous 1970 study of skid-row men follows this principle.

> Listening, watching, and allowing these men to become my teachers, I discovered a complex culture that gave shape and meaning to the lives of men most people wrote off as 'derelicts'. (Spradley, 1980: vi)

American sociology's 'first real research tradition', the 'Chicago School', emerged in the 1920s, led by W. I. Thomas and Robert E. Park. They applied principles anthropologists had used to study 'other' cultures to the study of their own (Collins, 1985: 199). They saw life as fluid and full of rapid changes, and, like reporters, watched events unfold in their natural setting and looked for sudden shifts and unanticipated developments. Spradley said ethnography was no longer relegated to 'cultures in far-off places', it had 'come home, to become a fundamental tool for understanding ourselves and the multicultural societies of the modern world' (Spradley, 1980:). Continuing in the Chicago tradition, Micaela di Leonardo says ethnography always *was* at 'home'. She studies 'home' communities and also media representations of anthropology. She says media often get it wrong, exoticising both anthropologists and the people they study.

> *Business Week*, for example, announces that anthropologists are now 'Studying Natives on the Shop Floor' ...
>   ... the *Chronicle of Higher Education* trumpets, 'Many Anthropologists Spurn Exotic Sites to Work Territory Closer to Home' ... (di Leonardo, 1998: 25–6)

She challenges media practitioners to stop misinforming the public.
    The Chicago School influenced the next major development – Symbolic Interactionism – which said the social order was negotiated, any institution could change and any society could be disrupted by revolution. Symbolic interactionists such as Herbert Blumer anticipated the journalist's need to expect the unexpected. This 'down-to-earth approach to the scientific study of human groups and conduct' had its

contradictions. Despite their subjective, interpretive approach, symbolic interactionists also sought 'an objective science of human conduct ... which would conform to criteria borrowed from the natural sciences' (Collins, 1985: 2). Similar contradictions permeate journalism – we emphasise subjectivity of a reporter's observations but seek a scientific 'objectivity' of verifiable facts.

The ethnographer asks the reporter's traditional five Ws and H (who, what, when, where, why, how) and, as James Clifford says, is an *active* participant who effectively tells the reader, 'You are there, because I was there' (Clifford, 1983: 118). There is a need to acknowledge both limitations and power. Inaccurate coverage comes less from ill will than from poor education, misplaced priorities, deadline-panic and inadequate research. Journalists are experts at becoming overnight experts. 'An anthropologist is a journalist with a two-year deadline' (Grindal and Rhodes, 1987: 11–13). I think the journalism of the future will be less elitist and will reflect and respect the multiplicity of cultures. Rick Salutin discusses the power differential in interviewer–interviewee dynamics.

> A reporter or film crew shows up at your house or workplace. It's already abnormal. They ask questions about who you are and what you're like. It's hard to respond – like those stilted lines people say in singles bars ... Who wants to spend loads of time feeling bad about a person freely giving you *their* time? Besides, there's something likable in almost everyone ... Insights of [the] murkier sort are unlikely to occur during the profile process. They're more inclined to come out incidentally, when people are just living their lives ... the best stuff happens when you turn off the tape or shut your notebook ... Everything important happens at the door ... you might miss those moments. They might not fit your story ... (Salutin, 1993)

Concerned that sociology had 'not gotten to the real bedrock of facts that we ought to be observing', Harold Garfinkel developed a discipline he named ethnomethodology (from ethnography – the 'observational study of' – and methodology – 'the methods that people use to make sense out of experience') (Collins, 1985: 211). The term is sometimes misused as a synonym for ethnography. It is especially useful in researching one's own home territory and in investigative work. Ethnomethodologists (nicknamed 'ethnos') criticised survey researchers for merely asking questions, saying they 'mistook the answers for the real ways people handled their lives' (Collins, 1985: 205). They said symbolic interactionists focused on the surface of interaction – a criticism also applied to journalists who rely on press releases, press conferences and survey and opinion polls instead of first-hand observation. Garfinkel's methods were extreme. He was (in)famous for sending

> students out to do 'experiments' that involved 'breaching' the taken-for-granted surface of everyday life. Students would be sent home to act like strangers in their own houses, politely asking if they could use the bathroom ... [They] would be told to go into a store, pick out a 99-cent tube of toothpaste and see if they could bargain the clerk into taking 25 cents for it. (Collins, 1995: 212–13)

Ethnos abandoned the principle of benign non-intervention, replacing the neutral or objective participant observer with an interfering observer who 'makes trouble' to increase knowledge.

> [I prefer] to start with familiar scenes and ask what can be done to make trouble ... to multiply the senseless features of perceived environments [and produce] bewilderment, consternation ... confusion ... anxiety, shame, guilt, and indignation ... disorganized interaction should tell us something about the way structures of everyday activities are ... produced and maintained. (Garfinkel, 1967: 38)

While many have criticised the ethics of this methodology, it is helpful for getting beyond surface impressions and assumptions. Janet Malcolm embraces Garfinkel's trouble-making principle wholeheartedly, saying the ways we conduct interviews are always 'morally indefensible', calling the journalist 'a kind of confidence man, preying on people's vanity, ignorance, or loneliness, gaining their trust and betraying them without remorse' (Malcolm, 1990: 3).

George Hicks took a gentler approach. In 1965, he went to learn about people in a US Appalachian mountain valley. He discovered that 'stores and storekeepers were at the center of the valley's communication system ...' (Spradley, 1980: 3). By visiting each store daily, he gradually pieced together the understanding he was looking for. For the official version, you go to municipal offices, courts and police headquarters. To learn what is going on, what people think – to get the *story* – you go to where people hang out or drop in.

As a reporter covering remote regions of the Canadian Arctic and the United States, I learned to loiter in general stores, pubs and coffee shops. Assigned to find out why a tiny Vermont town remained 'dry', I was stymied. My editors assumed the town was 'backward', driven by fundamentalist religious beliefs that postponed 'progress'. In vain, I sought information. Weary, I wandered into the general store for a soda, started chatting with customers and the proprietor – and got a very different, (front-page) story. It turned out that all of our assumptions were wrong.

Townspeople had spent years studying a politically, environmentally and economically tricky situation. Selling alcohol would have serious negative consequences for a delicate environment and the community's decision was based on complex political and social thinking, not unquestioned, old-fashioned beliefs.

I always tell students to start at the newsagent or general store. They never believe me and proceed immediately to somewhere official. They get frustrated. They come back and say, 'we went to the offices, but no one had any information and the interviews were boring. We found the real story at the general store'. The news happens in people's daily lives. For maximum information, you go to a place people frequent, where their guard is down and gossip flies. Then, you compare it to the information given by official sources.

As well as valuing gossip, journalists must learn to interpret culturally different meanings of space and time. A useful theory is Edward T. Hall's science of *proxemics* – the understanding of 'space as a specialized elaboration of culture'. Taking off from the work of Franz Boas, Edward Sapir and Leonard Bloomfield, Hall observed cultural differences in the use of space, identifying four levels of social distance: 'intimate, personal, social, and public'. Each culture has its own time frames and patterns. 'It is just as necessary to learn the language of time as it is to learn the spoken language' (Hall, 1983: 2). The North European system of doing one thing at a time is 'Monochronic' or 'M-time'. Polychronic or 'P-time' cultures (e.g. the Middle East and Latin America) stress personal involvement and 'completion of transactions' more than 'preset schedules'. Appointments are taken less seriously and are frequently broken; 'time is seldom experienced as "wasted"'. M-time cultures (e.g. Britain, Europe, North America) 'make a fetish out of management ...' (Hall, 1983: 46–7). A polychronic administrator assesses the job, lays out its component activities on elaborate charts and checks them off as they are completed, but the employee sets her/his own timetable. An M-time employer sets the timetable but leaves the actual structuring of the job to the employee.

Sometimes you need cross-cultural understanding just to find your way. In Japanese cities, intersections are named, streets are not and houses are numbered in the order in which they were built. In Tokyo, even taxi drivers must ask police for directions. Body language is equally important. The US media consultant William Boyd says white reporters often misperceive the everyday (high-energy, loud) talk and exuberant body language of African Americans as 'aggressive' (Boyd, 1992). Misinterpreting information isn't just bad practice; it can be a life or death matter. In Hartford, Connecticut, a crowd of about 100 attacked three policemen who were giving heart massage and oxygen to a woman having a heart attack. They thought the policemen were beating her. She died. The confusion may have been a cross-cultural communication problem. The police were white anglophones. The crowd were mostly Spanish-speaking residents of the neighbourhood, accustomed to rough police behaviour and perhaps unaware of CPR techniques (*Hartford Courant*, 1973: 6–7).

Another interpretive problem is what I call the 'double message interview'. In my research – especially in minority communities – the first reply to a question about a contentious issue is usually 'there's no problem'. When formalities turn to friendly talk, the interviewee starts to mention problems. I have learned to listen for the subtext – the spaces and gestures between words – and take my time (something journalists seldom do). I listen for shifts in meaning or tone and try not to take opening statements at face value. I don't see these contradictions as lies, but as evidence of 'front-' and 'backstage' behaviour in an interview in which trust and self-disclosure increase as it progresses. The journalist must decide what degree of involvement is appropriate to encourage deeper interviews. Journalists are taught to remain 'objective', distant and dispassionate – removed from their subjects. Anthropologists learn a wider range of possible levels of involvement. We must decide whether it is ever acceptable to withhold information in order to get information. Some ethicists say 'never', some journalists say 'often', others say it depends on the importance of the information to the public good.

Oriana Fallaci makes no pretence of objectivity. She is a copious describer of environment and personal characteristics, a masterful setter of scenes, a skilled observer of human behaviour. She makes moral judgements, a position more credible, perhaps, because she studies world leaders. She watches for shifts in tone or position, the methods and motivations of public people. She catches the smallest gesture. She takes control of interviews with people used to managing their interviews. To penetrate their carefully constructed public ('front-stage') personae, she must watch for the smallest detail.

> … I saw him arrive out of breath and unsmiling … he said, 'Good morning, Miss Fallaci.' Then, still without smiling, he led me into his elegant office, full of books and telephones and papers and abstract paintings and photographs of Nixon. Here he forgot about me, turned his back, and began reading a long typewritten report … it was a little embarrassing to stand there in the middle of the room, while he had his back to me and kept reading. It was also stupid and ill-mannered … However, it allowed me to study him before he studied me … After reading the … report – meticulously and carefully, to judge by the

time it took him – he finally turned to me and invited me to sit down on the couch. Then he took the adjacent armchair, higher than the couch, and from this privileged and strategic position began to ask me questions in the tone of a professor examining a pupil ... leaning back in the armchair with his right arm outstretched ... crossing his legs ... his jacket was so tight over his stomach that it looked as though the buttons might pop. (Fallaci, 1976: 20)

The details Fallaci accumulates, the positioning of herself in the interview, are not superfluous. They set the scene for her incisive portrait of Henry Kissinger. The ethnographer's tools are especially useful for dealing with a figure of such immense proportions. It is obvious to any journalist that Kissinger's words are carefully chosen. However carefully he constructs his persona and manages the interview, it is far more likely that he will reveal himself through body language, the architecture of his office, his passing behaviour. The ethnographer's role is that of private (and public) eye: she ferrets out the tiniest of clues, revealing the character of the man behind the words. Merely reporting the words would imply that the man equals his words and is no more, or less, than his rehearsed text. We see this kind of press conference-driven journalism all the time. It seldom tells us much about the issues, or the people behind them (except to the extent that we need to critically evaluate their 'front-stage' performances.

It is often hardest to apply ethnographic methods in one's own home. Many media and cultural studies scholars concentrate not only on 'home' but on audiences – on the consumers rather than the producers of information and culture. The American newspaper columnist and humourist, Dave Barry, explains why journalism cannot exist without an understanding of audiences:

The newspaper industry is in trouble ... We're having trouble attracting younger readers. They're not interested in the stories we put on the front page, about the ongoing breakdown of the Middle East Peace process, which has been breaking down for several thousand years now. (Barry, 2002: 20)

To get in touch with younger readers' interests, Barry subscribes to the America Online chat room and experiences culture shock.

As far as the America Online news department is concerned, [pop singer] Britney [Spears] is more important than nuclear proliferation. Recently, on the same day that there was a major development in the Middle East peace-process breakdown, the big story on America Online was that Britney broke up with Justin ... [There was] a poll where you could vote on what Britney should do next ... 'Learn to actually sing' was not an option ... (Barry, 2002: 20)

Barry's observations are supported by a good deal of research, including that of Dorothy Hobson, who was told by a female interviewee: '... I never watch the news, never ...' (Hobson, in Marris and Thornham, 1997: 309). Since the early 1980s, audience-focused research has suggested some of the ways in which people access and consume mass media.[2] The strengthening of links between entertainment and information is increasingly noted. The documented aversion of (especially female) audience members to violent television news (e.g. in Hobson, in Marris and Thornham, 1887) has accompanied the escalation and proliferation of violence in fictional works of television and film. It's not a question, then, of violence or non-violence – consumers want violence, but only if it isn't happening in the 'real' world. We are still a long way from knowing how to turn such observations into more ethical ways of producing information – if in fact that is a goal. If we seek to encourage both production and consumption of more informative and responsible journalism, we must learn much more about how to 'win' media consumers over to the side of reality. One way to make news more interesting, meaningful and accessible to audiences is to look beyond conventional sources. A producer for the Canadian Broadcasting Corporation (CBC) (and later for the BBC), William Law, found himself in a situation in which the usual sources were not telling the story. Months before the fall of the Soviet Union, while its instability was still being widely denied, he predicted the events to come by interviewing artists, not politicians. He wasn't even looking for a news story, he was making a documentary about theatre in Vilnius, titled 'There Is No Death Here'. He was making an arts programme. The world-changing information he learned did not appear in newscasts until months later. Because it was derived from 'arts' coverage, was produced by non-reporters and major political leaders were not interviewed, the CBC's news directors failed to take the information seriously. They were so bogged down in preconceptions about where news 'should' come from, they missed a major international story.

One of the finest examples of ethnographic journalism I have seen is a story by Mary Anne Weaver about a Pakistani bird, published in the *New Yorker* magazine. Her chronicle of the annual hunt by Arab sheiks and princes for the houbara bustard reveals global concerns through the tiniest of details. On the surface, it seems to be a small chronicle of regional environmentalism. Weaver unfolds a story of international politics and intercultural conflicts, unravelling many tangled strands of information. To understand the politics, we must understand the cultural reasons the bird is so highly valued (among Arabs, for its power-giving meat; among Pakistani, for its right to exist and its potential for revenue-production). We must understand the configurations of prestige and power in Pakistan, the economic tug-of-war that drives the hunt to its annual grim conclusion. Weaver takes us hunting, takes us to dinner, takes us into the realms of falconry and animal husbandry. Every detail counts.

> ... Saudi hunters would be led by one of the Prince's sons ... the Ambassador in Washington, or Prince Khalid, who had commanded Saudi forces during the Gulf War ... 'In the old days, we would hunt the houbara on foot or camelback ... try to outsmart it ... now customized vehicles have replaced camels, palaces have replaced tents. They use radar, computers, infra-red spotlights to find the bird at night ... The poor bird doesn't stand a chance anymore' ...
>
> Officials in Dalbandin had told me that the Saudi royal parties – which usually hunted two to three thousand birds during their monthlong stay – had no beneficial impact on the local economy ...
>
> ... 'The Prince doesn't want to meet any women this time.'
>
> 'I'm not a woman. I'm a journalist.'
>
> He shrugged. 'It's all the same,' he said.
>
> ... [In the dining tent] Prince Fahd, dressed in a camel-colored woollen robe embroidered with gold thread, sat cross-legged on an Oriental carpet, receiving his guests. The floor of the *chamiana* was covered with exquisite Kashan and Persian antique carpets ... In a far corner, there was a network of cellular phones, and other communications equipment hooked to a satellite dish. Behind the Prince, like a ceremonial guard, thirty-five hooded falcons stood at attention [perched on] stools etched with ivory and gold ... (Weaver, 1992: 60–1)

The ethnographer-journalist weaves a tale of intrigue, of a centuries-old quest for sexual and political power, of poverty and extravagance, deprivation and excess. We learn why a small bird in Pakistan is the subject of an international controversy the United Nations may have to resolve, with serious political consequences for us all. New information, new understanding, multiple perspectives: ethnography and journalism serving the Rashomon Principle and the reader.

Notes

1. This originates with the 1950 Japanese film *Rashomon* by Akira Kurosawa, in which the story of a murder (or death) and seduction (or rape) is told several times by different characters. Each time, the viewer sees 'truth' through one person's camera-eye. Each version of the story is different from all the others. In the end, we don't know which version is the 'real' one and Kurosawa turns his (and the audience's) attention from that problem to the more important reality of saving an abandoned baby. This new life, not the still unsolved death, is the only truth that matters.

2. For example, Ang, Ien (1985) 'The battle between television and its audiences: the politics of watching television', in P. Drummond and R. Paterson (eds), *Television in Transition*. London: BFI; Curran, J. and Gurevitch, M. (1991) *Mass Media and Society*. London: Edward Arnold; Grossberg, L. (1988) 'Wandering audiences, nomadic critics', *Cultural Studies*, 2 (3): 377–91; Hall, S., Hobson, D., Lowe, A. and Willis, P. (eds), (1980) London: Hutchinson; Lull, J. (1990) *Inside Family Viewing: Ethnographic Research on Television's Audiences*. London: Routledge; Moores, S. (1993) *Interpreting Audiences: The Ethnography of Media Consumption*. London: Sage.

Exercises

2.1 Observation role-play exercise: truth and accuracy in reporting

The tutor leaves the room. She or he re-enters the room and performs a five-minute activity of her or his choosing, using specific facial expressions, tone of voice, gestures and language.

The students are asked to write a detailed report of what they observe during the tutor's performance. Each 'reporter' should describe everything they see, hear, feel, etc. as vividly and completely as possible.

The students are invited to read their descriptions to the class. In the class discussion, consider the extent to which each person sees and hears a 'different event' depending on their skills, sensory observations and location in the room (or other location of the event).

2.2 Reading cultures: the journalist as ethnographer

1. Research and write a journalistic, 2,000-word story about people and/or a setting that is *unfamiliar* to you (a culture or activity very different from your own experience).

2. Research and write a journalistic, 2,000-word story about people and/or a setting that is *familiar* to you (a culture like your own, a

job, religion, neighbourhood like yours). Try to observe the people and activities as if they were alien to your experience (the ethnomethodologist's trick of making the familiar unfamiliar). Write the story presenting the subject as if it were entirely new to you and the reader.

Further reading

Blumer, Herbert (1969) *Symbolic Interactionism*. Englewood Cliffs, NJ: Prentice-Hall.

Clifford, James (1983) 'On ethnographic authority', *Representations*, 1 (2): 118–46.

Collins, Randall (1985) *Three Sociological Traditions*. New York: Oxford University Press.

di Leonardo, Micaela (1998) *Exotics at Home: Anthropologies, Others, American Modernity*. Chicago: University of Chicago Press.

Fallaci, Oriana (1976) *Interview with History*. Boston: Houghton Mifflin.

Garfinkel, Harold (1982) *A Manual for the Study of Naturally Organized Ordinary Activities*. London: Routledge & Kegan Paul.

Garfinkel, Harold (1967) *Studies in Ethnomethodology*. NJ: Prentice-Hall.

Goffman, Erving (1959) *The Presentation of Self in Everyday Life*. New York: Anchor.

Hall, Edward T. (1982) *The Hidden Dimension*. New York: Anchor.

Hall, Edward T. (1981) *The Silent Language*. New York: Anchor.

Malcolm, Janet (1990) *The Journalist and the Murderer*. New York: Vintage.

Spradley, James R. (1980) *Participant Observation*. New York: Holt, Rinehart & Winston.

Stone, I. F. (1970) *Polemics and Prophecies, 1967–1970*. Boston: Little, Brown.

Suggested viewing

For details see the annotated filmography in Appendix B at the end of the book.

Rashomon
Black Like Me
Bowling for Columbine
Gentleman's Agreement

3 Lies, truths and realities: the search for a responsible practice

In February 2002 – some five months after the destruction of New York's twin towers on 11 September 2001 – the Pentagon, home of US military operations in Washington, DC, launched a new initiative. Its weapons may have threatened as much destruction as a military initiative, yet its method was superficially benign. 'Pentagon is arming with words', read the front page headline in the *International Herald Tribune* (Dao and Schmitt, 2002: 1). After months of information control which many people suspected of continuing and deliberate falsification, the United States announced it was 'developing plans to provide news items, possibly even false ones' to media organisations around the world 'as part of a new effort to influence public sentiment and policymakers in both friendly and unfriendly countries' (Dao and Schmitt, 2002: 1). To facilitate dissemination of this questionable information, the US Defense Department created a bureau even George Orwell never dreamed of: the Office of Strategic Influence. While it may have looked like a new initiative, it was really nothing new.

Back in 1632 King Charles I shut down news publishing. During his rule, from 1649 to 1660, Oliver Cromwell closed most papers. In 1660, Charles II appointed Roger L'Estrange as Licensor. L'Estrange granted approval to a single publication: *The Royal* (court) *Gazette*, which towed the official government line. Things improved somewhat by 1688, when the 'Glorious Revolution' of the reign of William and Mary changed the government's approach to influencing the media. Realising the importance of public support, the Court sought writers who supported its policies and views. These early developments marked a shift from direct censorship to persuasion, or 'spin'.

Queen Anne was less enlightened. Daniel Defoe (born Daniel Foe) was punished for writing political poetry and satire. He was put into stocks and then imprisoned under an indefinite sentence, 'to lie in prison at the Queen's pleasure'. But the Queen knew the value of a good journalist. A minister was sent to offer Defoe a way to end his incarceration. He was told the government needed a writer who would present a neutral face while supporting all government policies. In exchange for his liberty, Defoe agreed to produce a news publication which would pretend to be independent but would never criticise or attack the government. From 1704 to 1711 he published the first modern journalistic publication, *The Review*. Ironically, he simultaneously deceived the public by presenting government 'spin' in the guise of journalism, and made substantial contributions to the techniques of modern journalism – inventing the Q & A form of interviewing and reporting and coining the term, 'eyewitness' (Steffens, 2001).

Deception in the gathering and reporting of news and information

In the light of Janet Cooke's dismissal for inventing 'Jimmy's World' and various outraged responses to plagiarism and invention over the years, how are we to understand the political communications that emerged from the offices of British Prime Minister Tony Blair in 2003. In its haste to support the US position on war with Iraq, Blair commissioned a dossier on Iraq, which was immediately dispatched to the world's media via Blair's website and released to the United Nations. It was titled *Iraq – Its Infrastructure of Concealment, Deception and Intimidation*. US Secretary of State Colin Powell was one of those who instantly praised and endorsed it. On 6 February, *BBC 4 News* and the public affairs programme, *Newsnight*, informed viewers that an unnamed Cambridge source had discovered more than half the document was plagiarised. Much of it was lifted verbatim (including typographical errors) from an article by US researcher, Ibrahim al-Marashi, 'Iraq's Security and Intelligence Network: A Guide and Analysis', published in the September 2002 issue of *Middle-East Review of International Affairs* (Associated Press, 2003: 3). Tiny changes were made in the government version to imply it was describing the current situation. Al-Marashi was neither consulted nor cited. In an interview with Associated Press, he said his research was based on thirty years of Iraqi history and some information was several years old. It did not take a great deal of detective work to discover the problem. 'Within three seconds of scanning the government's document ... the plagiarism software Copychecker ... revealed 36 clear cases of plagiarism' (*Guardian Education*, 2003: 11). The deception was all the more blatant because the government apparently used 'the spell-checker to take out all Americanisms ...' *The Guardian* maintained that any student who 'handed in an exam with this much plagiarism...would have been failed instantly' (*Guardian Education*, 2003: 11).

With enough egg on its face for several omelettes, the government might well have expressed an embarrassed apology. Instead, it insisted the document was accurate and squeamishly suggested it should have quoted the source.

In 2002, at the same time that the Pentagon launched its Office of Strategic Influence to 'inform' the world's media, the US State Department hired a former advertising executive to head its public diplomacy office, while under George W. Bush's presidency, the White House created a public information 'war room' to gather and disseminate its daily press feed (Dao and Scmhitt, 2002: 1). Under the direction of Air Force Brigadier General Simon Worden, the Office of Strategic Influence circulated 'classified proposals calling for aggressive campaigns' using both the Internet and covert operations (Dao and Schmitt, 2002: 7). Using the language of Hollywood portrayals of good and evil, Worden's programme includes 'black' campaigns featuring disinformation and other deliberately skewed communication, and 'white' public affairs campaigns featuring 'truthful news releases' and other honest presentations of transparently promotional material (Dao and Schmitt, 2002: 7). Such practices seldom stem from deliberate decisions to do evil deeds. The twentieth-century philosopher, Hannah Arendt, said: 'The sad truth is that most evil is done by people who never make up their minds to be either good or evil' (Rohmann, 2000: 26).

Activist-thinkers such as the nineteenth-century American Henry David Thoreau and the twentieth-century Indian leader Mohandas (Mahatma) Gandhi, believed that to combat evil, we must be willing to engage in what Thoreau called 'civil disobedience'. As Gandhi put it, 'Noncooperation with evil is as much a duty as is cooperation with good' (Rohmann, 2000: 63). Many religious and secular philosophies advocate versions of what Jewish and Christian tradition calls 'the Golden Rule'. In the first century BCE (BC), Rabbi Hillel said the Torah (Old Testament) prescribed: 'What is hateful to you, do not do to your neighbour'. In the New Testament (Matthew 7: 12 and Luke 6: 31) Jesus tells his followers: 'Do unto others as you would have them do unto you'. The twentieth-century German philosopher Immanuel Kant advocated the 'categorical imperative': 'Act as if the principle of your action were to become by your will a universal law of nature' (Rohman, 2000: 167). In China, K'ung Fu-tsu, better known as Confucius (551–479 BCE), prescribed his version of the Golden Rule: 'What you do not want done to yourself, do not do to others', which he saw as a 'Middle Way' of balance and harmony (Rohmann, 2000: 73–4). It can be argued that political 'spin' works against all of these efforts to enhance the public good, by creating an imbalance of benefit and power.

The political cartoonist for *The Independent* summarised the effects of spin doctors' campaigns in a drawing of the tools for doctoring information (newsprint words such as 'terrorist', 'chemical', 'poison'; scissors and glue) labelled 'WEAPONS OF MASS DECEPTION' and applied to a file labelled 'dossier on Iraq') (Schrank, 2003: 14).

Warren Beatty satirised this in his movie *Bulworth* (1998), in which a politician becomes absurdly hilarious simply because he starts telling the public the truth, 'a notion so outlandish that it's apt to sound incredible' (Solomon, 1999: 4). Solomon asks how viewers might react if TV news anchors rewrote the script.

> 'As usual, the script on my TelePrompTer is a scam ... written to make money...'
>
> 'From the somber tone ... you might think that our network is appalled by violence. Don't make me laugh. This network adores violence. We broadcast plenty of it – in prime time ...' (Solomon, 1999: 4)
>
> In law and in journalism, in government and in the social sciences, deception is taken for granted when it is felt to be excusable by those who tell the lies and who tend also to make the rules. (Bok, 1978: xvii)

Most codes of ethics, statements of principles and guidelines for journalistic practice (e.g. Russell, 1996: 34–5) consider it wrong to use hidden cameras, microphones and other techniques of information-gathering disguise – as a general principle for day-to-day practice. Yet despite these high-flown principles, few news organisations, editors or journalists insist on abiding by the (written or unwritten) rules one hundred per cent of the time. The main argument concerns serving the public interest. Sometimes important information can only be obtained through subterfuge. Especially where serious corruption or endangering public health or safety is concerned, such arguments are often credible. More often, the situation is ambiguous, and we must decide whether the quest for 'truth' is driven by the need for knowledge, the desire to increase readership or raise broadcast ratings, or blatant careerism.

Such decisions are supported in different ways by the moral philosophies of different times and cultures. Buddhists follow the 'Eightfold Path, or Middle Way' that recalls Aristotle's 'Golden Mean', based on categories of 'right' behaviour: right understanding, aspiration, speech, action, livelihood, endeavour, mindfulness and contemplation. At the centre is the idea that 'nothing is permanent'. While Hindus and Jainists believe that the soul passes from generation to generation by transmigrating from person to person, Buddhists see life as impermanent and ever-changing (Rohmann, 2000: 4).

The media and social change

The overarching principle of this book is that the media can play a major part in fostering positive social change. Consider, for example, Sheila Mullett's inherently activist feminist ethics. It contains three dimensions: 'moral sensitivity', 'ontological shock' – a new attitude that replaces passive acceptance of human misery with a commitment to 'reformulating our actions and thought', and 'praxis: a collective understanding of the transformative possibilities within a given social context' (Mullett, 1988: 115–16). The idea of praxis is founded on the principle of replacing the idea of unalterable 'fate' with the idea that, however limited the prospects and possibilities, social change is an omnipresent possibility.

The 'muckrakers' with their dedication and optimism are with us still. Like their predecessors, they still must fight reluctant publishers, public derision and efforts to censor their work.

The modern-day muckraker, Michael Moore, was asked to cut portions of his book *Stupid White Men* (2001). He held his ground, and after a long delay, the book was published. A century earlier, his publisher, Macmillan, had offered to publish Upton Sinclair's undercover investigation of the Chicago stockyards, *The Jungle*, provided he would 'cut out some of the objectionable passages' (Jensen, 2000: 52–3). He refused. After five publishers had rejected the manuscript, Sinclair published it himself in 1906. To cover the costs, he offered a 'Sustainer's Edition' at a higher price. He not only succeeded in selling his work and informing the public, he made more money in sales within the first two months than he had earned in the previous five years (Jensen, 2000: 53). Eventually, Doubleday decided to cash in on the book's success and agreed to issue a new edition.

Just as early twentieth-century publishers learned they could profit from the investigative journalism of early muckrakers such as Lincoln Steffens, Ida Mae Tarbell and Upton Sinclair, twenty-first-century publishers have learned and relearned the same lesson. Sometimes the muckrakers themselves are the publishers. In 1897, Lincoln Steffens 'got hold of' New York's oldest newspaper, the *Commercial Advertiser*.

> Editorially we were free … from any requirement beyond that of making the bankrupt a profitable property, which meant, at that stage, a good newspaper.
> … My reporters … were picked men and women, picked for their unusual, literary pose. I hated the professional newspaper man … I wanted none on my staff. I wanted fresh, young, enthusiastic writers who would see and make others see the life of the city. This meant

individual styles, and old newspaper men wrote in the style of their paper ... (Steffens, 1931: 311–13).

There was more to Steffens' method than the love of literary creativity.

> No one would be kept long in any department; as soon as a reporter became expert in one branch of work, he would be turned into another. This was not only for their sakes, but for ours also. When a reporter no longer saw red at a fire, when he was so used to police news that a murder was not a human tragedy but only a crime, he could not write police news for us. We preferred the fresh staring eyes to the informed mind and the blunted pencil...I declared that if any two reporters came to write alike, one of them would have to go. There was to be no *Commercial Advertiser* style...no lists of friends or enemies of the paper; no editorial policy; no 'beats'; and ... no insistence even upon these rules ... (Steffens, 1931: 314–15)

I. F. Stone, whose creative research methods were mentioned in Chapter 2, worked as a newspaper reporter and editorial writer from the 1920s to the 1950s. In 1941 he was banned from the National Press Club for bringing an African American judge to lunch. He was not re-admitted until 1981 (Jensen, 2000: 124). He spent his career challenging not only racism but government 'spin' on the Vietnam War, nuclear power and nuclear projects, and 'American imperialism' in South East Asia and Central America. His methods were considered unconventional at the time, but today they are in daily use by the world's investigative journalists. After years of trying to work within the bounds of existing media, he took his severance pay from a New York newspaper, a loan, his wife Esther and brother Marc, and launched the landmark *I.F. Stone's Weekly*. It accepted no advertising, and from 1953 to 1971 survived on subscriptions alone. Its charter subscribers included Bertrand Russell, Albert Einstein and Eleanor Roosevelt (Jensen, 2000: 125). He not only managed to survive financially, his independent, four-page, weekly newsletter influenced an international array of journalists, politicians and others, and his stories often made their way into the mainstream media.

Today, having stood his ground and kept his manuscript intact, Michael Moore and his publisher are (forgive the cliché) laughing all the way to the bank. Like his predecessors, Moore knows it is readers who make the difference.

> I'd like to acknowledge, first and foremost, those of you who have read this book. I hope you had a few good laughs. I hope it has inspired you

to go and raise a ruckus. You are the only ones who are going to change things. (Moore, 2001: 275)

Arundhati Roy originally trained as an architect in Delhi, India. She worked as a production designer, wrote film screenplays and in 1997 published her first book *The God of Small Things*. It won the Booker Prize for fiction, was translated into more than thirty languages and was said to herald the start of a brilliant career. Two years later, its author announced she was abandoning that career to devote herself to journalism and activism. In May 1998 India announced it had conducted a series of nuclear tests and 'declared itself a nuclear weapons state', followed within days by a similar declaration from Pakistan.

> I was in the United States on a reading tour ... My first response was one of disgust at the condescension ... hypocrisy and ... double standards of the reaction in the western world ... it took a few months for me to stop reacting to the international reaction and to begin to address what we had done to ourselves, to our lives, to our futures ... Nuclear bombs, we were told, were necessary as a deterrent. A deterrent to what? (Roy, 1999: Preface, unpaginated)

She then learned of plans to construct a massive dam, one of 3,200 on the Narmada River in central India, the largest such programme in history.

> These thousands of dams have been built in the name of National Development. Yet 250 million people have no access to safe drinking water. At least 350 million ... live below the poverty line. Over eighty per cent of rural households do not have electricity ... More than ten thousand people face submergence. They have nowhere to go. (Roy, 1999: Preface)

Like I. F. Stone and Michael Moore, Arundhati Roy has moved outside the world of mainstream media while managing to get her investigative research and opinion pieces published, first in smaller periodicals and then by major publishers. Having given up the path and perks of the successful, young, prize-winning 'star' novelist, she has managed to remain a familiar face and voice on television and radio, in public presentations and in print.

Making a living while making a difference

There is a moral within a moral here: it takes courage and persistence to uncover truth(s) and to find ways of bringing new and challenging information to the public. It is also possible to do some good in the world and, at the same time, to support yourself. Few of us are independently wealthy; most of us need to earn a living. You do not have to compromise your principles to do so. Ethical practice need not always mean a choice between starvation and survival, though it may sometimes mean a choice between basic economic survival and wealth – and in the worst of times, between life and death. Sometimes journalists, film-makers, musicians, broadcasters and writers of courage manage to make a fortune from their work. If that happens, you will have the opportunity to agonise over how many holidays to take, how much to leave your children, what charities and causes to support. My point is that, contrary to the claims of nay-sayers and intimidators, it is possible to sell your work without selling out.

Making connections

One of the most important services media practitioners can provide to the public is to clarify connections – from policy to practice, country to country, government to corporation, business to labour, profit to health and safety, and so on. In our daily lives we often see only the superficial effects of far-reaching policy and change. Sometimes this has been caused by deliberate corporate or government spin – the marketing of cigarettes without telling the public they contain added nicotine to encourage addiction; the marketing of war in Iraq without telling the public there was no evidence of weapons of mass destruction and no way of assuring the much-promised immediate success. Sometimes it is caused by the oversimplification of information and the absence of context – the reporting of a story about improved company profits with-out telling the public of the cost to health or the environment.

Editors and journalists often work from the assumption that readers, listeners and viewers are unable to cope with too much information and require the kind of tension found in works of drama and fiction to hold their interest. This leads to the conventional 'two sides to every story' approach. If you assume that most stories have many sides, it takes more skill to produce the stories in a coherent and accessible way, and more energetic research. The muckrakers have always known this. In 1903 *McClure's* magazine published a story by the US journalist Ida M. Tarbell titled 'The history of the Standard Oil Company: the oil war of 1872 – how the "Mother of Trusts" operated' (Weinberg and Weinberg, 1961: 22–39). In it, Tarbell untangled the strands of company history to reveal links between petroleum producers and oil barons, railways, refineries, pricing and financing, the US government, international trade and the public. Most of all, she showed the lengths to which the com-

panies would go to assure maximum profit at any cost, 'Unhampered ...
by any ethical consideration ...' (Tarbell, in Weinberg and Weinberg,
1961: 39).

Sixty years later, in Britain, Anthony Sampson published an update:
The Seven Sisters: The Great Oil Companies and the World They Made
(Sampson, 1975) and another portrait of entangled government and
corporate power, *The Sovereign State: The Secret History of ITT* (1973). In
it he reveals how the International Telephone and Telegraph Corporation (ITT), a nominally innocuous communications company, played
a central role in engineering some of the most shameful events in human
history. He shows how a simple desire for corporate profits linked to the
US government's power objectives led directly to the assassination of the
democratic President of Chile, Salvador Allende and thousands of his
supporters. They included journalists and bystanders from inside and
outside Chile, and the gentle poet, singer and co-founder of the 'New
Song' movement, Victor Jara. Their story is told in Jara's poem *Estadio
Chile* (Chile Stadium) and in the film *Missing* (Costa-Gavras, 1982). The
army rounded up university students and 'political' prisoners and took
them to the stadium. They broke the singer's hands, but not his spirit. He
sang for the others in the stadium, and shortly before machine guns
ended his life, Jara wrote and recited the poem:

> ... We are five thousand.
> I wonder how many we are in all
> In the cities and in the whole country
> ...
> They carry out their plans with knife-
> like precision.
> Nothing matters to them.
> ...
> How hard it is to sing
> When I must sing of horror
> Horror which I am living
> Horror which I am dying
> To see myself among so much
> and so many moments of infinity
> in which silence and screams
> are the end of my song.
> What I see I have never seen
> What I have felt and what I feel
> Will give birth to the moment ...
>   (Jara, 1973, English translation)

The poet and the journalist provide two windows onto a single story. In his account, Anthony Sampson unravels the tangled threads of international conspiracy. Even the explanation of how he became involved is surreal. He was invited to a strange and extravagant barbecue at a mansion in Brussels. Belgian waiters grilled steaks while corporate managers from around the world grilled each other.

> I was already interested in multinational corporations, and I had become specially curious about this conglomerate, with its astonishing jumble of world interests, from telephones to cosmetics ... I had been invited, as a solitary journalist, to attend this self-contained company function. (Sampson, 1973: 15)

There was much toasting and telling of jokes; the 'gathering was as emphatically masculine as a regiment or a football club ...' (Sampson, 1973: 18). One of the men told him the government should stop wasting time bothering about 'anti-trust' and support the corporations without question.

> As for these liberal newspapermen who attack big business, what do *they* know about making jobs? I interrupted him to say: 'Perhaps *I'm* a liberal newspaperman!' He looked at me in disbelief and roared with laughter ... We parted amicably, with mutual incomprehension. (Sampson, 1973: 18–19)

That was the start of a quest for knowledge and information. By the end of the book, we have learned how a company which, on the surface, merely provided jobs, products and services developed into a multinational octopus which captured innumerable governments and companies. In its insatiable quest for money and power, this company caused the deaths of thousands and the demise of democracy in Chile. Among the key players were the American CIA (Central Intelligence Agency) and government. Their hypocrisy was stunning: in the name of 'democracy', they killed a democratic leader and returned Chile to further decades of dictatorship. One of Sampson's most informative devices is a triple time-line of 'ITT's Wonder-Year, 1970–71'. He sets up events under three columns headed 'Chile', 'Anti-Trust' and 'San Diego'. The San Diego column ends with the decision to locate the Republican Party national convention in San Diego, at the Sheraton hotel owned by ITT. The Anti-Trust column ends with a decision in favour of allowing ITT to keep one of its companies. The Chile column ends in July 1971:

> (Sept 29) Allende appoints manager for ITT telephone company.
> (Oct 1) [ITT and government representatives produce] 18-point plan to bring down Allende.

The 'plan' worked. The world is still reeling from its effects. Thirty years after the assassinations and mass executions, Chile is witnessing a revival of interest in the plays, poems and songs of Victor Jara, produced and performed by the generation who survived him.

Truth is stranger than fiction is stranger than truth

Fact and fiction are interwoven in ways not often acknowledged. So-called works of fiction provide insights, not only into human behaviour and experience, but into factual storytelling and events. In Ian McEwan's novel *Amsterdam*, a news magazine editor discovers compromising photographs of a much hated politician cross-dressing – in potentially embarrassing postures but posing no harm to anyone. Much of the novel describes editorial meetings and discussions about whether to publish the photographs, and the results of that decision. There is an air of sanctimony about the meetings and in the thought process of Vernon, the editor.

> ... his sure hands were about to cut away a cancer from the ... body politic this was the image he intended to use in the leader that would follow Garmony's resignation. Hypocrisy would be exposed, the country would stay in Europe ... social welfare would survive ... the global environment would get a decent chance ... (McEwan, 1998: 111)

One of the questions McEwan implicitly asks is: does it matter whether the person who is exposed is 'good' or 'bad', loved or hated? We will revisit this in the discussion of *The Journalist and the Murderer* in Chapter 8. McEwan's resolution includes ironic twists and turns, and a moral warning. Thomas Keneally's novel *A Victim of the Aurora* describes a journalist's exploration of a scandalous British expedition to the South Pole.

> These days Victor would have been called a moral defective. He was charming ... he gave you the sense that you were the one person in a crooked world whom he respected ... It was just that he could see no reason not to sell you in the end. Betrayal was his medium ... (Keneally, 1977: 143)

As an avid reader of detective fiction, I have been surprised to discover how many of the writers started out as journalists, and how many detective novels feature media professionals and practices. On further thought, it makes perfect sense. As a journalist and researcher, I often refer to the 'thrill of the chase' in the research phase of a project.

Investigative journalism is detective work. Some detective novels offer insider glimpses into the journalist's world. Tony Hillerman's novel *The Fly on the Wall* (1971) (discussed in Chapter 2) is one of these. In *A Little Class on Murder*, Carolyn G. Hart spoofs and dissects journalists, universities, student newspapers, student journalists and university lecturers – and herself – via a character who lectures on women authors of detective fiction. A thinly disguised inquiry into media ethics, Hart's book considers questions of journalistic and academic responsibility in a case involving discovery of a guerilla warfare manual in a university library. The author's dedication of her book is another giveaway: to a professor 'who teaches the kind of journalism I believe in' (Hart, 1989: dedication page). Having long endured the pleasures and pitfalls of both journalistic and academic life, I finding it therapeutic to laugh and gasp at the intrigue, scandal and professional power-mongering in Hart's books. While being thoroughly entertaining, Hart manages to comment on the nastiness beneath the surface of 'respectable' academic life.

Elaine Viets writes a syndicated newspaper column and a detective series featuring her alter ego, the newspaper columnist Francesca Vierling. Among other things, she comments on inequalities in editorial decisions.

> Your paper will not print anything but bad news about our city schools, and we're tired of it. If your managing editor wants phone calls, he'll get them … We're sick of the rich kids in [the suburbs] … getting all the good stories, while our city kids are branded as hoodlums. (Viets, 2000: 19–20)

Viets offers a refreshing, if intolerant, critique of the fashionable US happy-talk craze for 'public journalism'. 'Its appeal to management was immediate: public journalism was cheap and noncontroversial. It was also shallow and stupid' (Viets, 2000: 42). In another novel, she takes on current fashions in media management – fashions, I might add, that are all too timely in challenging trends in managing all sorts of institutions, including British universities. In this scenario, part of the process of cutting the newspaper's precious budget involves allocating large sums of money to hiring jargon-happy consultants. In this case, 'Voyage Captain Jason' comes to (patronisingly and New Age-ishly) take the staff on a 'voyage' of discovery.

The only way to increase 'profit potential' is to reduce staff, 'first through attrition and then through agreements with the union', the 'captain' tells the newspaper staff.

He meant union-busting and forcing older employees into early retirement or, in the case of Monahan, early death ... 'And we will be bringing in a strong team of negotiators ... that specializes in negotiating pro-publisher newspaper contracts.' Translation: They break unions. (Viets, 1998: 188)

Having endured the consultant's 'voyage' the journalist sleuth, Francesca, speaks her mind. 'The publisher surrounded himself with yes-people. He needed to hear someone tell him what's really happening ... I was sure he'd want to fix it' (Viets, 1998: 190). She tells him there has never been a woman managing editor or department head, except in the 'female ghettos' of features and food. She challenges the publisher to learn more about readers' ages, and to realise (and remind advertisers) that middle-aged readers (whom he has abandoned for younger ones) have more buying power. She challenges him to find more creative – and profitable – ways to improve the financial picture than dismissing valuable staff. She also 'outs' one of the embarrassing secrets of the industry and university world.

'If Charlie [the editor] lost his job, no other newspaper would hire [him]. The best he could do was teach journalism at some godforsaken hole' (Viets, 1998: 209). Perhaps Viets went into novel-writing so she could comment on journalistic practice without fear of being fired. Having worked in media and academic institutions in three countries, I can attest to the truth of her observations in many cases and places. Journalism schools are often an uncomfortable mix of industry rejects, voluntary mid-career changers who enjoy research and teaching, and retired industry giants and treasures. Viets appears to have distilled the worst qualities of her most-hated editors into the fictional character of Charlie. Overall, her books offer a strong and thoughtful (if personalised) critique of media practice.

Another media critic-mystery writer is Carl Hiassen. Like Viets, he is a working journalist. His books are both funny and wickedly critical of media and environmental hypocrisy. Some of them describe the blurry line between journalism and public relations. *Native Tongue* is a (fictionalised) comic textbook of ethics in public relations and promotion. In it, a Florida theme park (one of the favourite targets of Hiassen's derision) develops an elaborate campaign to attract the public to one of its animal exhibits, masterminded by a career-minded publicist named Charles Chelsea. His writer is a disaffected journalist trying to make a better living (publicists almost always outearn journalists). The fictional Amazing Kingdom sets up an exhibit of endangered animals – two rare voles called Violet and Vance. When they are kidnapped, the whole project is threatened.

... all of us are on red alert ... We mishandle it, and it blows up into a story about crime at the Amazing Kingdom. If we can spin it around, it's a story about a crime against Nature ... The annihilation of an entire species. (Hiassen, 1991: 16)

As in most Hiassen novels, nothing is as it seems.

Like everything else at the Amazing Kingdom, the Vole Project had begun as a scheme to compete with Walt Disney World. Years earlier, Disney had tried to save the dusky seaside sparrow, a small marsh bird whose habitat was being wiped out by overdevelopment ... With much fanfare, Disney had unveiled a captive-breeding program for the last two surviving specimens ... Unfortunately, [they] were both males ... (Hiassen, 1991: 21)

Although the project was doomed and the sparrow became extinct, the Disney spin doctors managed to gain positive publicity for their organisation's 'conservation efforts'. Eventually journalist Joe Winder's investigative instincts take over, the bad guys get their come-uppance and, many laughs later, Winder redeems himself and a tiny corner of the world is saved.

By writing as a detective novelist instead of as a journalist or historian, the former reporter and editor Nancy Pickard is able to bring important concerns to different audiences. Her novel *The Truth Hurts* challenges tabloid journalism and journalism–government relations. At the same time, she provides an incisive and timely portrait of government and vigilante intimidation in the early days of the US Civil Rights movement. From the moment when writer-protagonist Marie Lightfoot sees her face in a supermarket tabloid with the headline: 'Best-Selling Author Hides Her Racist Past', she is plunged into a series of life-threatening events. The tabloid reveals none of its 'sources' but offers 'Cash for Tips!' and takes care that its accusations are 'ambiguously close enough to a truth' to be un-actionable. The more serious effects are not the legal ones.

... did they just make this up, assuming they could link it to some kind of truth? It hardly matters now. If there's damage, it's been done. Maybe the worst of it is how they've trivialized my life ... Why didn't these people have the decency to call me first? (Pickard, 2002: 21)

In a novel-within-a-novel, 'true crime writer' Marie Lightfoot investigates her past, returning to events of 1963. The US government under President John F. Kennedy announced initiatives to integrate the University of Alabama and work to end racial segregation across the US.

Kennedy branded civil rights a moral issue ... Enraged by the speech, a bigot in Mississippi hopped into his car and raced through the dark streets to assassinate the black civil rights leader Medgar Evers in his driveway. Evers's wife and children were in their living room, having just watched the president's speech, when they heard the gunshots that killed their husband and father. (Pickard, 2002: 39)

Pickard positions herself clearly in Marie Lightfoot's story by dedicating the book 'with awe and respect, to all of the known and unknown heroes of civil rights movements everywhere' (Pickard, 2002: dedication page). In her own way, Nancy Pickard is carrying on the tradition of muckraking and media criticism, and calling for a responsible and ethical media practice.

Exercises

3.1 Lies, truths, and information control

Using examples from current newspapers and events discuss the following (or organise a classroom debate, pro and con):

1. 'Journalists do not have special privileges or rights ...' (Russell, 1996: 35).
2. '[Journalists] need flexibility and occasionally must break the rules' (Russell, 1996: 35).

3.2 Detecting media ethics

Read any of the detective novels mentioned, or other relevant works by these writers or others (e.g. Sue Grafton, Sara Paretsky). Outline the ethical issues raised and discuss them. How might these issues and their treatment inform guidelines for an ethical media practice?

Further reading

Bok, Sissela (1978) *Lying: Moral Choices in Public and Private Life*. New York: Pantheon.

Russell, Nicholas (1996) 'Lies, damned lies and journalism', in Valerie Alia, Brian Brennan and Barry Hoffmaster (eds), *Deadlines and Diversity: Journalism Ethics in a Changing World*. Halifax: Fernwood, pp. 30–9.

Sampson, Anthony (1973) *The Sovereign State*. London: Hodder Fawcett.

Also novels by Sue Grafton, Tony Hillerman, Carolyn Hart, Carl

Hiassen, Thomas Keneally, Sara Paretsky, Nancy Pickard, Elaine Viets and others concerned with media practitioners and practice.

Suggested viewing

For details see the annotated filmography in Appendix B at the end of the book.

Missing
The China Syndrome
The Day the Earth Caught Fire
Hearts and Minds

Suggested listening

CD

Manifiesto (Victor Jara: Chile, September 1973)

4 The ethics of accuracy and inclusion: reflecting and respecting diversity

A recent issue of my local newspaper carries a splashy new 'lifestyle' supplement. At its centre is a two-page, full-colour, lavishly photographed spread headlined, 'Celebrating the Difference'. With the city experiencing bouts of harassment, assault and generalised intolerance of cultural difference, I was thrilled to see the paper offering readers some positive intercultural coverage. Or so I thought. On closer inspection, I saw … seven sweet-looking, pale-faced girls, all but one of them blonde. I doubt that the editor meant to make a 'racial' statement with the cutely punning captions ('Sari, sari night', 'Bolly good show', and so on). But like her companions, the girl whose photograph is captioned 'ALL WHITE HERE' is indeed 'all white'. So where's the 'difference'? It's all in the subheading: 'Bollywood comes to South Hylton'. The girls are playing *dress-up*.

The story contains information about a special programme at a local primary school in which members of Indian and other cultural communities have brought their music, food, clothes and art to the school. But where are those people's children? Certainly, not in the photographs or the clothes. The writer called it 'a true taste of India' and gushed: 'The girls felt like little princesses as they dressed in silks …' (Colling, 2003: 6). There were clearly well-intentioned thoughts behind the week-long celebration. But there is no hint of dialogue between students of different ethnic backgrounds. The 'all white here' girl – and the editor – appear not to know that in India white is generally a funereal colour. Nobody seems aware that girls from India and Indo-British communities are not all 'little princesses'. Or that our city is home to significant numbers of people with variously hued hair and skin. Here is a prime example of a missed opportunity for the media to truly celebrate difference and promote intercultural tolerance and understanding.

The principle of inclusivity is an essential requirement of any ethical media practice. There are two essential aspects of inclusivity which concern us here – media participation and media representation.

Participation refers to the people who create and maintain writers, editors, broadcasters, film-makers, artists, technician managers. Ideally, an ethical media practice would include equa ticipation by women and men at every level of an organisation, and participation roughly proportional to their numbers in the general population of members of all minority groups. These groups would be represented in the media in appropriate proportions, with appropriate respect and treatment equivalent to that of the majority population. I don't have to tell you that we have not yet reached this ideal world.

Women and children ... first?

Just in case you thought women had become media equals in Britain, Catherine MacLeod, political editor of the *Herald*, explains how it works in the parliamentary gallery. 'Women at Westminster are already up against it in the promotion stakes'; they must also endure male colleagues' sexist and homophobic comments. According to *Daily Mirror* columnist Paul Routledge (whom she quotes), some male parliamentary journalists call their female colleagues 'the lezzie lobby'. Some male colleagues are genuinely friendly, she writes, 'but it's not enough.'

> [To] advance real change, the newspaper editors and broadcasting managements need to take an interest. Nearly 20% of the 200 journalists at Westminster now are women, and I suppose that should be applauded, but surely it is reprehensible that the bosses have failed miserably to achieve any notion of gender balance among their parliamentary reporters.
>
> Most national newspapers include one woman on their parliamentary team. Few employ more than one, and the others [are] male-only ... Not one London-based daily paper has a woman political editor, and in the entire parliamentary gallery there are only three: the *Sunday Express* (my newspaper), the (Glasgow) *Herald*, and the *Western Mail*.
>
> Broadcasting is no better ... While Elinor Goodman, the political editor of *Channel 4 News*, breached the male preserve of political editors years ago, Martha Kearney of *Newsnight* followed only last year. (MacLeod, 2003: 8)

When the media refer to children, it is generally in relation to their victimisation (rape, murder, abuse), their cuteness (photographed for food, holiday or fashion features), their secondary role as children of ... (mothers, fathers, doctors and scientists creating 'designer babies' or saving lives). They are seldom portrayed as newsmakers and agents in their own right. A delightful exception is a story in *The Independent* given top-of-page prominence. Headlined 'Children who set up art studio win £200,000 Lottery grant', it describes students in a Scottish primary school who created a studio for artistic production and intellectual reflection. The children at Caol Primary School in Fort William

> elect their own leaders, keep the accounts and appoint the artist in residence. The project's managing director, Denielle Souness, aged 11, said that pupils believed the expression of their individuality was 'essential to the wealth and health of the wider community'. (Beard, 2003: 8)

It is notable that the school's head teacher and other adults are quoted only secondarily, and that the children's faces and voices dominate and receive full credibility and authority. The story is accompanied by an attractive full-colour illustration with a caption identifying the girl in the photograph as 'Lindsay Martin, one of the artists from Caol Primary School …' Not 'one of the children' or 'one of the child artists' but 'one of the artists …' Here is an example of appropriate and laudable choices by the writer, the photographer, the cutline (caption) writer and the headline writer.

Seeking asylum (from the press?)

In representing different people and groups, the media progress and regress – sometimes in equal measure, and sometimes within the same outlet and time-frame. In late May 2003, *The Independent* devoted its front page and most of an inside page to educating readers about the experience of asylum seekers and minorities in Britain. It was headlined, 'Asylum. The facts (or why you shouldn't believe everything you are told by the Government, the Tories, and the right-wing press)'. Attempting to set the record straight, it included such information as, 'According to an opinion poll … the public believes that the UK hosts about 23 per cent of the world's refugees, although the real figure is 1.98 per cent' (*The Independent*, 23 May 2003: 1). To increase the impact on readers, the paper printed the misinformation in small black type and the correct information in large red type. Clearly, the editors' objective was to increase public awareness and understanding. Yet just two weeks later, *The Independent* repeated one of the major offences of a racist press by including irrelevant, culturally identifying information in the headline of a story about violence in London.

'Tamil beat man to death through "sheer cruelty"', the headline reads (Clarke, 2003: 8). It could have appeared in any of several tabloids instead of this generally literate, left-of-centre paper. The story concerns ongoing conflict and killings among different gangs of people who appear to be British citizens of Sri Lankan ancestry. I say 'appear to be' because the story never makes it clear whether they are asylum seekers, recent immigrants or long-time citizens. We are told what part of London the perpetrators and victims came from and what court they attended (the Old Bailey) but not the historical and social context in which the actions took place. By emphasising ethnicity and brutality over clarity, the reporter gives readers too little information to understand what has taken place. To compound the problems, the editor approved and sent the article to press without correcting the problems in either the headline or the report. There is space on the page for further information, but the editor has chosen to print a mug-shot-style photograph of the convicted man, underscoring the racist presentation of the story. The photograph has neither news value nor artistic merit and could easily have been omitted.

Such treatment runs counter to the paper's own efforts to challenge racism in the press. It demonises people as 'Tamil' and 'Sri Lankans' as people who beat people to death 'through "sheer cruelty"', representing an entire civilisation as cruel and a community of British citizens (or refugees) as barbaric outsiders. This is the first story I have seen in at least a year about Tamil or Sri Lankan people. I cannot recall having read any stories about Britons of Sri Lankan origin. How am I to understand one horrible episode in the context of an entire cultural community that remains invisible to the broader public? The media have great responsibility here – not only for correcting misinformation, fact by fact, but for placing each story in context and making sure the headline accurately and fairly represents the story.

The 11.15 p.m. ITV news broadcast on 4 October 2002 described the Queen's annual visit to Canada. With a mix of misinformation and half-truths, the audience was shown pictures of 'Baffin Island', where Her Majesty 'was greeted by some of the local Inuit Indians'. Baffin Island is Canada's largest island, the size of many a small country. Its main community is Iqaluit, which – since it has the only real airport – is probably where the Queen landed. Since 1999, Iqaluit has been the capital of Nunavut – a Canadian territory similar to the provinces. Nunavut (which the report did not even mention) covers nearly two million square kilometres – about one-fifth of Canada.

There was a second and far worse blunder: there is no such thing as 'Inuit Indians'. Inuit are people whom outsiders used to call 'Eskimos'. In Canada and the US, some non-Inuit indigenous people are called 'Indians' – an error dating back to Columbus's arrival in 1492, when he thought he had found India. Those people – who are entirely unrelated to Inuit – are variously referred to as Native Americans, First Nations, indigenous or Aboriginal people, or by one of the hundreds of culturally specific names such as Ojibway, Cree, Tlingit, Lakota, Cherokee. Except for an occasional immigrant to the region, none of these 'Indian' people live in Nunavut. 'Inuit Indians' is something the writer made up and the editor failed to correct.

A 2003 science article in *The Independent* refers to 'Inuits' – the equivalent of referring to male residents of England as 'Englishmans' (Burne, 2003: 8). Any reader would consider 'Englishmans' absurd; any editor would correct the error. In the case of 'Inuit' (which is the correct plural form – the singular being 'Inuk') the editors, like countless others, missed the error. There is a tendency to assume that all such errors appear in the tabloid press. Sometimes the broadsheets are even worse because readers take their greater accuracy and integrity for granted.

The situation is further complicated by the fact that even when conscientious writers and editors think they are doing their homework, the sources they consider authoritative are themselves providers of misinformation. The venerable *Oxford Dictionary for Writers and Editors* declares Inuit to be 'Canadian Native American people', their language 'Inupiaq', 'Inuk' to mean '(a member of) a Canadian or Greenland Native American people …' and 'Iñupiat … (a member of) an Alaskan Native American people, or the language of this people' (Ritter, 2000: 172). The *Oxford English Reference Dictionary* defines 'Inuit' (which is in fact a plural!) as 'an Inupiaq-speaking Eskimo, esp. in Canada' (Pearsall and Trumble, 1996: 739). The *Oxford Colour Spelling Dictionary* informs us that the plural of 'Inuit' (remember, this is only a plural form) is 'Inuit *or* Inuits' and the plural of 'Inuk' (a singular form!) is 'Inuk *or* Inuks' (Waite, 1996: 277).

Let us unpick the inaccuracies in this maddening mess. Most Iñupiaq-speakers live in Alaska and Siberia. 'Inuit' cannot refer to 'an' anybody because it is a plural. 'Native American' refers to indigenous people of the United States, sometimes including Iñupiat and Yup'ik Eskimo (Inuit) of Alaska but not including people from Canada. Inuit live mainly in Arctic and subarctic Canada, Alaska, Greenland and Siberia. Iñupiat constitute only one of the Inuit subcultures; Yup'ik are also Inuit and have their own language. Inuvialuit are Inuit who live in the western Canadian Arctic. The generic for the language is *Inuktitut*, though there are several related languages. I have heard Inuit jokingly or ironically call themselves 'Inuks', when speaking in English to *Qallunaat* (non-Inuit people), anglicising the pural – as when Deborah Evaluardjuk expressed resistance to assimilation by saying: 'We were not going to be turned into white Inuks' (Alia, 1995). But there is no such thing as this plural in the

Inuktitut language. And no Inuit, even jokingly, call themselves 'Inuits'. That is an invention of the British 'scholars' who misinformed Oxford's publications – and consequently much of the media public.

It appears that nobody in the chain of editorial responsibility bothered to check proper usage with Inuit themselves. Here is one instance in which the research results are more accurate on the Internet than in reference works. A quick computer search reveals several websites with accurate information on proper usage, including those representing Inuit organisations easily contacted to check that information. One of the clearest explanations appears on the website of the University of Oregon Yamada Language Center:

People
(Singular:) … inuk … Note: The term 'Eskimo' is no longer used
(Plural:) … inuit … Note: The term 'Inuits' does not exist
(Yamada, 2003)

You may think this is a big fuss about a small issue. But it reflects a kind of carelessness that, however unintentional, borders on racism. Such mistakes are made about minority people in faraway places. A reporter assigned to cover a story in an unfamiliar place is supposed to research the facts and the place. Can you imagine a newscast from Newcastle Airport saying: 'The Queen visited Tyne and Wear and was greeted by some of the local English Italians'? How silly! Everybody knows Italians come from Italy and natives of Newcastle-upon-Tyne are English (or British, or Geordie). We need to avoid such double standards. Journalists must do their homework regardless of where they are and who they are reporting about. Anything less is insulting, not only to the people concerned but to the news organisation and media consumers.

Media depictions of the Arctic are steeped in the language of conquest and colonisation. Despite centuries of change and decades of progress, that language persists. Explorers are depicted as quasi-military conquerors who launched 'assaults' on the Pole. Indigenous people are seen as aiding in those assaults and increasing the comforts of the conquerors, ignored, or treated as exotic items for study or observation, in need of 'civilisation'. In 1991 *The Daily Telegraph* sent a team for a brief visit to Holman Island and published a photo-essay in its magazine supplement that infuriated members of the Holman (Uluqsaqtuuq) community and many others. Headlined 'Dressed to Kill: Hunting with the Eskimos of Holman Island', it presented a distorted and racist picture. In a letter to the editor which *The Telegraph* declined to publish, Holman Mayor Gary Bristow, Holman Community Corporation Chairman Robert Kuptana and anthropologist Richard Condon wrote:

thousands of … readers have had their opinions and attitudes about the Canadian Arctic falsely influenced by individuals with no understanding of even the most basic aspects of Canadian Inuit culture … (Condon, 1992; Bristow, Kuptana and Condon, 1992)

Among the most 'grotesque' of *The Telegraph*'s errors:

'Among hunters there is no code of honour,' the article proclaims … apparently measuring Inuit hunting against aristocratic English fox hunts. 'The hunter … is merciless and self-interested, gathering food only for himself and his family' … The unsuccessful hunter and his family could go hungry only steps away from someone else's well-stocked tent. (Thompson, 1992: A3)

The Holman writers explained the Inuit food-sharing system, which *The Telegraph* did not take the trouble to research. The writer told of 'Eskimos' who eat 'boiled duck and grease soup flavoured with feathers'. Duck soup does not contain feathers – unless one accidentally falls in. The remark about 'grease' is gratuitous – it could as easily be said of Yorkshire pudding. The *Telegraph* writers presented a portrait of fictional, 'wild' indigenous people much like the 'wild Indians' of the fashion catalogue described below. Even the efforts to place Inuit in the current century were misleading. Readers were told that Inuit track caribou by satellite.

Perhaps the author is of the opinion that each snowmobile includes a satellite dish and computer screen? … wildlife biologists … track the wanderings of caribou on Victoria Island, making use of satellite technology. This technology is *not* used by Holman hunters … (Bristow, Kuptana and Condon, 1992)

The community was further offended at the publication of 'quaint photographs' of unnamed community members. The newspaper would never publish photographs of British people without identifying them. Yet two of Holman's most respected elders, Jimmy and Nora Memogama, were presented with no identification. Some of the errors were amusing, but should have led to the sacking of the writer and the editor who sent the story to press. 'All of us in Holman were amused to hear about the community's 'richest villager' who … decided to order a steam roller … one does not purchase a steamroller to make gravel roads in the Arctic'.

Most amusing of all is the story, repeated to *Telegraph* readers, of a 'young white man who stepped off a train to stretch his legs; his frozen body was discovered the following spring' (*The Telegraph Magazine*,

1991). It is possible that, realising his ignorance and gullibility, someone had a joke at the journalist's expense. No one has ever stepped off a train at Holman. The nearest railhead is more than a thousand miles away, near the Alberta border. 'Perhaps, in the author's imagination, this is the same train which brought the steam roller and the satellite equipment for hunting caribou?' (Bristow, Kuptana and Condon, 1992).

I tell this story often, and it always gets a laugh. Judging from its continuing errors, *The Telegraph* still doesn't get it. The photo-essay is not just an amusing example of journalistic ignorance. It is

> representative of a disturbing trend in journalistic coverage of the North ... Each year ... Holman is visited by journalists who desire to write or photograph the definitive article about an isolated Inuit community ... the community has no way to ... monitor or comment upon their finished works ... [the] worst harm is not the offence they give to northern residents but the distorted view they present to thousands of readers about northern life and northern people. In an age when Inuit culture is being attacked by numerous animal rights groups, articles like 'Dressed to Kill' ... perpetuate prejudice. (Bristow, Kuptana and Condon, 1992)

Worse even than the writers' attempts to exoticise and demonise Inuit is the fact that the newspaper's editors chose a headline which exaggerated the story's worst offences, made no apparent effort to check the facts, and then refused to publish the letter from Holman community members correcting the errors. Such treatment suggests a deplorable absence of ethical standards at one of Britain's major national newspapers.

Changing media, changing voices

The inadequacy of mainstream media has led minority groups to develop their own news outlets. They are using satellite, digital, cable and the Internet to strengthen their culturally and linguistically diverse voices and disseminate information to a rapidly expanding global audience. Ien Ang describes the 'progressive transnationalization of media audiencehood' (Ang, 1996: 81). However, I think 'transnational-isation' is too limited a term because it implies a one-way crossing of national boundaries. I have extended it to refer to a fluid movement in which people and media keep crossing from boundary to boundary and place to place. In my work on indigenous media, I have called this *inter*-nationalisation of *indigenous* media audiencehood and media production the New Media Nation (Alia, 2003: 36).

Indigenous people have centuries of media problems to correct. In the early twentieth century, advertisements and films were filled with images of 'Indian princesses' and other imaginary people. 'Indian' is a term used to sell things – souvenirs ... cigarettes ... cars ... movies ... books. 'Indian' is a figment of the white man's imagination, says the Ojibway storyteller and writer, Lenore Keeshig-Tobias (1990). The woman known as Sakajawea or Sakakawea, an Hidatsa word meaning 'bird woman', inspired a 1920s cleaning and dyeing advertisement of an '"ageless" and shapely Indian princess with perfect Caucasian features, dressed in a tight-fitting red tunic, spearing fish with a bow and arrow from a birch bark canoe suspended on a mountain-rimmed, moonlit lake'. Another indigenous damsel promoted Chippewa's Pride Beer (Valaskakis, 1995: 11).

Consider whether things have improved, in the twenty-first century. In 2002, an ash-blond boy in a generic headdress promotes a Japanese car with 'ample space for *braves* and *big chiefs ... young Hiawatha ...* needn't leave *his headdress* behind, which could avoid some ruffled *feathers*'. The puns suggest fun, presumably at no one's expense (Suzuki, 2002). A Swedish designer tells readers of her spring 2003 catalogue that her collection was inspired by 'wild, colourful Native Americans'.

> Squaw, Pawnee & a little Kickapoo. Sometimes you just feel like doing something wild ... my rebellious artistic soul ... loves the unexpected and surprising ... And so the Native American theme was born ... It's so exciting, don't you think? Yee-haa!

Fake 'Indian' feathers are combined with fringes, beads and geometric patterns. The text (in the designer's own voice) and footnotes give the work an academic air. The multilayered misinformation is difficult to disentangle. 'Red Indians prefer to be called "Native Americans" ...'; 'Chippewa' is 'The highest leader (Chief) in the Algonquian tribe'; 'Squaw' is 'A Native American woman'. A blonde model with feathers in her hair, identified as 'Squaw Hanna', 'dances wild in a native American-inspired tunic ... and pretty ikat-weave silk scarf ...'. But ikat is an *Indonesian* weaving technique, and 'squaw' is a term many Native American and other indigenous people have long considered offensive (Sjöden, 2003).

Ironically, the designer is a descendant of Sámi people and her catalogues are more generally notable for their inclusivity. They are among the few fashion catalogues to regularly feature models of all colours, shapes, heights and ages.

Such images and texts are being challenged – not only through letters to the editor and efforts to improve mainstream media coverage.

Increasingly, people are taking portrayals of their communities into their own hands. There is a strong and growing international body of indigenous films and an international network – the First Nations Film and Video World Alliance – with members from Canada, Vanuatu, Mexico, the United States, Greenland, Australia, New Zealand and the Solomon Islands (First Nations Film and Video World Alliance, 1993). In 1991 the world's largest aboriginal television network was born. Television Northern Canada (TVNC) broadcast in English, French and several indigenous languages, via satellite, to an audience of approximately one hundred thousand. In 1999, it expanded to become a national television service – the Aboriginal Peoples Television Network (APTN). Indigenous and other minority people are working in Australia, New Zealand, Greenland, Sweden, Norway, Finland and other countries to develop similar networks and expand existing print, broadcast and new media services.

Taking steps: initiatives to improve inclusivity and diversity

For years, I kept hearing that 'white' journalists were afraid to go into indigenous communities to research stories first-hand, a fear derived from stereotypes that were often perpetuated by the news media themselves. While living in the Yukon I was repeatedly warned not to go into First Nations communities. Yet my experiences in these communities were crucial to the accurate understanding of people and issues. Frustrated by the inaccuracies and misunderstandings, Bud White Eye (a journalist from the Moraviantown Delaware First Nation in Ontario) and I organised an annual programme to bring university journalism students and members of First Nations together. We designed a one-day immersion experience that introduced future journalists to the history of Canadian first peoples, to some of the current issues they might end up covering, and to the diversity of indigenous languages, cultures and concerns. We chose speakers from several cultures, communities and professions.

Many students said they had never met any indigenous people before. They expressed surprise at the 'friendly', 'fair' and 'open' exchange and the widely divergent points of view, saying they had been led to believe (by journalists, among others!) that any dialogue with First Nations people would be driven by specific (and predictable) political agendas. Later, at Western Washington University, I worked with Pete Steffens, who had developed an outreach programme and several collaborative projects with minority journalists, educators and community leaders. The objective was to improve media coverage and public awareness, and recruit Native American and other minority students and faculty. In Canada the Nation of Immigrants Project, aimed to develop diversity training resources and improve diversity in news media. 'We have to be trustworthy to gain trust', said broadcaster and co-founder of the multi-cultural, multi-faith Vision TV, Rita Shelton Deverell (Deverell, 1996: 68–9).

The Canadian government guidelines provide a good starting point for media practitioners. Here are some of the key points:

> Words, images and situations are the tools of journalists. In our coverage of ... events, issues and personalities, it is very   important that we do not reinforce erroneous preconceptions or suggest that all or most members of a racial/ethnic group or nation-state are the same.

> VISUALS
> [Visible minorities should be seen] at all levels in a broad range of occupations ... in pursuit of a wide range of interests, sports and hobbies ... portrayed as equally capable, resourceful, self-confident, intelligent, imaginative and independent ... as both observers and participants in mainstream cultural events ... as well as in festivities focusing on multiculturalism per se ...

> LANGUAGE
> Avoid words which cloud the fact that all attributes may be found in all groups and individuals. Avoid qualifiers that reinforce racial and ethnic stereotypes. A qualifier is added information that suggests an exception to the rule. [Watch for] language [with] questionable racial or ethnic connotations ... Be aware of the self-identification preferences of racial and cultural groups, e.g. 'Inuit' is preferable to 'Eskimo'. [Actors, interviewers and interviewees should not be excluded from being hired] because of an accent, so long as the message can be understood. [Avoid using] accents which may reinforce stereotypes ... Use gender-neutral words [wherever possible]. (Roth, 1996: 85–6)

To check a story's fairness, I suggest applying what I call the 'test of parallels'. If the story concerns a woman, try substituting a man. 'Female lawyer wins case' is not acceptable unless we would also use the headline, 'Male lawyer wins case'. 'Tamil beat man to death' is not acceptable unless the newspaper would also print the headline, 'Anglo-Celtic' or 'White Englishman beat man to death ...'

These techniques for combating ethnocentrism are essential. But improving media representation is only half the battle. The other half concerns the participation of people from the broadest spectrum of society as media practitioners. People with disabilities, people of many colours and cultural origins from various minority communities, women and men of various ages and sexual preferences, should be hired to present the news, create, edit and produce the programmes, head the newspapers, magazines, advertising and public relations agencies, film companies, and radio and television stations. They should not be ghettoised. As Rita Shelton Deverell said, some people of colour may choose to focus on issues relating to people of colour or minority communities, while others have entirely different areas of expertise. Because Deverell's expertise is in the arts, much of the programming she produced for Vision TV was arts-related. The fact that she is a woman of African-American descent does not make her an expert on women, African-Americans or African-American women.

Case study: A conflict of interest

A US newspaper editor made a controversial decision to participate in the 1995 'Million Man March' on Washington, DC. Some of his colleagues said this would suggest alignment with Nation of Islam leader Louis Farrakhan's anti-Jewish and racist views. The editor defended his decision by saying his participation was personal, not political. I do not consider journalism inherently neutral or journalists value-free receptacles of information. I believe deeply in fairness and accuracy in reporting and editing and in the public's right to get the broadest possible picture of an event. In writing my opinion of this case for an Associated Press study, I consulted the *Statement of Principles* Dan Smoke and I had written for Native News Network of Canada (see Appendix D). As I see it, the editor had the right to attend the event as a citizen acting from personal convictions and conscience. However, he was obligated to make certain that his participation did not affect the content, slant or overall coverage by his news organisation of that or other events. He was obligated to disclose his involvement in the march to his employer and the public, and to remove himself from any professional task which might involve a conflict of interest.

I do not think such participation constitutes commitment by the news organisation to a particular perspective, event, politics or movement. Journalists are people. In their daily lives, people make many judgements – some public, some private – and have many preferences, most of which are never revealed to their employers. Despite those convictions, I was deeply concerned about the

Million Man March's link to Louis Farrakhan, many of whose views and statements I find intolerant and intolerable. However, many men of conscience, from all walks of life, attended the march and I believe they were fully within their rights to do so. (Alia, 1997: 1, 12)

What can individuals do?

No matter how determined, an individual in a large media organisation has limited opportunities to affect policies, broadcasts and publications. Nevertheless, there are many ways to affect and effect change. Each of us must decide what we can do in our everyday work and lives, and how and when we might take on bigger challenges to structures and systems. My own career has bridged journalism and academe. As a journalist, I found numerous small opportunities to write about diversity, sometimes in small and relatively inoffensive ways, sometimes in more challenging and risky ways. I found opinion columns especially appealing. Below are excerpts from two of the columns.

The powwow is more than just a carnival of color

… [The London, Canada], Free Press coverage of the heritage celebration was full of respect and detail. Yet like so many other powwow stories, in so many other newspapers, it focused on 'contests' and omitted the spirituality at the core of the celebration.

I wonder how Christian readers would feel if news media treated the music, art and soul of church services as pop-culture entertainment …

At a powwow, people are asked to stand for the Grand Entry 'in respect for the Creator and this sacred way of life.' They may record the Grand Entry, the honor dances, or the accidental falling of an eagle feather 'only with eyes, ears and heart.' People must respect the sacred fire (which burns throughout a celebration) and the medicines of sweetgrass, cedar, tobacco and sage used by different peoples. A sunrise ceremony welcomes each day …

… While no news story can fully capture an event, accuracy requires that we research the cultural context. … (Alia, 1991: A7)

The following piece was an attempt at a more subtle way of countering racism. This was a (non-kosher) cafe in a predominantly Jewish Toronto neighbourhood. When a Vietnamese immigrant took over its management, there were whisperings and wonderings. How would she keep the (albeit secular) flavour of the original place? How would she relate to the customers, many of whom had been coming here for years? Would she 'fit in'? I was looking for a way to demonstrate the possibilities of fostering tolerance and understanding and the social impact of maintaining small businesses, while expressing a very personal appreciation of the proprietor and the place.

A restaurant with a franchise on kindness

By Valerie Alia

This is a going-away present to someone I barely know, yet count among family. It is at once a celebration and a lament. In hard times, there are many quiet casualties; this is about one of them.

On Eglinton Avenue West, you can still find a handful of staunch holdouts against the creeping glitz-and-pretension that threatens to overwhelm the neighbourhood. One of the holdouts is a tiny restaurant called Bagel Paradise. It sits on an unobtrusive corner, its wide windows overlooking a collage of pedestrian and automotive traffic, architectural turbulence and stasis.

Although food is its business, it is far more than a place to eat. For me, this place – and other small businesses like it – has come to mean community. And community is crucial to the continuing life of a city ...

I wrote much of my [doctoral] dissertation and major chunks of a couple of books in Bagel Paradise, finding respite from the challenges of single-parenthood in the quiet off-hours when I could command a double table and settle in, without harming business.

My sons grew many years and inches here ...

Today in North America, the small, personal, family-run business has not yet died. But as scholars have said in more abstract ways, it is an increasingly endangered species. Places like Bagel Paradise are small treasures in a world of depersonalization and replication. You can franchise to your heart's content ... guarantee identically shaped and flavoured meals, served up in lookalike locations across the continent. You can't franchise kindness.

It may be that the restaurant will outlive its proprietor's lease.

Perhaps it will continue to offer solid meals, reasonable prices, wildly imaginative milkshakes and Toronto's sweetest carrot juice. It won't have Wan Lam Ha's special warmth, her smile that kept us going through some of the hardest winters. It won't have someone who, after my six-year absence from Toronto, remembers not just my face, but precisely what I like for breakfast.

Until she said she was leaving, I didn't realize how much this meant. Gently, carefully, we had spoken (as caring strangers do) of difficulties and improvements, pleasures and privations. I remember when she arrived, a newcomer to an old business in a rather insular neighbourhood. I admired the courage and staying power it must have taken to enter a new neighbourhood and find, and give, welcome.

In two weeks she will go ... Today, it is business both usual and unusual. Friends are gathered in a corner, sharing animated talk and breakfast. Newcomers and regulars arrive. Babies are coddled and admired. Grandparents dote on toddlers, young adults dote on grandparents. A man sits in the middle of the room, oblivious to everything but his newspaper. Several women take over a large table ... Patiently, Wan Lam Ha takes and retakes their swiftly shifting orders and remembers (as I can't) the final version. Remembers, too, to wish them a pleasant meal.

It is winter. The wind lashes and howls around the windows ... As always, it feels like sanctuary – cheerful yellow walls and a tolerance for difference. Loud or quiet, solo or ensemble, denim or silk, you are welcome. I think of the place as sunshine. In her next venture, I wish Wan Lam Ha much sunshine. (Alia, 1995: A20)

Exercises

4.1 Case study: A conflict of interest

A newspaper editor has decided to attend a public demonstration opposing Britain's involvement in the conflict with Iraq. The demonstration takes place on a day when the editor is not at work. The editor has told her employer of her intent, and has explained that she is attending the event on a non-work day, as a private citizen, and will in no way identify herself as a member of the news organisation.

Discuss this decision in class, or in a debate, considering the ethical implications of the editor's decision. For one opinion on such actions, see the case study *A conflict of interest* above.

4.2 Group discussion

As a group, or in small-group discussions, examine some current media representations of women and minorities. Discuss the problems, and outline a plan for improving diversity, fair and accurate representation and participation in the media.

Further reading

Alia, Valerie (2003) 'Scattered voices, global vision', in K. H. Karim (ed.), *The Media of Diaspora*. London: Routledge.

Alia, Valerie (1999) *Un/Covering the North*. Vancouver: UBC Press.

Deverell, Rita Shelton (1996) 'On subjectivity', in Valerie Alia, Brian Brennan and Barry Hoffmaster (eds), *Deadlines and Diversity*. Halifax, NS: Fernwood, pp. 59–71.

Hall, Stuart (1980) 'Race, articulation and societies structured in dominance', in *Sociological Theories: Race and Colonialism*. Paris: UNESCO, pp. 305–45, at 339.

Roth, Lorna (1996) 'Cultural and racial diversity in Canadian broadcast journalism', Valerie Alia, Brian Brennan and Barry Hoffmaster (eds), *Deadlines and Diversity*. Halifax, NS: Fernwood, pp. 72–91.

White Eye, Bud (1996) 'Journalism and First Nations', in Valerie Alia, Brian Brennan and Barry Hoffmaster (eds), *Deadlines and Diversity*. Halifax, NS: Fernwood, pp. 92–7.

Suggested viewing

For details see the annotated filmography in Appendix B at the end of the book.

Gentleman's Agreement
A Bell for Adano
A Cry in the Dark
Lakota Woman
Skokie

5 The empire strikes forward: internationalisation of the media

> We are beginning to learn that de-colonisation was not the termination of imperial relationships but merely the extending of a geopolitical web which has been spinning since the Renaissance. The new media have the power to penetrate more deeply into a 'receiving' culture than any previous manifestation of Western technology ... (Said, 1994: 353)

> Who or what, exactly, is a foreigner? Annoyingly to the Brits, only non-British people are likely to ask this question. The English, you see, believe that they know the answer instinctively, feel it in their bones. (Shah, 2000: 3)

In his challenging and irreverent *The Englishman's Handbook*, Idries Shah – a humourist and also a leading interpreter of Sufism to the West – dissects British identity and discovers all manner of travels and ethnicities, domestic and foreign. The very word, 'foreigner', is derived from the French and probably arrived with the Norman invasion. Shah also offers instructive observations on the cross-cultural experiences of media practitioners.

> I vividly recall my daughter Saira, born and brought up in England, returning to culture-shock in Britain. She had been with the *Mujahidin* warriors inside Afghanistan under Soviet rule, and in the Afghan refugee camps.
> 'The thing about there,' she said, despairing at some seemingly intractable delay, 'is that there you can't get much done without a tip or bribe. But it gets done. Here they won't take bribes, but they won't do it, either!' (Shah, 2000: 48)

In 2001 Saira Shah returned to the family's native Afghanistan, under cover, to make a remarkable television documentary, *Inside Afghanistan: Behind the Veil*, about the Taliban's treatment of women. This time, she experienced not only culture shock but media shock. When her crew were told they could only film inanimate objects, they decided to go under cover. They were helped by the Revolutionary Association of Women of Afghanistan (RAWA), a women's movement that runs secret schools for girls. Faced with total cover-up in the *burqa* or inability to film, she wore the garment – and found herself crossing not just a cultural but a journalistic line. 'I suddenly wasn't an objective reporter anymore; I was someone actually participating in this; I was actually being subjected to the same restrictions' (Shah, 2001). The relationship between Britain, 'foreigners' and British people at home and abroad, has long been particularly complicated for the media. At issue is always the balance of power and control.

In the 1930s Britain's Press Office was born. During the First World War, the Ministry of Information was run by British press barons who subordinated their obligation to inform the public to unquestioning support of the official government line. News management techniques became increasingly sophisticated. The Second World War saw the use of the rapidly expanding documentary film industry as a medium for distributing government propaganda to a swiftly growing mass consumer market. In September 1939 the Ministry of Information started operating as soon as war broke out, but this time it was no longer run by press barons. Its staff grew exponentially and its central distribution and services devolved into a collection of regional offices.

During the Second World War the British government increased its censorship of media in new and extreme ways as a result of concern about growing radicalism as well as the war. While there is no question that the situation was desperately dangerous, we must question the assumptions underlying decisions to control both the media and public access to information. Fearing German invasion, the government instituted a repressive regulation, which continues to have chilling implications for our own time in the wake of British and US efforts to control information and access in the 2003 conflict in Iraq. In 1940, the government gave the Home Secretary, Sir John Anderson, the power to single-handedly control the British press. At the heart of this power was Regulation 2D, which granted the Home Secretary unprecedented, personal power to ban any publication that might be seen as encouraging opposition to any aspect of any war in which Britain was a participant. Not only could the Home Secretary arbitrarily shut down the publications of his choosing, but publications were explicitly denied the right of appeal or any other access to the law courts.

In 1941, amid a climate in which the government Committee on Communist Activities persistently attacked the left press, which faced increasing intimidation and harassment, two Communist newspapers –

.. HE'S A WAR CORRESPONDENT!

War reporting has always been a risky business. (Ron Walton)

The Daily Worker and *The Week* – were shut down. More moderate and less successful forms of intimidation were applied to less radical, left-of-centre papers critical of the government. The government did not lift its ban on *The Daily Worker* and *The Week* until 1942, more than a year after the Soviet Union had become one of Britain's closest allies. It was a turning point in British media history. Henceforth, proposals for press censorship were rejected, and Regulation 2D was never invoked again. Still, we have to wonder whether government and its spin doctors will someday want to resurrect it.

Since the late 1940s, various organisations and structures have been put in place in an effort to limit government control of the media and improve media responsibility. In 1947, the National Union of Journalists (NUJ) successfully pressurised the government to convene the First Royal Commission on the Press. Though its effectiveness must be questioned in the light of today's media empires, they sought to study and challenge the ever-increasing concentration of media ownership, the profit-based information machinery that ultimately limited and distorted news and information. In the name of expanding opportunity and a 'new information universe', the reality is that the media empires have narrowed the information universe. Only by consciously and energetically seeking an array of information through a variety of media and online sources can the public obtain adequate and uncensored information.

Developed and subsidised by publishers, the First Royal Commission on the Press had no legal status and was destined to end up supporting media industries and failing the public. It found evidence of ethical problems and recommended the creation of a national press council. In 1961 the Second Royal Commission on the Press was convened. When the government threatened to legislate change, it brought in members from outside the newspaper industry, as well as the Monopolies and Mergers Act of 1965. Despite the mandate to limit concentration of media ownership, we again must question the effectiveness of such measures in the light of contemporary developments and practices. The 1974 Third Royal Commission on the Press once more criticised both the Press Council and the press, made a series of recommendations for improvement, produced a written code of conduct, but decided against outside interference in the regulation of the press. Thus it remained an industry-driven and largely ineffectual agency, resistant to regulation or change.

Based on their 'propaganda model', Edward Herman and Noam Chomsky say the media have become too independent and powerful for the public good.

> The mass media serve as a system for communicating messages and symbols to the general populace. It is their function to amuse, entertain and inform, and to inculcate individuals with the values, beliefs and codes of behavior that will integrate them into the institutional structures of the larger society. In a world of concentrated wealth and major conflicts of class interest, to fulfill this role requires systematic propaganda ... the propaganda model focuses on inequality of wealth and power and multilevel effects on mass-media interests and choices – it traces the routes by which money and power are able to filter out the news, marginalize dissent and allow government and dominant private interests to get their messages across to the public. (Herman and Chomsky, 1994: 297)

Jeremy Tunstall challenges the often-heard claim that the media have little power.

> Newspapers and their owners and editors tend to understate the extent of their power for two sound, and potentially embarrassing, reasons. First, there is the issue of whether it is compatible with, or healthy for, democracy to have so much power residing in so few unregulated hands. Secondly, most daily newspapers ... have local monopolies or semi-monopolies; here is the embarrassing question of whether a democratic press and the market-place of ideas are

compatible with unregulated local private private press monopoly. The British press is an extreme case within Europe in the extent to which it is dominated by national newspapers published in one city (London) ... (Tunstall, 1996: 2)

Sometimes a journalist's work and career is itself internationalised because of unexpected assignments or decisions. In 1951, Anthony Sampson went from the rarefied atmosphere, stimulation and shelter of Oxford to the danger and chaos of Johannesburg, South Africa, where for four years he edited the black magazine, *Drum*. It 'opened all doors into the vibrant and exciting world of black writers, musicians and politicians' and gave Sampson 'a front seat from which to observe the mounting black opposition to the apartheid government which had come to power in 1948'. Soon after arriving, he met Nelson Mandela. This series of events and decisions – some of his own making and some beyond his control – led to his authoring the definitive biography of Mandela (Sampson, 1999). Sampson attended the African National Congress (ANC) conference which launched the Defiance Campaign of 1952.

> I watched Mandela organizing the first volunteers, and mobilizing resistance in 1954 to the destruction of Sophiatown, the multi-racial slum where I had spent many happy evenings. (Sampson, 1999: xiii)

Returning to Britain, he commuted to South Africa. He covered the 1960 Sharpeville crisis for *The Observer*

> and interviewed Mandela in Soweto just after the massacre. My last, poignant sight of him was in 1964, when I was observing the Rivonia trial in Pretoria, which gave me a chance to see the final speech he was then preparing ... As a journalist I could not see Mandela during his twenty-seven years in prison, but I revisited black South Africa and kept in touch with exiles in London and elsewhere. (Sampson, 1999: xiii)

In 1986, the apartheid government banned him from returning to South Africa, where he was researching a book on black politics and business (*Black Gold*). The ban was temporarily lifted 'just in time for me to return before Mandela's release from jail in February 1990' (Sampson, 1999: xiv). The chain of events and decisions enabled Sampson to help expand international public awareness of South African politics and society, at a time of extreme suppression of information and repression of non-white South Africans. Happily, he was able to chronicle the demise of apartheid government as well as its rise.

John Pilger sets out to bring hidden voices and faces to an unaware public. He uses the term 'Unpeople' to refer to the millions worldwide who are marginalised or omitted entirely from media coverage.

> The children of Iraq are Unpeople. So, too, are the half a million children who, according to UNICEF, die beneath the burden of un-repayable debt owed by their governments to the West … Unpeople are the heroes of this book. Their eloquent defiance and courage are as important as the secret histories of their neglect. (Pilger, 1998: 3)

In Herman's and Chomsky's 'propaganda system', the media are said to follow this practice by portraying people 'as worthy or unworthy victims' (Herman and Chomsky, 1994: 37). In the film *Manufacturing Consent*, Chomsky presents a case study of media monopoly and 'unworthy victims' and what he calls 'media complicity in genocide' in the case of Indonesia and East Timor. Here, he showed that an effective media blackout by the United States had worldwide impact.

In today's reality, 'British' media are no longer strictly British; press barons and corporate structures cross geographic, organisational and other borders. While this chapter focuses on these issues, they enter into most other chapters as well. Understanding media internationalisation requires a consideration of the people who create and sustain it.

The new media cyber barons: Bill Gates and company

The villain of the James Bond movie *Tomorrow Never Dies* is a caricature of a power-mad, mega-press baron who creates and controls a multi-media global news corporation. The character seems a composite of Microsoft founder-owner-director Bill Gates and the international media mogul Rupert Murdoch. Much as the early press barons squeezed out the competition when production costs went up, today's mega-media barons limit consumers' access to the Internet, virtually force PC users to employ Microsoft products, and control front-line information, advertising and purchasing sources by providing selected (and paid for) gateway access to the company's choice of business and information services. The consumer who wishes to reach a wider array of choices can technically do so, but will find it costly and time-consuming. Thus the barons and their empires succeed in intimidating consumers and business competitors by distancing, limiting or killing off the competition.

Even when the news media try to challenge the power and controlled information, there are ironies. *The Guardian's* coverage of the November 1999 Microsoft trial in the US was limited by available newspaper space. As is often the case with major stories, the paper offered fuller, expanded coverage to its readers on its *Guardian Unlimited* website, along with an additional a website providing the judge's findings. But despite the outcome – in which a Microsoft monopoly was outlawed – most people who sought access to this information had to use Microsoft's Internet Explorer to access *The Guardian* websites, which informed them of the decision to keep Microsoft from monopolising access!

After 9/11 …

Contrary to all of the political communication and most of the media, John Pilger contends that September 11, 2001 did not 'change everything'; it only 'accelerated the continuity of events, providing an extraordinary pretext for destroying social democracy' (Pilger, 2002: 2). At the heart of the matter are the media conglomerates. They have 'unprecedented power'. The modern-day media barons own newspapers and magazines, radio and television, book publishing houses, film production companies, Web and Internet resources and other instruments and outlets of local, regional, national, transnational and global communication. 'The "global economy" is their most important media enterprise … They have transformed much of the 'information society' into a media age where extraordinary technology allow the incessant repetition of political 'safe' information …' (Pilger, 2002: 3).

Julie Bradford, a university lecturer and former journalist with the French news service *Agence Presse*, talks about the near-impossibility of reporting for an international media service. 'It's a clash of world views. You have to write stories that are acceptable in many different countries. The same story has to work for the U.K. and Saudi Arabia.' On the other hand, in an instant-access, interdependent world, no story is entirely self-contained, and most so-called 'national' stories are ultimately international. Explicitly international reporting is a peculiar mix of ethnocentric, voyeuristic tourism, cross-cultural communication and interpretation, and everyday journalism. As we saw in Chapter 2, ethnocentrism and cross-cultural misunderstandings can endanger the research, comprehension and production of news – and ultimately, human lives.

Ros Coward observes the effects of ethnocentric tourism and the need for responsible reporting in a discussion of the post-September 11, 2001 attack on nightclubbing tourists in Bali. She questions the behaviour of travel companies that present and promote holiday destinations as if they exist in an apolitical vacuum. The website, Party towns.com, described Kuta beach as 'an exotic gem … a real party town all the year round …' Such descriptions perpetuate 'a staggering lack of awareness among these travellers that their lifestyle could be seen in any other light than the one they shed on it ...' (Coward, 2002: 15). A responsible media must help educate the public – not only in the name of intercultural tolerance, but in the interest of public safety.

> There can never be any excuse for indiscriminate killing ... but I do despair of the cultural ignorance and chauvinism that these young people have grown up with ... Television continues to promote the world as a series of tourist destinations ... Even after the ... attack ... in Bali, no one has discussed the problems western lifestyles pose to a region marked by poverty ... No one has talked about the need for westerners to travel with more grace and more modesty. (Coward 2002: 15)

She calls this kind of tourism a 'form of casual imperialism that looks for warm places to party where the beer is cheap, the view is good and the locals are tolerant enough not to cause too much trouble' (Coward, 2002: 15).

The ITN war correspondent Michael Nicholson was accused of journalistic tourism and breach of professional detachment in his coverage of 1992 Bosnia. In his own account and the Michael Winterbottom film *Welcome to Sarajevo*, he (and the actor who plays his lightly fictionalised role in the film) attempts to justify his humanitarian-driven actions. Filing nightly reports from Sarajevo, he discovered a group of children, orphaned or separated from their families, coping with the daily horrors of life and death in the war zone. Abandoning his role as journalist-observer, he became personally involved in helping to smuggle children out of Bosnia. He became so deeply involved that he and his wife eventually adopted one of the children and brought her home to live in England (Nicholson, 1994; Winterbottom, 1997).

Early in the last century, Lincoln Steffens was invited to join a delegation of American business people on a chamber of commerce-sponsored tour of Europe.

> My exercise on that trip was baiting those business men and politicians who had come along to learn. I said they could not learn. They said they wanted to see what things were done better abroad so as to do them that way at home. I told them that the best they aspired to was to be good men, not to make better cities. I was told ... that I was an offense all through that grand tour of England, Belgium, Germany, Switzerland, France, and back. I could not ... point out the facts and the views to these commercial-political tourists and let them take or leave what they saw ... (Steffens, 1931: 649)

Steffens wanted them to take away from Europe the value of national-ising public utilities. He told the mayor of Denver that 'the privately run companies were more in politics than those that were publicly run ...' (Steffens, 1931: 649–50). He wrote about the inseparability and inter-dependence of nations decades before 'globalisation', and before Nadia Martinez and Mark Engler called the failed but posthumously persistent US corporation Enron a 'toxic export' (Martinez and Engler, 2002: 28). Writing in the campaigning 'red-green' coalition magazine *Red Pepper*, they cautioned against the dangers of exporting damaged and damaging global trade and investment to the vulnerable developing world. '... Enron Global Services has a long history of pushing industry de-regulation and avoiding oversight' that threaten to develop ecologically sensitive areas such as protected indigenous lands in Bolivia.

Johan Galtung identifies two kinds of violence, 'direct' or 'personal' violence and 'structural' violence. 'Direct violence' is equivalent to the conventional meaning of 'violence', in which someone is injured or killed. Pressure from a dominant group for a subordinate group to assimilate – for example, the government-sponsored renaming of thou-sands of Canadian Inuit in 1970 (Alia, 1994) is a form of 'structural violence'. Although the effects of structural violence are often less visible or immediate, it is destructive and often leads to direct violence. Galtung emphasises that 'there is no reason to assume that structural violence amounts to less suffering than personal violence' (Galtung, 1980: 7). One of the results of structural violence is what is sometimes called cultural genocide, whose consequences sometimes include waves of suicides. The late anthropologist Eleanor Burke Leacock considered the high rates of suicide among indigenous peoples, internationally, to be a form of indirect genocide, and thought it ought to be studied and reported in that way (Leacock, 1982). In an earlier study, I began to develop the model which has been updated in Figure 5.1, in an effort to help clarify these concepts.

Journalistic intervention can affect the violence continuum at any point. Journalists and mass media are omnipresent players in the esca-lation, or the defusing, of conflicts. Journalistic practice can reside with structural violence, by limiting or controlling access to information or by providing inaccurate or damaging information (e.g. the 'disinformation' distributed by US spin doctors during and after the attacks on Iraq). It can also fall into the category of direct violence. A journalist's (mis)judgements can lead to danger and even death. Media coverage of the 1995 conflict between US federal agents and cult leader David Koresh at Waco, Texas and the behaviour of individual reporters and editors may have helped to escalate the conflict, which resulted

Decisions and behaviour of journalists and editors; media representations:

→   →   →   →   →   →   →   →   →   →   →   →
←   ←   ←   ←   ←   ←   ←   ←   ←   ←   ←   ←

Non-violence	Structural violence			Direct violence
	Oppressive or repressive structures (disempowerment) War	Cultural genocide	Culture-wide suicide or state-sanctioned murder	Genocide Legally-sanctioned execution

(Adapted and updated from Alia (2000: 278).

Figure 5.1 A model (continuum) for examining levels of violence

in the deaths of the people barricaded inside Koresh's compound.

Addressing the 'Non-violence' end of the spectrum, William Coté and Roger Simpson caution that, without professional training in psychology, psychiatry or social work, journalists should not reach beyond their capabilities and responsibilities. The journalist's 'prime job is to inform – not diagnose, treat, and heal physical and mental ills'. Nonetheless, they believe that 'journalism can be one of the "helping professions"'. One way is, as physicians pledge, to 'seek to do no harm' (Coté and Simpson, 2000: 223). Another way – which they do not identify – is to work actively to counter dangerous and damaging policies and activities. The world media that ignored people, conditions and developments in South Africa under apartheid contributed directly to the structural violence of apartheid, and indirectly to direct violence. Conversely, the contributions of journalists such as Anthony Sampson helped to inform a wider international public and support black journalists and activists within South Africa, and ultimately helped to undermine the apartheid regime.

The flip side of internationalisation: empowering the people

The South African magazine *Drum* gave voice to a new generation of black journalists and artists and provided a forum for coverage of political and social movements and developments. Working both for *Drum* and later for *The Observer*, Anthony Sampson was able to create a bridge between South Africa and Britain and from there to disseminate news to the rest of the world. In the 1960s, Pete Steffens worked in Israel as an editor on *New Outlook*, an English language monthly produced by an egalitarian team of Palestinian and Jewish–Israeli journalists, another example of a cultural and political bridging project. The British monthly magazine *Red Pepper* (mentioned above) is one of many alternative media outlets that work to challenge mainstream, corporation-driven media. While its focus is British, it covers international issues, movements and events. *Adbusters Magazine*, founded by Canadian 'culture jammer' Kalle Lasn, disseminates its news, features, and satirical and provocative visual materials via a colourful and stunningly designed slick magazine and a free-for-all website. Lasn describes his project as

> a loose global network of media activists who see ourselves as the advance shock troops of the most significant social movement of the next twenty years. Our aim is to topple existing power structures and forge major adjustments to the way we will live ... We believe culture jamming will become to our era what civil rights was to the '60s ... (Lasn, 1999: xi)

Such efforts help to counter the chauvinistic, US-dominated international media universe.

> ... why don't other countries see the world the way Americans do? News coverage is a large part of the answer ... the 'liberal' US media are strikingly conservative – and [in the case of the 2002–3 conflict in Iraq] hawkish ... Most people ... get their news from television ... the difference is immense. (Lasn, 1999: xi)

Anti-war rallies in February 2003 were taken seriously by British and European television and trivialised by US television news. News anchors on Fox described the demonstrators in New York as 'the usual protestors' or 'serial protesters'. CNN's website read: 'Anti-war rallies delight Iraq' and showed pictures of marchers in Baghdad but not in London or New York. Paul Krugman posits two possible explanations for the 'great trans-Atlantic media divide'. Either European media are driven by a 'pervasive anti-American bias' or some US media outlets '– operating in an environment in which anyone who questions the administration's foreign policy is accused of being unpatriotic – have taken it as their assignment to sell the war' (Krugman, 2003a: 7).

John Merrill is concerned that we tend to view internationalisation as a technological more than a socio-political problem.

> Modern technology has created of the world a small house, and human beings are locked together in the same tiny room where everyone is forced to share the consequences of one another's action. Physical means of communicating news and disseminating it throughout the world are well developed ... [but as] governments

become more sensitive and cautious ... the universe of frank and open news reporting is restricted ... (Merrill, 1991: 3)

As a combined effect of technological, social and political change, Seán Ó Siochrú, Bruce Girard and Amy Mahan say we must seek changes in global governance, with particular attention to governance of media and communications:

> The institutions and system of global governance ... will never again be the concern simply of governments ... behind ... closed doors ... and indeed they never really were. In all areas of global governance including media and communications, other actors, especially the private sector ... are making their presence felt ...

They envision 'a civil society movement organised at the global level, but acting at' the national level as well, to ensure the development of a 'governance system of media and communication with people at the center' (Ó Siochrú, Girard and Mahan, 2002: 179–80).

The 'New Media Nation' discussed in Chapter 4 is part of a growing international media movement of indigenous peoples. As indigenous people around the planet organise their own media 'empires' (though without the kind of capital and power associated with mainstream empires) other minorities and disadvantaged groups are developing their own media organisations and coordinating their interventions into existing media. Thanks in part to new media technology (discussed in detail in Chapter 10), minority voices are becoming global choruses and reaching an ever-expanding audience.

Exercises

5.1 The new media barons

Discuss the idea of Bill Gates as media cyber-baron. How does he create and control information?

5.2 Debate: costs and benefits of media consolidation and media empires

Bring in a variety of the day's newspapers. Discuss the impact of media empires and media barons on information access and people's daily lives and well-being. Divide the class into two groups. Each group gets copies of (the same collection of) newspaper cuttings and other briefing materials, and appoints two people to present its views. One person presents the argument; the second person makes the rebuttal.

- *Group A* presents the Affirmative ('for') position: benefits to consumers – readers, journalists, labour, business, society – of media consolidation, activities of current press barons and their media empires.
- *Group B* presents the Negative ('against') position: dangers to consumers – readers, journalists, labour, business, society – of media consolidation, activities of current press barons and their media empires.

PROCEDURE

1. *20 minutes.* Groups A and B meet, read their briefing notes and plan their arguments.
2. *30 minutes.* Debate takes place:
   Introductory arguments:
   (a) Group A – first person presents the Affirmative argument.
   (b) Group B – first person presents the Negative argument.
   Rebuttal:
   (a) Group A – second person challenges Group B's position and continues the Affirmative argument.
   (b) Group B – second person challenges Group A's position and continues the Negative argument.
   General discussion. Which argument is more convincing?

5.3 International crisis reporting: when the journalist becomes the story

View the film *Welcome to Sarajevo* (optional reading: Nicholson, *Natasha's Story* (later retitled *Welcome to Sarajevo*)). Discuss the ethical and unethical behaviour of the different journalists portrayed in the film, and outline the different positions they take. Discuss the decisions made by the main character (a representation of the real-life television reporter Michael Nicholson) and the ethical implications of his decisions. What would you have done? What do you think he should have done?

5.4 Adbusting

Look at one or more issues of *Adbusters* magazine or browse the *Adbusters* website. Outline some of the tactics and techniques used to challenge the advertising industry, and globalisation. Discuss the effectiveness or lack of effectiveness of, for example, the annual 'Buy Nothing Day', and Kalle Lasn's long-term goal of destroying the tobacco industry.

Further reading

Alia, Valerie (2003) 'Scattered voices, global vision: indigenous peoples and the new media nation', in Karim H. Karim (2003) *The Media of Diaspora*. London: Routledge, pp. 36–50.

Alia, Valerie (2000) 'The boundaries of liberty and tolerance in the Canadian North: media, ethics, and the emergence of the Inuit homeland of Nunavut', in Raphael Cohen-Almagor (ed.), *Challenges to Democracy*. Aldershot: Ashgate, pp. 275–94.

Alia, Valerie *Un/Covering the North: News, Media and Aboriginal People*. Vancouver: UBC Press.

Herman, Edward and Chomsky, Noam (1994) *Manufacturing Consent*. New York: Vintage.

Pilger, John (1998) *Hidden Agendas*. London: Vintage.

Tunstall, Jeremy (1996) *Newspaper Power: The New National Press in Britain*. Oxford: Clarendon Press.

Suggested viewing

Films

For details see the annotated filmography in Appendix B at the end of the book.

Manufacturing Consent
Tomorrow Never Dies
Welcome to Sarajevo
The Year of Living Dangerously
Before the Rain
Cry Freedom
Foreign Correspondent
Gandhi
Salvador

Video

Episodes from *The Prisoner*

6 Struggle and spin: politics, politicians and the media

> ... politics is business. That's what's the matter with it ... The politician is a business man with a specialty. When a business man of some other line learns the business of politics, he is a politician, and there is not much reform left in him. Consider the United States Senate, and believe me.
>
> The commercial spirit is the spirit of profit, not patriotism; of credit, not honor; of individual gain, not national prosperity; of trade and dickering, not principle ...
>
> But there is hope, not alone despair, in the commercialism of our politics. If our political leaders are to be always a lot of political merchants, they will supply any demand we may create. All we have to do is to establish a steady demand for good government ... It is idiotic, this devotion to a machine that is used to take our sovereignty from us. [If people express dissatisfaction] the commercial politician would feel a demand for good government and he would supply it.
> (Steffens, 1904: 5, 6)

Lincoln Steffens believed that public pressure would lead politicians to lead better governments more responsibly, because they would see it in their own interests to meet public demand. He admitted it might take a generation or two. What he failed to fully account for was the range and extent of variation – the fact that every society is composed of publics, rather than a single 'public'. We have to wonder what he would make of the non-election of 'President' George W. Bush. The majority of American voters did not choose him, and even the electoral college vote was manipulated by decisions to discount, disqualify and ignore large numbers of votes. There is growing dissatisfaction with the Bush Jr presidency, following what many say was an illegal (non)war against Iraq and an array of unpopular domestic policies (e.g. on taxation, the economy and the environment). Perhaps Steffens will turn out to be right after all, and the American public will force Bush out of office, to be replaced by better government. Perhaps public dissatisfaction with Tony

Blair will force a change in Britain. Whatever happens, you can be sure the media will be there, front and centre.

Paying for our crimes ... or someone else's

Ian McEwan's 1999 novel *Amsterdam* (discussed in Chapter 3) criticises media practice in which 'news and information becomes a commodity to sell to the highest bidder' (Keeble, 2001: 4). As we have seen, this is nothing new. It was the subject of Upton Sinclair's landmark 1920 study *The Brass Check*.

> What is the Brass Check? The Brass Check ... is the price of your shame – you who take the fair body of truth and sell it in the market-place, who betray the virgin hopes of mankind into the loathsome brothel of Big Business. And down in the counting-room below sits the 'madame' who profits by your shame ... (Sinclair, 1920: 436)

The journalists in *Amsterdam* are a deeply cynical group. We are told that their publication, *The Judge*, is known as 'a decent, fighting paper'. They struggle to maintain this image and their self-respect in the midst of the crass commercialism of deciding to publish embarrassing photographs of a politician, they print 'denunciations by those opposed to publication' and 'sponsored a televised debate on the need for a privacy law'. They also portrayed the politician, Garmony, as representative of a government that 'had been in power too long and was financially, morally and sexually corrupt'. Without opposing publication of the compromising photographs, the paper's various editors protected their self- and public images for the record. The 'editor was ... arguing into silence from his senior editors rather than protests; secretly they all wanted him to go ahead as long as their principled dissent was minuted'. Go ahead they did, and in 'a week, sales were up by a hundred thousand' (McEwan, 1998: 100).

With a primary objective of increasing sales, *The Judge's* editors pass judgement on a government and one of its leaders, while sanctimoniously convincing themselves they are helping to end corruption and serving the public interest. Such behaviour is part of the intricate dance that has long been part of the uneasy relationship between journalists and politicians, media and government.

Controlling the media, *spin*ning out of control

The US government of President George W. Bush has attempted to intimidate and censor films, articles and broadcasts critical of its practices and policies. In 2003, the actor Tim Robbins challenged journalists to keep their courage and convictions, and refuse to allow such intimidation and censorship (or self-censorship) to prevent them from doing their work. In an address to the National Press Club he talked about the fear of questioning government policy, which he saw reflected in the behaviour of his children and their teachers. He said:

> Today, prominent politicians who have decried violence in movies ... voted to give our current president the power to unleash real violence in our current war. They want us to stop the fictional violence but are okay with the real kind. And these same people that tolerate the real violence of war don't want to see the result of it on the nightly news. Unlike the rest of the world, our news coverage of this war remains sanitized, without a glimpse of the blood and gore inflicted upon our soldiers or the women and children in Iraq ... We want no part of reality in real life. (Robbins, 2003: 3)

He called upon journalists to 'insist that they not be used as publicists by this administration'. Echoing Oriana Fallaci's belief that journalism is 'an extraordinary and a terrible privilege', Robbins said:

> Any acquiescence or intimidation ... will only lead to more intimi- dation. You have ... an awesome responsibility and an awesome power: the fate of discourse, the health of this republic is in your hands ... We lay the continuance of our democracy on your desks, and count on your pens to be mightier ... Our ability to disagree, and our inherent right to question our leaders and criticize their actions define who we are. To allow those rights to be taken away out of fear ... to limit access in the news media to differing opinions is to acknowledge our democracy's defeat. (Robbins, 2003: 4)

These are not new developments. Back in 1920, Upton Sinclair's pub- lisher wrote:

> If it gets any publicity, it will be only because of a libel suit or something sensational ... If the great mass of the people ever hear of the book, it will be because you, the reader, do your part ... If your experience is the same as mine, you will find nearly everybody distrustful of Capitalist Journalism, and willing at least to consider the truth about it. (Sinclair, 1920: 444)

The link between media and politics was established long before Steffens and Sinclair.

> The newspaper press became increasingly prominent in English political life after 1760, due largely to the part it played in various

extra-parliamentary campaigns. Newspapers were also influential in deciding the fate of individual politicians. (Barker, 2000: 169–70)

> [The] world of clubland and the lobby system ensured that journalists and politicians became increasingly intimate towards the end of the nineteenth century ... It was now impossible to imagine the political world operating without newspapers. (Barker, 2000: 227)

Not since the days of overt media censorship have so-called democratic governments placed so much pressure on the press. Government control in the earlier Gulf War has been widely criticised and documented. The 'war' on Iraq makes it look like a preparatory exercise. In 2003, having thumbed its nose at the United Nations and determined to go to war against Iraq no matter what, the ill-gotten US presidency of George W. Bush spun a web of media-capturing lies, half-truths and 'disinformation' aimed at assuring unquestioning public support. Britain's Prime Minister Tony Blair bought the programme and followed the plan. The plan, which many argue had as its main objective the securing of Iraqi oil for US business interests, was to tell the public pretty much anything that would assure support (or at worst non-resistance) to the (illegal and undeclared) 'war'.

David Miller considers 'embedded' journalists 'the greatest PR coup of this war'. Their entrance was heralded by much fanfare and jargon. 'Dreamt up by the [US] Pentagon and Donald Rumsfeld the 'embeds', as they are now routinely described, are almost completely controlled by the military'. To gain access to the front lines, 'embeds' gave up 'most of their autonomy'. More sinister even than information control was the hidden threat, which said, in effect, 'If you are not embedded, we cannot (or will not) protect you'. Each embedded reporter was required to sign a contract with the military and was 'governed by a fifty point plan issued by the Pentagon detailing what they can and cannot report'. There were about 900 embedded reporters, about 130 of them with UK forces.

> The PR genius of the embed system was that it allowed unprecedented access to the fighting and, also, unprecedented identification by the reporters with the military. (Miller, 2003: 3)

Eating and drinking together and sharing the high-level front-line risks led journalists to identify with the soldiers – an intimacy that almost guarantees media self-censorship. Who needs to shut down the presses when the journalists are speaking out of government-sponsored military mouths? The insiderness was underscored by media reports linking journalists to soldiers with words like 'we' and 'our'. Those who sought more distance were expelled, or 'found their satellite phones blocked for unexplained reasons'. A reporter for the US military magazine *Army Times* said some embeds were 'hounded by military public affairs officers' who stayed with them as they conducted interviews. 'All of the … misinformation coming out of Iraq in the first two weeks' was 'fed out by the US/UK global media operation' (Miller, 2003: 4).

The effects of such pressures were evident in the scarce coverage of widespread international opposition to the 'war'. Public demonstrations of unprecedented scale (e.g. in London and Rome) were minimised and many were not covered at all. The opposition got more coverage on British television than on American TV. But even there, it was usually presented as a blip on the screen of the main news day – a little spice added to the pro-war stew.

As we go to press, none of the weapons of mass destruction cited as a major argument for going to war have been found. No one argues that Saddam Hussein was a tyrant. Removing him by US/UK force, and garnering public support by making unproven claims, is another matter. Stephen Dorril was perplexed to find that instead of blaming intelligence services, media blamed the apparent misinformation on political spin.

> The idea that the politicians 'over-hyped' the intelligence and forced the services to 'politicize' their intelligence has become the standard and accepted explanation … The evidence suggests, however, that the reason for [MI6's] reticence in releasing intelligence-derived material was that the services knew that it was, at best, weak. (Dorril, 2003: 1)

Whether we blame political spin doctors, government officials, or intelligence organisations, we are left with the conclusion that someone, following someone's plans and orders, spent a good deal of time, ingenuity and money to restrict media access, circulate dubious information, limit and shape the words and images that were allowed to reach the public. All this, while proclaiming the urgency of replacing an unquestionably repressive and dictatorial regime with a supposedly exemplary 'democratic' government. Perhaps the most sinister piece of the puzzle is the chilling reality that thirty-six journalists were killed on the job in 2003, thirteen of them in Iraq (Reuters, 2004: 5).

One of those was Terry Lloyd of ITV News. Witnesses said that US soldiers fired on his vehicle; the US military agreed to an inquiry. It is hard not to ask just how much distance there was between military warnings of non-protection for unembedded journalists and open fire by 'friendly' forces. If it's open season on journalists in a 'democracy', how are we to understand the relationship between media and government?

And who are we to insist that such governments must oversee creation of a new 'democracy' in Iraq?

It isn't the first time a democratic government has tried to intimidate or silence its much-touted 'free press'. In *Alien Ink*, Natalie Robins chronicles the systematic surveillance, intimidation, interference, and character assassination by the US Federal Bureau of Investigation (FBI) of an astonishing roster of American writers. The list reads like a 'who's who' of twentieth-century letters. There are poets, novelists, short story writers, playwrights and humourists – Ezra Pound, Ernest Hemingway, Richard Wright, Archibald MacLeish, Katherine Anne Porter, Carl Sandburg, Muriel Rukeyser, Dorothy Parker, Truman Capote, Arthur Miller, Theodore Roethke, James Baldwin, John Steinbeck, Jack London – and muckrakers such as Jessica Mitford, Upton Sinclair, and Lincoln Steffens. Although Steffens published *The Shame of the Cities* in 1904, the FBI did not investigate him until 1917:

> when the muckraking movement – of which he was the prophet – reached its crest. The term 'muckraking' was first used in 1906 by Steffens's friend, President Theodore Roosevelt, who had also first proposed the idea of creating an FBI. (Robins, 1992: 41–2)

In 1917 he went to visit the 'New Russia'. His remark, 'I have seen the future and it works' is remembered far more widely than the fact that Steffens neither joined the Communist Party nor advocated a new American revolution. He was a reformer, not a revolutionary. Yet for much of his life, the FBI followed his footsteps, checked his mail, heard his speeches, read his writings and (in the guise of friendly visits by falsely identified people) entered his home. It similarly 'investigated' his wife, the writer Ella Winter, and their young son Pete (Robins, 1992: 42–3; Pete Steffens, personal communication).

The surveillance – which as far as anyone knows continues today in various forms – did not stop at writers on the political front lines. Some are 'indexed by the FBI' simply for having signed petitions or participated in civil rights and anti-war protests during the 1960s (Robins, 1992: 409–12). This list includes literary critic and satirist Frederick Crews, cartoonist Jules Feiffer, philosopher Susan Sontag, journalist I. F. Stone, artist Andy Warhol and playwright Arnold Wesker.

The financial costs of such surveillance must surely be astronomical; the social costs cannot be measured.

Bark, bite or roll over: media watchdogs

Brian McNair contends that sometimes government 'controls and constraints' are required to support 'good government' and 'social cohesion'.

Other times, such limits to media freedom are simply the product of government self-interest.

> Journalism, as the 'watchdog' profession, plays an important role in defining where that line is drawn ... journalists must constantly struggle against the political apparatus for their freedom to report and analyse events ... This frequently puts them in the front line of political debate and conflict. (McNair, 1998: 83)

Throughout history, the press has actively challenged as well as supported governments and political leaders. The *Leeds Mercury* criticised government war expenditures and the elitism of economic and political policies. The *Manchester Times* protested the governing aristocracy's greed in creating laws doubling the price of food, lowering people's

> wages by excluding the produce of their labour from foreign markets, ... [carrying] off their hard-earned savings in taxes ... [and denying] them, when it is required, a portion of that abundance which has been produced by their labour. (Barker, 2000: 199)

Radical papers campaigned against the elitism and detachment of government from the realities of nationwide poverty. According to Barker, print 'formed the backbone of radical politics', confirming the fears of conservatives 'that newspapers would challenge the very existence of the old order' (Barker, 2000: 223). More recently, Richard Keeble has observed that 'the dissenting voices of feminists, peace campaigners, environmental activists, anarchists, lesbians and gays ... have been marginalized or even demonized ...' (Keeble, 2001: 5).

One of the major challenges for journalists is to maintain their autonomy as they cover political campaigns, elections and government. Politicians hire increasingly elaborate teams of 'spin doctors' – 'a clique of unelected, though immensely powerful officials' ... (Keeble, 2001: 4–5) whose job is to cast them and their policies in the best possible light, and to persuade the media to present their version of 'reality' to the public. While it is true that politicians consciously and carefully manipulate journalists, it is equally true that journalists manipulate politicians. Both sides of this awkward equation require access to each other and to the public(s) they serve – who in addition to being served also pay the bills. 'In election campaigns the information that becomes news emerges from a kind of closed system in which journalists are dependent for information on a small circle of sources in each of the political parties' (Fletcher, 1996: 143). Bob Franklin is concerned that the 'spheres of journalism and government increasingly overlap as journalists and politicians have grown mutually reliant ... Contra the image of journalists as independent of government, many observers ... describe their relationship as collusive' (Franklin, 1997: 30).

Frederick Fletcher maintains that information trading among journalists, and between journalists and political sources, is not unethical, provided 'information is properly verified and confidentiality is maintained.' He says, 'It is an axiom of political journalism that the best questions in news conferences come from reporters who already know the answers' (Fletcher, 1996: 144).

Politics makes strange, bad fellows

Covering politics takes vigilance and persistence, dedication to maintaining the 'watchdog' role, avoidance of government spin and seduction, and a good sense of where to draw the boundaries.

There was a time when newspaper owners and politicians were often the same people and no one batted an eye. Although official attitudes and principles have changed, journalism careers are seldom as pure as some would have us believe. Before and after (and, less often, during) their journalistic lives, they are employed as speech writers, political advisors and sometimes even politicians. Former politicians become journalists or owners of media organisations. Ideally, political reporters are expected to be politically neutral. Political columnists and editorial writers, on the other hand, may express strong opinions, and news organisations (particularly major newspapers) may themselves take a strongly partisan position overall. At the extreme, some journalists decide (or are pressured by their employers to decide) to refrain from voting. At the other end of the spectrum, they become known as party insiders who have nearly unlimited access to party leaders and spokespeople, but whose credibility is suspect by virtue of that very access.

In the 1970s, in his ground-breaking ethnographic study *The Boys on the Bus*, Timothy Crouse described the perils and pitfalls of 'pack journalism':

> ... this group was as hierarchical as a chess set. The pack was divided into cliques – the national political reporters ... the campaign reporters from the big, prestige papers and the ones from the small papers; the wire-service [reporters]; the network correspondents ...

All of them 'fed off' the same reports, handouts, speeches. 'After a while, they began to believe the same rumors, subscribe to the same theories, and write the same stories' (Crouse, 1973: 7–8). The question implicit in Crouse's study is: why does pack journalism persist, given its bad reputation?

> Everybody denounces pack journalism, including the men (*sic*) who form the pack. Any self-respecting journalist would sooner endorse incest than come out in favor of pack journalism. (Crouse, 1973: 8)

That he refers to 'the men' is indicative both of the limits of Crouse's imagination and the fact that in the 1960s and 1970s – and all too often today – there were few female political correspondents. Still, some of the 'boys on the bus' were girls.

Caryl Rivers says that sometimes 'the media can be the wolf pack, going for the jugular ...' but 'the species is more often *Sardinius canned* [tinned sardines] than *lupus* [wolves] ... The news media are more often passive than predatory ...' (Rivers, 1996: 214).

> The laziness of pack journalism allows cultural stereotypes to multiply like bacteria on the locker-room floor ... Being in the middle of the pack is comfortable, risk free and – too often – rewarded. Journalists have to show more willingness to break free ... to risk the ... scorn of their colleagues and editors when the story they are pursuing is not trendy or in line with the conventional political wisdom of the moment. (Rivers, 1996: 224)

'Journalists occupy an ambiguous position in the political world, in which they are very influential actors but not full-fledged members,' observes the French sociologist Pierre Bourdieu. Too many journalists do little research and documentation, and are thus unable to help the public understand politicians, political policies and decisions, and events. Especially television journalists tend towards short-term, oppositional thinking.

> No doubt, they are encouraged to act as they do by politicians, and especially by government officials ... [who] like to stress the short-term effects of the decisions they make and announce to the public ... This vision is at once dehistoricized and dehistoricizing, fragmented and fragmenting. (Bourdieu, 1996: 4–6)

Just as the priest is an intermediary between the parishioner and God, the journalist serves as intermediary between citizen and politician (who in this way becomes godlike, untouchable and unchallengeable).

> The world shown by television is one that lies beyond the grasp of ordinary individuals. Linked to this is the impression that politics is for professionals, a bit like high-level competitive sports with their split between athletes and spectators. (Bourdieu, 1996: 8)

Hugo Young, of the London *Sunday Times* and *The Guardian*, said it is important that journalists 'know their limits. In the end we are not players ... We criticise decisions but never make them' (Young, 2003: 6). He recalled the time in 1964 when US President Lyndon Johnson visited the journalist Walter Lippman at home and asked him for advice on the Vietnam War. Decades earlier, Lincoln Steffens entertained a friendship with President Theodore Roosevelt, who consulted, respected and insulted him by labelling Steffens and his colleagues 'muckrakers'. Today it is customary to be critical of journalists who cozy up to presidents. Young thinks it is impossible to maintain distance, but essential to maintain *critical* distance.

> ... we can't avoid talking to politicians. We need to have relations with them. ... The line they're spinning is at least half the story, and the [political] columnist ... has the advantage of being able to expose the spin ... But he obviously has to talk around to be able to do that. He must sup with the devil constantly ... Though writing ... as an outsider, he must discover as an insider. (Young, 2003: 7)

There is 'a limit to the intimacy,' Young says, adding that there are 'no more than three politicians I've regarded as friends' (Young, 2003: 7). For some journalists, that is three friends too many.

Critics and court jesters

Some writers push non-friendship to its extremes. The political humourist and modern-day muckraker Molly Ivins writes some of her columns for *The Texas Observer*, a 'scrappy little magazine' that proudly declares: 'We will serve no group or party but will hew hard to the truth as we find it and the right as we see it ... we will take orders from none but our own conscience ...' Ivins and her co-author, *Texas Observer* editor Lou Dubose, cannot resist adding, 'Of course, it has never paid much' (Ivins and Dubose, 2000: vii). Their book *Shrub* is subtitled – optimistically – *The Short but Happy Political Life of George W. Bush*. Before rubbishing the Bush, Jr Presidency with a litany of horrific policies and decisions, they remind the reader:

> Young political reporters are always told there are three ways to judge a politician. The first is to look at the record. The second is to look at the record. And third, look at the record. (Ivins and Dubose, 2000: xii)

Following the record, they find Bush a 'wholly owned subsidiary of corporate America' who is 'weak on the governance side of politics' and who, as Governor of Texas (with the help of his oil industry and other corporate friends), helped make Texas 'number one' in:

1. overall toxic releases;
2. recognized carcinogens in the air;
3. suspected carcinogens in the air;
4. developmental toxins in the air (affecting brain and nervous-system development in children);
5. cancer risk (Ivins and Dubose, 2000: xvi, xvii, 107–8).

Another writer who is not likely to find friends among the ranks of politicians is the political satirist, writer, film-maker and stand-up comic Michael Moore. In his book, *Stupid White Men* and his documentary film *Bowling for Columbine*, he takes on US social policy, gun-and-violence-obsessed culture, government in general and the Bush, Jr Presidency in particular.

> Welcome to your Century 21 Nightmare!
> A man no one elected sits in the White House …
> Oh, and aren't *you* lucky! You're working two jobs, and so is your wife … and next month you're going to make the last payment on that student loan you've had for the past twenty years, but *then* … SUDDENLY, your company has announced it's moving to Mexico – without you! (Moore, 2001: xi–xii)

Moore is more than a media practitioner and social critic. He is a dedicated reformer. Like reformer-muckrakers Ida Tarbell, Upton Sinclair and Lincoln Steffens before him, he wants to see things changed. No friend to presidents, he addresses his investigations, challenges and calls to action to citizens. An investigative reporter first, he carefully outlines his account of Bush's record, the apparently illicit capturing of the White House and the frightening implications for the future of American people, American society and the planet as a whole. He calls George W. Bush the 'Thief-in-Chief' and 'President' of the United States, placing quotation marks around 'President' to underscore his contention that the Bush 'win' was illegal.

> Al Gore is the elected President of the United States. He received 539,898 more votes than George W. Bush … It used to be that politicians would wait until they were in office before they became crooks. This one came prepackaged … I have sent a personal request to UN Secretary General Kofi Annan to hear our plea. We are no longer able to govern ourselves or to hold free and fair elections. We need UN observers, UN troops, UN resolutions! (Moore, 2001: 2–3)

Another political journalist who is not likely to be invited into the corridors of power is Paul Krugman. In June 2003 he wrote in *The New York Times* that 'Bush bamboozled the United States into war [in Iraq]'. British Prime Minister Tony Blair received similar criticism from an array of journalists pointing out both deception of the British public and complicity with US deception. Starting a war on false pretenses 'is, to say the least, a breach of trust'. Krugman says journalists have 'a moral obligation to demand accountability'. To do so in the face of

> a powerful, ruthless political machine [and] in the face of a country not yet [prepared] to believe that its leaders have exploited Sept. 11 for political gain [is] a scary prospect. (Krugman, 2003b: 9)

Anthony Sampson laments the replacement of 'news about the world' with columnists offering 'news about *themselves*: opinions, reminiscences and details of their domestic lives …' The main casualty, he thinks, 'has been Parliament, the traditional citadel of democracy which newspapers had stormed with such difficulty' (Sampson, 2000: 54).

> The newspapers' neglect of Parliament brought its own dangers. The more journalists competed to provide their own political news and debates, the more they pursued short-term stories which turned out to have little significance. (Sampson, 2000: 55)

Sampson contends that such short-term news is easier for spin doctors and lobbyists to manipulate and distort. Although the newspapers have returned to a modest amount of parliamentary reporting, 'Parliament is still only shown as a kind of side-show to the main political debate conducted by journalists' (Sampson, 2000: 56). Thus journalists have gone from being government bedfellows (or at least dining table-sharers) to being detached commentators and observers at best, and at worst to *becoming* the story.

My own position is that it is impossible to be value-neutral, and in an election that uses secret ballots, the idea of not voting is absurd. I also think media practitioners must stay out of politicians' pockets. If this means losing some access, so be it. Great journalists, such as I. F. Stone, have always found ways to get information not provided to them and often, information gotten the hard way is more accurate and detailed. I think one of the major responsibilities of political journalists is to help decode and demythologise political behaviour for the public. The news conference simulation exercise that accompanies this chapter demonstrates just such a process, helping to illuminate the relationship between spin-doctored information, insider- and outsider-journalists, news organisations and the public.

As Rita Shelton Deverell points out, 'events have several sides, not just two' and ethical journalism reveals as many sides as possible (Deverell, 1996: 59). She also calls for reporting of 'the view from the losing side' (Deverell, 1996: 62) and 'rich reporting' from an array of sources – not just the official ones – that 'requires time to find out how many stories are within the story'. This means balancing the reportorial distance needed to observe and evaluate events and positions with the empathy and close observation of an inside view. 'Putting ourselves inside gives us greater, not less, access to information. It gives us a vantage point from which we can see many sides. Then we give others an opportunity to see with us and we increase the amount of information, accuracy and truth in the world' (Deverell, 1996: 63).

Deverell advocates thoughtful subjectivity instead of the convention-ally approved (but seldom achieved) objectivity. She is referring here, not to politicians and others with power, but to those with less power and often more information about a range of constituencies and perspectives. Her dedication to using the media to empower the disempowered echoes the words of Anishinabe (Ojibwe) environmentalist, community leader and human rights activist Winona LaDuke:

> I believe that, in its foundational ... ethical sense, democracy is about the need for public policy to fill the needs of the poorest people in this country, not the richest – the right for those who are the most silent to have a voice, the right for all of us to be able to participate in political discourse and dialogue. (LaDuke, 1998: 69)

Exercises

6.1 News conference simulation

This exercise is a simulation of a familiar format in which politicians and other public figures present information to the public through media intermediaries. The press or news conference sometimes varies in form, but the main structures and objectives are the same. 'Spin doctors' specialise in preparing material and grooming leaders to 'handle' the media. Media practitioners are taught the techniques of trying to elicit a statement that is off 'the programme'. This exercise should be enjoyable, and is an excellent way to consider some of the problems and principles of political communication and political reporting. As preparation, students should be encouraged to watch television news conferences such as BBC2's *Newsnight* in the UK.

The tutor chooses an issue, decision or event that is currently in the news, and prepares briefing notes. I usually bring in an array of press cuttings from various magazines and newspapers and whatever additional data and materials I can find.

The class is divided into two groups: the politician and her/his entourage, and the journalists. Each group is given an instruction sheet (see below) and a set of briefing notes (cuttings, etc.).

The groups meet separately (preferably in spaces where they cannot hear each other) for a designated time (30 minutes to an hour should suffice). They assign roles, as specified, and prepare their agenda, operational method and position.

The class reconvenes and becomes a news conference, following the format specified in the instructions below.

INSTRUCTIONS FOR GROUP A: *THE POLITICAL PARTY*
In a meeting of (30 minutes, 45 minutes or 1 hour):

1. *Select one person* to be the Politician.

    Politician: You are your party's public face and voice. You have called this press conference – it's your show.

    Your assignment: In consultation with your Spin Doctors and Party Leaders, write down four or five main points the press conference will address. *You must stick to these points, no matter what the reporters say or do.*

    At the news conference:
    – Make an opening statement (3–5 minutes).
    – Open the floor to questions from reporters (about an hour).
    – Respond to the questions, trying to stay within the boundaries your 'party' has set.

2. *Appoint two people* to be the Spin Doctors.

    Spin Doctors: You are the press contacts and PT managers.

    Your assignment:
    – Guide the Politician, Moderator and Party Leaders.
    – Read the package of press cuttings (sharing key information with everyone).
    – Advise – help set the agenda and strategy (how to present things in the best light, to the press).
    – Help write the politician's briefing notes and introductory statement.

At the news conference:

- Check the setup of the room. Sit beside or behind the politician – stay close (remember to let them have the spotlight).
- Make sure they stay on track (you may pass notes or whisper in their ear if necessary).

3. *Appoint one person* to be the news conference Moderator.

Moderator: You will host the news conference.

Your assignment: Follow the guidance of Spin Doctors, Politician and Party Leaders.

At the news conference:
- Welcome the media.
- Introduce your esteemed leader.
- Maintain order.
- Be vigilant – if reporters put pressure on issues you want to avoid, try to keep them in line and calm things down. (Try to cut off discussion if your agenda is threatened or the press is gaining too much control.)
- When questions have been addressed to your satisfaction, you will call the press conference to a close.

4. *Other group members* are the Party Leaders.

Party Leaders: You will help set priorities, write the agenda and develop a strategy for controlling the press conference in the party's interests.

Your assignment: Try to figure out what questions you think the reporters will ask, and help prepare the politician to respond effectively.

At the news conference:
- If you see things getting out of hand, intervene (by speaking; trying to influence a reporter you have identified as friendly; sending a note to the Politician, Moderator, or a Spin Doctor, etc.).

Group A's objective: Stay with your chosen agenda. Control the debate and the try to control the journalists' questions. Try to make your candidate look good on camera and sound good on microphone and in print. Look for ways to defuse controversy or conflict and keep things on track.

The Politician's task: Stay in control and 'manage' the event. Don't let journalists trap you into answering questions you don't want to answer or addressing issues you don't want to address. Stick to the points your party decided to raise and avoid all others. Decide what basic tone you will take with the media (friendly, authoritative, kind and gentle, generous, terse, informative, conciliatory, aggressive). Keep your public personality within these bounds and avoid allowing the journalists to steer you off course or provoke you to change your demeanour or tone.

INSTRUCTIONS FOR GROUP B: *THE JOURNALISTS*
In a meeting of 30 minutes, 45 minutes or 1 hour:

1. *Select one person* to be Moderator.
   Moderator: You convene the group meeting, help set the journalists' agenda and keep the press conference focused on the public's right to know and the reporter's right to provide information.

   At the meeting: Facilitate the group discussion; be sure each person gets a chance to provide input.

   At the news conference:
   – Be sure the journalists get their questions asked, heard and responded to.
   – Watch the reporters and make suggestions about appropriate behaviour, as needed (you may pass notes, whisper to them, or in extreme cases, disrupt or interrupt the proceedings).

2. *Select two to five people* to be Reporters for *major national newspapers, radio or television.*

   National Reporters: Try to dominate the questions and debate – to make your editors happy and inform your audience.

   At the news conference:
   – Place yourself strategically in the room, in view of the Politician and their entourage.
   – Try to get called on to ask the first question; keep getting your questions heard and answered.
   – Redirect vague answers to specifics.
   – Try to get the Politician to relinquish control of the press conference; get the Politician off-balance, away from their agenda so they will answer deeper questions and address key issues.
   – Your three main objectives are: (a) provide readers with nationally and internationally significant information; (b) further your career (keep your job, get promoted, win prizes, etc.); (c) sell newspapers or capture air time.

3. *Select two to five people* to be Reporters for *local newspapers, radio or television.*

Local Reporters: Try to get your questions answered without letting *either the politician or the national reporters dominate.*

At the news conference:
 − Try to get called on to ask the first question.
 − Focus attention on the issues that most affect your region.
 − Try to make the Politician relinquish control and let reporters control the press conference.
 − Try to get the Politician to make specific comments and responses instead of platitudes; get them off-balance and away from the party's predetermined agenda.
 − Your three main objectives are: (a) provide locally and regionally relevant information; (b) further your career and position in the community (get promoted, win prizes, etc.); (c) sell newspapers and air time.

4. *Appoint two people* as Heads of News Organisations.

Heads: You will advise reporters on the main points which should be covered.

At the group meeting:
 − Suggest key questions for reporters to ask.
 − Help devise strategies for getting the questions answered.

At the press conference:
 − Watch the action − keep things on track.
 − If you think the Reporters are getting submerged in the Politician's and Party's agenda, try to force a shift.
 − You may pass notes to the Reporters or whisper suggestions to them.
 − In extreme cases, if things are getting out of hand, try to interrupt or disrupt the proceedings.
 − Your two main objectives are: (a) to sell newspapers, radio and television; (b) to provide the best possible information.

Group B's objective: Plan a strategy that will force the politician to give precise answers and substantive information, not the party-controlled official version.

The Journalists' task: Take notes and plan how you would write the story for your newspaper and readers (what introduction, headline, illustrations?), for your radio or television station (what visuals? what audio?).

6.2 Browsing assignment

Go to your community or university library or newsagent. Look for newspapers and magazines you have never read which you consider to represent different views from your own. If you regularly read *The Guardian* or *The Independent*, read *The Sun* or *The Telegraph*. If you generally read magazines or newspapers representing labour or the left, find a more right-wing or centrist publication. If you consider yourself more Conservative, centrist or right-wing, read an issue of Red Pepper (a 'red-green' coalition magazine) or *The New Internationalist* or another left-of-centre publication.

Bring your notes and, if possible, a copy of the publication to class. In class, discuss students' choices and what has been learned from reading the unfamiliar publications. Were there any surprises? Consider whether your assumptions were correct, and what you have learned from reading material written from a different perspective. Would you read this publication again? Is any of the information persuasive enough that it might change your mind about an issue?

Further reading

Frederick, Fletcher J. (1996) 'Journalism in a fish bowl: ethical dilemmas in campaign coverage', in Valerie Alia, Brian Brennan and Barry Hoffmaster (eds), *Deadlines and Diversity: Journalism Ethics in a Changing World*. Halifax, NS: Fernwood, pp. 140–50.

Frank Howard, 'Conflicts of interest and codes of ethics in the parliamentary press gallery', in Valerie Alia, Brian Brennan and Barry Hoffmaster (eds), *Deadlines and Diversity: Journalism Ethics in a Changing World*. Halifax, NS: Fernwood, pp. 121–31.

Moore, Michael (2001) *Stupid White Men*. New York: HarperCollins.

Suggested viewing

For details see the annotated filmography in Appendix B at the end of the book.

Bowling for Columbine
Bulworth
Wag the Dog
The Prisoner (TV series)
The West Wing (TV series)

7 A picture is worth a thousand … : ethics and images

The camera was invented in 1839. It is generally attributed to Louis Daguerre, although he may just have been the most skilful self-promoter among several inventors. Another Frenchman, Hippolyte Bayard, invented a photographic process at the same time, as did the Englishman, Henry Fox Talbot. As we will see below, Hippolyte Bayard was deeply resentful of Daguerre's greater popularity. Whatever the reasons, it was Daguerre's name that became synonymous with early photographic images – daguerrotypes – and was extended to refer to professionals (daguerrotypists). When the technology spread worldwide, it was further extended to '*daguerromanie*' (daguerromania).

The first affordable, popular camera appeared in 1888. Within thirty years, photography was in daily use across the social spectrum – for 'police filing, war reporting, military reconnaissance, pornography, ency-clopaedic documentation, family albums, postcards, anthropological records, sentimental moralising, inquisitive probing, aesthetic effects, news reporting and formal portraiture' (Berger, 1980: 48). The first daguerrotypes were one-of-a-kind images and therefore as singular as paintings. Specialists in this early form of photographic production proliferated rapidly. By 1853 there were ten thousand in America; in 1861 there were two thousand photographers registered in Britain.

The new technology showed its sinister side early on. In 1871 the Paris police used photographs to help capture activists of the Paris Commune, and soon 'photographs became a useful tool of modern states in the surveillance and control of their increasingly mobile populations' (Sontag, 1977: 5).

In 1876 in Philadelphia, George Eastman left his job as bank clerk to manufacture cameras; within five years, 90,000 cameras were in the hands of ordinary people (Briggs and Burke, 2002: 165–6). His legacy is with us still, in Kodak cameras, films and processing. The democratis-ation of the camera contributed to its image as an instrument of reality and daily life. The camera was ubiquitous. Its role in illustrating media stories was a natural outgrowth of its role in illustrating the events of people's lives. The distance from photographing a family wedding to photographing a royal wedding was only a matter of personal versus professional use of the same technology. Press cameras were larger than family cameras and may have produced sharper images, but they were familiar objects producing images that were reproduced more or less faithfully, on film. The very familiarity of the camera kept it from being seen as an intruder or a manipulator.

It is important to place these observations in an international and multicultural context. This account of photographic history refers only to societies that welcomed the camera and its images. In parts of the Middle East, in Amish communities of Canada and the United States and in numerous other societies, such image-making is considered harmful and unacceptable. Eager photographers have come into uncomfortable contact with the need for transcultural sensitivity. You may note, for example, that many of the photographs of Amish people seen in travel brochures, newspapers and other media show people from the back (usually dressed in traditional clothing and travelling in horse-drawn buggies). Other 'authentic' Amish images are created by actors wearing Amish costumes.

'The predatory side of photography is at the heart of the alliance ... between photography and tourism ... tourists invaded the [Native Americans'] privacy, photographing holy objects and the sacred dances and places ...' (Sontag, 1977: 64). For the past twenty years I have worked as a journalist, photographer and academic conducting research in the Arctic and with Inuit and other indigenous peoples in various parts of North America. With very few exceptions, my photography has concentrated exclusively on landscape. There are aesthetic reasons that I prefer landscape photography, but the main reason I avoid photographing people has to do with my discomfort with that role. The fascination with unfamiliar landscapes also fits the tourist profile (and is also a potential interference with homelands and private or sacred space) but at least it avoids the literal 'in your face' invasion of other people's lives. The exceptions have been occasions on which I was asked to take photographs of specific people, at specific occasions or locations.

When a stranger brings a camera into a community, the intrusiveness is obvious. But what about the instances in which the camera and the photographer are invited, even welcomed? Is a friendly camera still an 'invader'? And what about the hidden camera? Is it intrusive, if no one knows it is there?

... photographs are not, as is often assumed, a mechanical record. Every time we look at a photograph, we are aware, however slightly, of the photographer selecting that sight from an infinity of other possible sights. This is true even in the most casual family snapshot. The photographer's way of seeing is reflected in his choice of subject … our perception or appreciation of an image depends also upon our way of seeing. (Berger, 1972: 10)

Any time a camera is used – no matter how sensitively and unobtrusively – it is intrusive. 'There is an aggression implicit in every use of the camera' (Sontag, 1977: 7). Subjects are 'captured'; images are 'shots' – a camera session is a 'photo shoot'; and in a sense, photographs kill their subjects by freezing them in time and space onto paper that can be pinned and printed wherever we like. Filmed and videotaped moving images do this as well; despite the appearance of motion, the subjects are nevertheless restricted and framed in films or news clips, their movements locked in a permanent loop.

Photographs alter and enlarge our notions of what is worth looking at, and what we have a right to observe. They are a grammar and, even more importantly, an ethics of seeing … they fiddle with the scale of the world … get reduced, blown up, cropped, re-touched, doctored, tricked out. (Sontag, 1977: 18–20)

Photographs also glamourise. The most horrific of scenes can be inadvertently beautified by the very skill that enables the photographer to create the image. Few people would claim a rat-infested slum, or bloody battle field, or the face of a person in pain, is beautiful. Yet countless well crafted photographs show as much attention to composition and craft as to depiction of those realities. I think it is not irrelevant that (in 1841) Fox Talbot named his patented photograph the 'calotype', from the Greek word, *kalos*, meaning 'beautiful'.

In the early 1900s police used hidden cameras to snap pictures of activist members of the Women's Political and Social Union.

… these techniques of covert surveillance were first developed nearly a century ago by Scotland Yard to tackle the then novel direct-action tactics of the militant suffragettes battling for votes for women … it was the police rather than the press who first developed the snatch tactics of the modern-day paparazzi. (Travis, 2003: 8, 9)

In using photographs in the media, John Hulteng cautions that the journalist must always consider the extent to which the photographic intervention is necessary or important. The journalist must weigh 'whether the obvious newsworthiness … justifies use of photos … is it worth the transitory exploitation of newsworthiness? Not only that, but we must consider the image's potential impact in the light of the proliferation of images that can *de*sensitise as well as sensitise viewers. Images can 'anesthetize':

> The quality of feeling, including moral outrage, that people can muster in response to photographs of the oppressed, the exploited, the starving, and the massacred ... depends on the degree of their familiarity with these images ... the ante keeps getting raised – partly through the very proliferation of such images of horror. (Sontag, 1977: 19)

Images can help to promote or discourage moral conduct. These days we tend to assume that moving images carry the greatest impact. But film-makers know otherwise. The 'freeze-frame' was once an innovative technique; after many years and movies, it has become something of a cinematic cliché. Nevertheless, the idea that *stopping* motion can be stronger than continuing motion persists in both fictional and factual television and film. A still photograph is often more powerful than full television coverage of an event-in-motion. Filmed or televised (moving) images may have less impact than still images. If viewers are over-whelmed, they sometimes 'shut down' and move on, unable to process anything. Most important, however, is the viewer's access to context. 'What determines the possibility of being affected morally by photographs is the existence of a relevant political consciousness.'

> Photographs like the one that made the front page of most news-papers in the world in 1972, of a naked South Vietnamese child sprayed by American napalm, running down a highway toward the camera, her arms open, screaming with pain, probably did more to increase the public revulsion against the war than a hundred hours of televised barbarities. (Sontag, 1977: 18)

In *About Locking*, John Berger notes that such images are 'discontinuous with normal time' (Berger, 1980). Whether an image is horrifying, amusing or simply serious, it is this temporal discontinuity that most affects the viewer. We freeze events into single-frame moments or 30-second clips. The viewer can only guess at what went before and after. No matter how meticulous the reporting or how faithful to the journal-ist's understanding of the event, we see it *out of context*. The event burned on the viewer's retina will remain *the event*, regardless of how fragmented or distorted it may be. At their most conscientious, photojournalists still cannot be neutral: the images they purvey still shape the viewer's understanding of people and events. The lessons of *Rashomon* must be remembered: we must learn to question *pictures* as carefully as we question *words*.

'Seeing is believing'?

> A photograph passes for incontrovertible proof that a given thing happened. The picture may distort; but there is always a presumption that something exists ... (Sontag, 1977: 5)

That presumption may not reflect reality. Increasingly, photographs are not 'incontrovertible proof', or even evidence of what exists. Many discussions of images and ethics are based on the premise that photographs can be separated into two basic categories, of 'manipulated' and 'honest' images. If we consider the nature of photography – from its origins to the digital present – we must acknowledge that there are no such categories.

> ... photography ... is an inherent manipulation – a manipulation of light, a process ... subject to the biases and interpretations of the photographer,   printer, editor, or viewer. Photography is not absolute 'reality.' It is not unqualified 'truth'. (Wheeler, 2002: 3)

This means that our discussion of ethics and images must be shifted, from a discussion of 'truth' versus 'lie' to one of degrees of truth-telling or falsification. Not only are all photographs 'manipulated' to one degree or another, but conscious image manipulation is nothing new.

The simplest means of altering a photograph is by *cropping* – cutting portions off the borders, or enlarging the central image and allowing the borders to disappear. It is possible, even with this most straightforward technique, to place an image out of context. The other main pre-digital techniques are called *burning* and *dodging*, which involve increasing or decreasing exposure of an area of a photograph to enhance or alter its effect. Usually applied to black and white photographs, these techniques are not generally ethically problematic, except perhaps when they alter the mood of a scene or the perceived character of a person. Earl Winkler gives an example of a woman and a policeman who are having a friendly conversation. The policeman raises his right arm to wave to a passing motorist; at the same time, the woman is startled by the sudden sound of a factory whistle. If one section of the photograph is enlarged, 'you find an image of a burly policeman, seen three-quarters from the rear, with his arm raised; a woman watches him from the side, leaning away with a look of fear on her face'. If that image is published without explanation or context, it conveys a 'truth' entirely at odds with the reality experienced by the two people concerned (Winkler, 1996: 19).

The first known faked photograph was apparently Hippolyte Bayard's 'Portrait of the Photographer as a Drowned Man, 1840' – produced just a year after photography began. Bayard's doctored photograph of his own 'suicide' was apparently meant to challenge the fact that government and the public had ignored him (in favour of the more prominent and publicised Daguerre) (Wheeler, 2002: 15). In 1919, a photograph of Vladimir Lenin in Red Square was published with several figures painted out – including that of Leon Trotsky (Wheeler, 2002: 21). In the 1970s, one of my own newspaper stories – a review of a ballet performance by Rudolf Nureyev – was accompanied by a photograph of the great dancer. Concerned that his Boston readers' delicate sensibilities might be offended by the noticeable 'bulge', the editor ordered the photographic department to airbrush Nureyev's crotch. The flattened photograph was a source of mirth among newspaper staff for a long time after.

In 1996, *The National Geographic* magazine published an advertisement for its online site, with a photograph of a polar bear. The only problem was that the magazine called it a photograph of 'Antarctica', and there are no polar bears there. Polar bears do live in the *Arctic* – at the other end of the planet – and 'also in the Ohio zoo where this particular animal was photographed' (Wheeler, 2002: 45). While editing his film *Zoolander* – shot before the September 11, 2001 attack on the New York World Trade Center, but released several months later – director Ben Stiller had the now destroyed World Trade Center twin towers digitally removed from the film (Wheeler, 2002: 30). Along with current trends in news photography and television, Stiller's actions point to one of the major shifts of media responsibility – from cameraperson and photographer to director and editor. It is always the case that movie images are subject to editing – the director's and editor's decisions have always mediated between cameraperson and audience. But (except in cartoons and science fiction movies) the editors chose, deleted and (re)ordered scenes rather than deliberately altering the basic images. In news media, the photojournalists decided what images to shoot, developed their film and brought in their printed contact sheets. The editor then chose which images to print. The decision-making chain has collapsed.

> The photographer ... knew that the photograph was going to be manipulated. I said, 'Do you know what is going to happen?' and he said, 'No.' ... There was a sense that photographers had lost control of this process and a more centralized authority would make those decisions' ... (Abrams, 1995: 43)

There are indications that the more sophisticated the technologies of manipulation and the more centralised the decision-making becomes, the less the public trusts the images. It is not so much that technology has changed the possibility of altering images, but that the quantity of

(a)

(b)

Figure 7.1 Digitally manipulated photographs. (Rik Walton)
(a) What do these people seem to be doing? Where do they appear to be?
(b) What does this image imply about the relationship between these people, as compared with the same people in (a)?

(a)

(b)

Figure 7.2 Where is this woman relaxing? How can you tell? Which is the 'original' image, (a) or (b)? (Rik Walton)

altered images and scale of the problem has changed. It may soon be that the *un*altered image will be the anomaly. We must consider carefully what this means for the prevalent wisdom that photojournalism provides an 'eyewitness to history' (Arnett, 1998: [no page]). Edgar Huang warns that the loss of credibility threatens to change not only public faith in the 'truth' of photographic images but ultimately the media's ability to carry out its watchdog role. Huang uses the example of the 1989 killings at Tiananmen Square. The Chinese government spokesperson Yuan Mu 'impudently denied the fact that ordinary citizens were killed ... as shown in the news photographs carried in the Western media'. His argument was based on the assumption that 'the veracity, or the witness function, of those news photographs' was questionable in the age of digital imaging and manipulation. Huang worries that in the future, 'governments may be less afraid of the documentary evidence of photography' and therefore less likely to be intimidated by the media's watchdog role (Huang, 1999: 11).

The thorny path ahead contains some possible safeguards. The public has become so accustomed to manipulated images that media credibility is compromised. In turn, the media are trying to win back the public's trust. Some media outlets are adopting protocols for image-taking, image editing and disclosure. Earl Winkler cites cases 'in which digital manipulation is justified'. One is the story of a twelve-year old Californian boy who was photographed receiving an award. When the newspaper editors discovered his trousers were unzipped, they contrived to digitally 'zip' them before publishing the photograph (Winkler, 1996: 19).

'Ways of seeing', ways of feeling: the ethics of photojournalism

In his book *The Press and Its Problems*, Curtis MacDougall proposed an easy 'solution' to the 'problem' of reluctant subjects. If a subject kept trying to hide her or his face, MacDougall's advice to the photographer was to cry, 'Fire!' Hearing such a cry, he said, would often cause people 'to uncover long enough for a speed flash'. His advice for photographers of children or single women was to tell the women, or the children's mothers, that they 'are to be entered in beauty or intelligence contests' (MacDougall, 1964: 342). Today, few people would consider such methods acceptable, let alone ethical.

Despite her deeply felt moral concerns and dedication to a pro-active, social change-oriented photographic enterprise, Susan Sontag is pessimistic about the predominance of consumerism in the field.

Whatever the moral claims made on behalf of photography, its main effect is to convert the world into a department store or museum-without-walls in which every subject is depreciated into an article of consumption, promoted into an item for aesthetic appreciation. Through the camera people become customers or tourists of reality ... (Sontag, 1977: 110)

The quintessential question of photojournalistic ethics is: given the choice of recording an event or intervening to prevent pain or save lives, what should the photojournalist do? In the case of the 'evergreen lady', the Quebec television journalists Pierre Mignault and Alain Picard decided they had a moral obligation to abandon their cameras and intervene to avert human suffering. They also decided to continue filming the story and to produce it, despite the subject's request to be left alone. They took her to hospital despite her protests. They continued to film her, despite her protests (Mignault, 1996: 8–9). In the first instance, they cited her welfare as justification for their actions – she had gangrene and they felt they were acting to save her life. They made a judgement that 'our moral duty was to intervene ... We acted not as journalists but as private citizens' (Mignault, 1996: 9, 11). In the second instance, they justified their actions in terms of the public good. As Sontag sees it, photographing 'is essentially an act of non-intervention' – an act made horrific by

the awareness of how plausible it has become, in situations where the photographer has the choice between a photograph and a life, to choose the photograph. The person who intervenes cannot record; the person who is recording cannot intervene. (Sontag, 1977: 11–12)

Some photographers operate as if they are 'scientists', others as moralists; the scientists make an inventory of the world; the moralists concentrate on hard cases (Sontag, 1977: 59). As Sontag sees it, both kinds of photographers can do good in the world, but the 'pseudo-scientific neutrality' of the scientist-photographer is a fiction.

In the late nineteenth century, Jacob Riis pioneered the use of photographs to illustrate and underscore stories of the plight of people living in poverty. Riis was a reporter for the *New York World*, and Lincoln Steffens's mentor (see Figures 7.3 and 7.4).

Jake Riis was a Danish American who 'covered' police headquarters, the Health Department ... and 'the East Side,' which was a short name for the poor and the foreign quarters of the city. And he not only got the news; he cared about the news. He hated passionately all tyrannies, abuses, miseries, and he fought them. He was a 'terror' to

Figure 7.3 Lincoln Steffens, the great 'muckraker' and first investigative journalist (used with permission of Pete Steffens).

Figure 7.4 Jacob Riis, pioneering journalist and photojournalist. Photograph by Davis Garber, inscribed to Lincoln Steffens (used with permission of Pete Steffens).

the officials and landlords responsible, as he saw it, for the desperate condition of the tenements where the poor lived … (Steffens, 1931: 203).

Riis's book *How the Other Half Lives* was one of the first 'documentary' texts to bring photographs and words together. He felt that words were insufficient to move people to change the conditions of people living in New York's slums. He wanted to affect the public, politicians and policy-makers. As a reporter and reformer, Riis 'forced the appointment of a Tenement House Commission' whose investigation resulted in the destruction of some of the worst places, regulation of the tenements, and creation of a collection of small parks – green spaces providing relief from the concrete urban jungle (Steffens, 1931: 203).

> The writer of nonfiction is only a renter, who must abide by the con-ditions of his lease, which stipulates that he leave the house – and its name is Actuality – as he found it … The writer … is under contract to the reader to limit himself to events that actually occurred and to characters who have counterparts in real life, and he may not embel-lish the truth about these events or these characters. (Malcolm, 1990: 153)

Christopher Harris finds Janet Malcolm's description relevant to the photojournalist's role.

> The potential loss of the public's trust in visual journalism is of vital concern … The challenge … in news photography is to treat the 'house of Actuality' as though it were indeed being rented. Ethically we owe our photojournalism audience factual visual evidence of news occurrences. Such is implied, if not written into, our photojournalis-tic lease with our audiences. (Harris, 1991: 165)

Exercises

7.1 Class debate on case study: Photojournalism under fire

Divide the class into two teams, one 'for' and the other 'against':

Resolved: a journalist should only document and should never intervene as a private citizen, even to save lives.

BACKGROUND

A photojournalist was sent to a war zone in a country he had never been to. His editor had heard that the country's army was torturing and killing civilians but the army kept denying the charges and the story could not be confirmed. Preparing for the assignment, the photojournalist said he would not get involved in the action, no matter what happened, but he would wear a soldier's uniform to avoid attracting attention.

When he arrived, he found a group of soldiers destroying villagers' homes and raping and torturing children, women and men. He had two choices: to intervene and stop at least some of the atrocities, or to keep taking pictures. He kept taking pictures. He later explained his actions as an essential part of the journalist's duty to witness and document. He said if he had intervened, he would have been unable to record the events and bring the information to the public.

(Adapted from a case study by Deni Elliott in
FineLine, October 1990: 2)

NOTES FOR INFORMATION AND DISCUSSION
Visual images: bring examples of still photographs and videotape.

Issues, principles and guidelines: Oriana Fallaci says that the journalist is also a historian who records events for posterity. In deciding whether to photograph or film, the photographer or videographer should consider:

1. Is this a newsworthy event? If so, can the story be told without pictures, or are pictures essential or important?
2. If visual images are important, how can I minimise negative impact on the subject(s)? Can I shoot from a distance and avoid 'getting in someone's face'? What is the best possible way to relate to the subject to avoid hurting them?
3. Is the subject a prominent figure accustomed to being photographed or an 'ordinary citizen' unaccustomed to being in the public eye? What special problems and obligations do I have in each of these cases?
4. If the person has experienced a trauma, must I photograph them at this moment or can I wait? Is it important that this be made public? Is it essential? Am I taking the picture only to further my career, or is it to inform the public and perhaps aid the subject?
5. The camera is always intrusive. If I use it in this instance, do I risk causing further injury or trauma? If so, can it be avoided?

Question: What is the role of the journalist as citizen here? Are there any cases in which you would consider it appropriate to put down the camera and intervene?

For further information, see Bryant (1987).

CLASS DISCUSSION

'It has been said that photographs furnish evidence that something happened, and even if they are distorted, they prove something exists.' Do you think this is an accurate statement? Explain. When isn't an image 'true' or 'reliable'?

Further reading

Berger, John (1972) *Ways of Seeing*. London: Penguin Books.

Berger, John (1980) *About Looking*. New York: Pantheon Books.

Bryant, Garry (1987) 'Ten-fifty P.I.: emotion and the photographer's role', *Journal of Mass Media Ethics*, vol. 2, no. 2, Spring/Summer, 32–9.

Elliott, Deni (1990) 'As life passes by', *FineLine*, October, 2.

Lester, Paul (1991) *Photojournalism: An Ethical Approach*. Hove and London: Lawrence Erlbaum Associates.

Sontag, Susan (1997) *On Photography*. New York: Farrar, Strauss & Giroux.

Wheeler, Thomas H. (2002) *Phototruth or Photofiction? Ethics and Media Imagery in the Digital Age*. London: Lawrence Erlbaum Associates.

Suggested viewing

For details see the annotated filmography in Appendix B at the end of the book.

Broadcast News
Man with a Movie Camera
Network
Rear Window
Tomorrow Never Dies
The Truman Show

8 'Trust me, I'm a friend': the ethics of interviewing

At the heart of journalism is the *interview*. At the heart of the interview is the (usually short-term) relationship between interviewer and interviewee. Media studies texts often devote modest attention to the nature and impact of interviews. Journalism texts almost always include some information on the basics of how to conduct an interview, without which journalism could scarcely exist. Few of the texts address the issues in depth, or provide engagement with the ethical issues that make interviews so challenging and so potentially dangerous. The interviewer–interviewee relationship involves a degree of trust. The trust between the journalist and the 'source' is often unjustified, and manipulated in unethical – and sometimes unnecessary – ways. In a sense, Janet Malcolm *begins* her discussion of the ethics of interviewing by *ending* it. She tells us there is no alternative but to behave immorally.

> Every journalist who is not too stupid or too full of himself to notice what is going on knows that what he does is morally indefensible. He is a kind of confidence man, preying on people's vanity, ignorance, or loneliness, gaining their trust and betraying them without remorse. (Malcolm, 1990: 3)

> We went on like that for a half hour, and then when I'd asked all the polite questions, I started in on the impolite ones. It's an old journalist's trick to save the worst for last. That way if you're thrown out, you still have most of your interview. (Viets, 2000: 105)

Types and techniques of interviews

Arthur Barron identifies three basic kinds of journalistic interview: the 'repertorial', the 'adversarial' and the 'open' interview. Each of these has its strengths and weaknesses; each has its particular ethical dilemmas.

In a *repertorial* interview, the interviewer behaves as a reporter who asks questions only in order to gather 'factual information'. The interviewer adopts a 'neutral tone' and an objective of 'accuracy, balance and objectivity' (Barron, 1999: 10–11). In discussing the reportorial inter- view, Barron treats it as if there were no relevant ethical concerns or questions. But there are crucial ethical questions that *should* be asked. Since no one is free of values and opinions, what problems might arise from the pretence of neutrality or objectivity? Is this not a form of journalistic deception? How might it influence the interviewee's responses? Oriana Fallaci is one of those who consider reportorial neutrality both an impossibility and a misguided objective. Most of her interviews are with the world's major political figures – of all nationali- ties and persuasions. She adopts an interview style composed of several techniques, but the one she ignores – or, more accurately, opposes – is the 'repertorial' technique. In Chapter 2 she is cited as an exemplary ethnographer, an illuminating and incisive revealer of large truths through small details. She is also a participant observer, and a participant as *herself*. A muckraker to the core, deeply committed to social change, she sees no point in conducting an interview that is not grounded in her own moral and political judgements.

> I did not go to these … people with the detachment of the anatomist or the imperturbable reporter. I went with a thousand feelings of rage, a thousand questions that before assailing them were assailing me, and with the hope of understanding in what way, by being in power or opposing it, those people determine our destiny. (Fallaci, 1976: 9)

An *adversarial* interview raises more visible ethical questions. Here, the interviewer takes on the role of 'investigative reporter, detective or prosecutor', adopting a tone of scepticism or even confrontation. There is no pretence of trust – quite the opposite, the interviewer behaves as if she or he trusted nothing that the interviewee says. The objective in this method is to reveal deception or inconsistency in the responses to questions. Barron cautions about the dangers of entrapment and bully- ing. To this we should add a third concern, of possible deception – in the interviewer's pretence that she/he disagrees or mistrusts the interviewee entirely. This method is used most often with public figures – politicians or celebrities whose self-interest and willingness to deceive the public is often assumed.

In an *open* interview, the interviewer takes on the role of 'caregiver, therapist or cleric' and the interview becomes a sort of confessional exercise. Such interviews tend to be 'lengthy, probing and open-ended'. The interviewer behaves in a non-judgemental way, striving to create an atmosphere of trust, empathy and support. To do this, the interviewer sometimes shares her or his own feelings and opinions. The goal is 'to encourage people to reveal their emotions, attitudes, beliefs, and generally, behaviour that is usually kept private'. The ethical risks of 'open' interviews include manipulation, in which the interviewer creates a false climate of trust and betrays that trust through the deceptive use of phoney empathy. Caught off guard, the interviewee may reveal information that they had intended to keep private. There are psychological risks in this method. 'By probing for material kept private or repressed, the interviewer can stir overwhelming emotions' and problems that only a proper therapist can deal with. The other ethical risk is that of jeopardy. Once the interview is broadcast or published, the person is left to cope with the effects of the interview. This can mean negative responses of viewers and readers, or even criminal prosecution (Barron, 1999: 10–11).

Lynn Barber takes a different position. She says there are as many interview techniques as interviewers. She groups these into four main techniques: the 'minimal question' school of interviewing (her favourite); the 'conversation or debate'; the 'sisterly confession' school; and the interview in which 'the interviewer does all of the talking'. Ideally, she thinks the subject should 'do all the talking, with only occasional interruptions from me'. Thus, she prefers the *minimal question* method. She sees each method as having particular strengths and weaknesses. The *conversation or debate*-style of interview is good for encouraging interviewees to voice their opinions. It is less effective in illuminating character. As Barber puts it, 'It can produce an awful lot of hot air'. The *sisterly confession* school indulges the interviewer's ego. Interviewers 'talk about their own disastrous childhoods, love lives, drink problems, etc., in the hope that the interviewee will ... say, "Oh, me too!"' This method is fraught with dangers, including the accusation of malpractice for impersonating a therapist, and the danger of eliciting information which can lead to personal crisis. The case of the *interviewer doing all of the talking* requires little explanation. Here again, the interviewer's ego is paramount and the source's own story gets lost in the shuffle. The journalist is egomaniac, sycophant, or both.

> The earliest interviews tended to be of the 'Tell me, Famous Person, what brings you to London?' variety ... they featured a deferential and unsceptical tone – they were designed to elicit information but not evaluate it ... (Barber, 1999: 197)

Barber's vote for all-time best interview is Lillian Ross's profile of the writer and former journalist Ernest Hemingway, 'How do you like it now, gentlemen?' published in the *New Yorker*. Ross interviewed Hemingway in New York, over a two-day period in the spring of 1950. Her intention was to adopt a non-judgemental position with which she produced what she considered to be 'an affectionate portrait'. Hemingway expressed no problems with the finished piece. Contrary to accepted journalistic practice, she allowed him to read the article before publication but he did not ask her to rewrite it. Ross and Hemingway became lifelong friends. Nevertheless, the article

> produced a storm of outrage when it was published. Many readers ... said they were 'devastated' by its cruelty; others congratulated Ross on exposing Hemingway as a fraud. (Barber, 1999: 198)

This goes to prove that no matter how careful you are, any interview using any technique is liable to misinterpretation and abuse. Regardless of the chosen technique, or combination of techniques, an interview with a celebrity is likely to be controlled by the marketing department. It is difficult to gain access to a celebrity without being joined by a public relations entourage. Often, you must submit questions in advance and try to sneak in an occasional impromptu query on the sly.

Barber takes issue with Janet Malcolm's idea of the interview as a betrayal – 'as if two people have met and had a friendly private conversation, and then one has gone out and published the other's secrets to the world'. She says that in reality interviews do not work that way. 'Famous people ... know that this nice friendly woman coming to see them is not a long-sought soulmate or a kindly psychotherapist but a journalist intending to write a piece for publication.'

The problem with Barber's analysis is that, by focusing on the celebrity interview, she conveniently omits most of the interviews journalists do and trivialises or minimises the ethical dilemmas. Even celebrities are sometimes caught off guard. I can vouch for this myself. Over the years, I have obtained a good deal of personal information about performers and others during interviews and sometimes in informal pre- or post-interview sessions. This usually happened in the course of conversation, and I have never published 'off the record' information that was not freely given as part of the interview itself. (In case you think this a high and mighty position to take, let me assure you that in Chapter 9, I confess to various imperfections and ethically embarrassing decisions and behaviours.)

Barber says that both interviewer and interviewee should use a tape recorder. It is a good idea, and two tape recorders are surely better than one. Nevertheless, it is crucial to take notes as well. High-tech interviews cannot replace the careful and thoughtful framing and asking of questions or careful and accurate note-taking. The tape recorder is 'libel insurance' and a way of improving accuracy. It should never replace a notebook. Barber argues that interviewees must be quoted verbatim, grammatical errors and all. I think this is a matter of judgement, though it is a generally appropriate rule. If verbatim quotation gives the flavour of a person's speech, it can be very effective. If it becomes unnecessarily cumbersome (as when the subject says 'well' or 'uh' or 'hm' over and over, taking precious space from the substantive comments) it can be cut. The most careful way to do this is to use ellipses (...) to indicate omissions. Whatever perspective is adopted, it should be thoughtful and attentive to accuracy and integrity. I am dismayed by the rampant rewriting of quotes seen so often these days. It has become too facile and too unquestioning.

Barber claims the journalist has all the power – limitless opportunities for 'slanting' the interview ... (Barber, 1999: 196–205). I think the power runs both ways, especially with celebrity and politician interviews. For one thing, she oversimplifies 'the journalist' in the equation. There is also an editor, and another editor who decides where and how to place the interview; there are photographs (flattering or un-) and headlines and all sorts of other intervening facets of publication. And no matter how naive the subject, 'sources' are as highly motivated as journalists and as likely to manipulate the interview for their own ends. In reality, the interview is a tug-of-war. When it works well, the reader, listener or viewer wins – or everybody wins.

Methods, motives, murders

The ethicist Edmund Lambeth calls Oriana Fallaci the 'greatest political interviewer of modern times'. She 'brings a formidable amount of background knowledge to each interview. She knows her history' and 'infiltrates, goes behind the lines and sketches from life ... she breaks many rules we're teaching and gets in' (Lambeth, 1986: 6). Her interviews are always designed to correct the imbalance between highly powerful subjects, the interviewer and the readers she serves. She has interviewed Henry Kissinger, Yasir Arafat, Golda Meir and countless other world leaders. Invited to interview the Pakistani leader, Ali Bhutto, Fallaci accepted, with care. She mistrusted his motives because he had *invited* her. Although she decided to accept his invitation, 'I let him know that being his guest would not keep me from writing about him with the same independence of judgment that I applied to everyone without distinction ...' (Fallaci, 1976: 182).

Not all interviews are with the famous or the powerful. John McPhee sometimes interviews both, but he specialises in interviewing ordinary people in extraordinary ways. McPhee has the ability to take the most mundane of subjects and turn it into magic, capturing the reader's interest and managing to be thoroughly entertaining, while teaching the unsuspecting reader things they never even thought of learning. The 1968 story 'Twynam of Wimbledon' is a fine example of his method and his art. Unlike many of the ethically problematic interviews cited elsewhere in this chapter, this one is wholly respectful of its subject.

> A weed – in the vernacular of groundsmen in England – is known as a volunteer, and there are no volunteers in the Centre Court at Wimbledon. Robert Twynam, who grows the grass there, is willing to accept a bet from anyone who is foolhardy enough to doubt this … When Twynam describes tennis players, he is less likely to call them touch players or power players than … toe-draggers, sliders, or choppers … Twynam is not a horticulturist or a botanist … his approach … goes some distance beyond science. He is a praying man, and at least part of the time he is praying for the grass. (McPhee, 1968: 175, 176, 177, 179)

Once you have read McPhee's essay, watching Wimbledon can never be the same. The art and science of grass, the vagaries of nature and the cares of Twynam are inextricable from the game and skill of tennis and its players – users, destroyers, protectors and appreciators of grass.

> Nearly all the greatest stars of tennis have played under his scrutiny, and – while he knows a great deal about the game – his appraisals of all of them seem to have been formed from the point of view of the grass. 'When [a player] puts his foot down, he is stepping on forty or fifty plants.' (McPhee, 1968: 176)

The interview is neither romantic nor cynical. With deceptive simplicity and a respect for the subject's own voice, McPhee tells us a great deal about tennis, its players, Wimbledon, horticultural care and conservation, Robert Twynam and ourselves.

In contrast to this dignified and gentle interview, consider the mood and method of Martin Bashir's treatment of a celebrity, the singer Michael Jackson. In 2003, the reclusive and self-protective American performer allowed British broadcaster Martin Bashir to interview him and film a television documentary at his Neverland ranch home, based on apparent flattery. The case echoes issues raised in Janet Malcolm's *Journalist and the Murderer* study of journalist–source friendship and betrayal. In questioning Jackson for his documentary, Bashir said kind things concerning Jackson's highly controversial ways of caring for children (his own and others). Those words are recorded in a documentary produced as rebuttal by Jackson's own television crew. Bashir's kind words were omitted from his documentary. In Jackson's film, Bashir is heard to say: 'Your relationship with your children is spectacular. It almost makes me weep when I see you with them because your inter-action with them is so natural, so loving, so caring' (Mills, 2003: 7). In a leader following the two documentaries, *The Guardian* called Bashir's programme

> strongly critical, and convincingly so, about the singer's relationship with the children he entertains at his Neverland ranch, which [Bashir] described as a 'dangerous place' for vulnerable children ...
>
> ... Either Mr Bashir believed this when he was saying it or he did not. If he did not, then he would have been in breach of the highest journalistic ethics by lying ... to get a better story. If he did believe it, then either he changed his mind in the light of later evidence – which was not obvious to viewers – or decided for other reasons to have an ending ... inconsistent with his earlier comments ... (*The Guardian*, 2003a: 21)

The Guardian makes the power relationship between journalist and source transparent: 'Both have made a lot of money from their respective films' (*The Guardian*, 2003: 21). John Pilger tries to correct the imbalance of journalist–subject power by concentrating his interviews with the people he refers to as 'Unpeople' – those in poverty, in unpopular or unpowerful countries, those whose politics or circumstances have left them voiceless. In Australia, he interviewed 'many of the stolen children ... moved and angered by what I have heard' (Pilger, 1998: 242). In Burma he interviewed the political dissident, Aung San Suu Kyi, under house arrest, and found

> a striking, glamorous figure who ... appeared at first to carry her suffering lightly. It was only later when I looked at film of her taken just before her arrest that I realised her face had changed ... (Pilger, 1998: 204)

In *The Journalist and the Murderer* Janet Malcolm documents an altogether different journalist–subject relationship.

> In the deal that was presently struck ... McGinniss [the journalist] would receive not only total access but also a written promise of exclusivity and a release from all legal liability ... For his part, MacDonald [the murderer] would receive twenty-six and a half per cent of the advance and thirty-three per cent of the royalties. (Malcolm, 1990: 19)

The arrangement is dangerous from the start. As the relationship develops, McGinniss allows MacDonald to think he is a friend who believes in his innocence and whose book will help to exonerate him. On the other hand, McGinniss gradually comes to believe MacDonald is guilty – a view upheld by the jury. However horrific MacDonald's crimes, Janet Malcolm asks whether the journalist's deception is not a murder of another kind. As is apparent from the passage quoted at the opening of this chapter, she is cynical about the entire enterprise. She concludes that journalism does not just *tolerate* such compromising behaviour, it *requires* it for its very existence. And she insists that the interviewee is complicit in her or his own compromise, not the unwilling victim of a predatory interviewer.

> My whole life, I've been a great eavesdropper … The nuances of ordinary speech interest me, but what really fascinates me is the person who is so caught up in what he's saying that he tells more truth than he intends to …

> What gives journalism its authenticity and vitality is the tension between the subject's blind self-absorption and the journalist's scepticism. Journalists who swallow the subject's account whole and publish it are not journalists but publicists. (Higgins, 1999: 10)

As for the interviewees, 'human nature guarantees that willing subjects will never be in short supply'. In assessing what she believes to be the inherent interviewer–interviewee relationship, Malcolm makes no distinction between murderers, celebrities, politicians and other leaders, and ordinary people. She compares all interviewees to the Aztec people who 'lived in delightful ease and luxury' while awaiting (their own) sacrifice. Journalistic subjects

> know all too well what awaits them when the days of wine and roses – the days of the interviews – are over. And still they say yes when a journalist calls, and still they are astonished when they see the flash of the knife. (Malcolm, 1990: 144–5)

What are we to make of Malcolm when there is no knife? Before we take her at face value, we must consider the separate universes of McGinniss's Macdonald and McPhee's Twynam, Fallaci's political villains and heroes and the silent non-interview of Pierre Mignault's Eva the Evergreen Lady' (Mignault, 1996).

Guidelines for ethical interviewing

Coté and Simpson title their chapter on interviewing, 'The interview: assault or catharsis?' They stress the importance of considering the consequences of a particular approach or of conducting an interview at all. They question whether it is necessary to interview people who have experienced trauma immediately after the event. 'What is the value of intruding on people when they are grieving, disoriented, shocked, and frightened?' And what is required for a traumatised person to grant informed consent (Coté and Simpson, 2000: 83–4)? In their view, an ethical media practice requires careful reconsideration of some of the basic operating assumptions (e.g. it is always best to 'grab' an interview as soon as possible, whatever the nature of the situation and the people involved). With a goal of minimising violence and preventing its escalation, and preventing unnecessary trauma to interviewees, they call upon responsible media practitioners to think carefully about their work, and follow the guidelines summarised below.

1. Watch what you say.
2. Set the stage. 'Ask a "when" question: When did you hear the news? When did the police arrive?'
3. Explain the ground rules: '… gain informed consent by identifying risks to the interview subject'.
4. Share control with the interviewee.
5. Anticipate emotional responses. Just because people may have difficulty communicating does not mean they do not want to tell their stories. 'Interrupting them may be experienced as patronizing … if you terminate an interview … because you find it upsetting … you may be re-victimizing the victim'.
6. Listen.
7. Review with the interviewee what you have learned.
8. Think through what you have heard and seen. (Coté and Simpson, 2000: 83–101)

Lincoln Steffens addressed this last point (and its limitations) in examining his experience of interviewing James B. Dill, author of trust laws for the state of New Jersey, which 'had the right to pass any laws it pleased'. Mr Dill had managed to get this legislation passed 'quietly, almost secretly' – legislation that supported 'plain financial crimes' (Steffens, 1931: 193). 'Wall Street', of course, refers to the New York Stock Exchange, located on that famous street.

> … to my amazement he opened up the criminal inside of the practices … a picture of such chicanery and fraud, of wild license and wrong-doing, that I could not, I dared not, take it all down; I was too confused …
>
> '… you must write what I tell you. Don't quote me …' I did not

Respect the other person's efforts to regain balance after a horrible experience.
(Ron Walton)

write all that Dill told me … I was too imbued with the Wall Street spirit and view of things … I was a Wall Street man myself, unconsciously … That's how I came finally to understand what corruption is and how it gets a man … (Steffens, 1931: 194)

Exercises

8.1 Class discussion: the interviewee – complicit egomaniac or innocent victim?

View the film, *Absence of Malice*. Discuss Janet Malcolm's position on the interviewer–interviewee relationship in the light of the relationships between the journalist and the people she interviews, and the various consequences of her decisions about interviewing technique and approach.

8.2 Simulation exercise: experimenting with Barron's typology of journalistic interviews

INTRODUCTION TO BARRON'S TYPOLOGY OF JOURNALISTIC INTERVIEWS
Students should reread the discussion of Barron's typology in Chapter 8.

PREPARING THE SIMULATION EXERCISE
Select six volunteers. Organise them in three pairs. Each pair has an interviewer and an interviewee.

SIMULATED INTERVIEWS
Using Barron's criteria, pairs conduct interviews in front of the class. Each pair takes one interview style. Each interviewer asks the same two questions:

1. What are your career objectives after graduation?
2. Why study ethics?

CLASS DISCUSSION
Discuss the interviews in terms of interviewers' behaviour, interviewees' responses, ethical implications of the methods and the way these particular interviews developed. The exercise can be extended by considering and experimenting with other interview techniques discussed in the chapter. It can be varied by changing the interview questions.

8.3 Case study: False confidants: truth, lies and trust – the journalist–interviewee relationship

BACKGROUND OF THE CASE

A man accused of murdering his wife and two small children is on trial. Several years ago, while he was serving in the Army, an army tribunal found him not guilty. But pressure from the murdered woman's step-father led the Justice Department to reopen the investigation. Now, after several years, there is enough evidence to bring the man to trial. A newspaper columnist interviews the man.

At this point, the journalist has no strong opinion concerning the man's guilt or innocence. Near the end of the interview, the man invites the journalist to attend the trial, live with the defence team and write a book from the defence team's perspective. The arrangement would allow the journalist exclusive access to people and information.

ETHICAL PROBLEM A

The agreement the journalist is offered includes a written promise of exclusivity and a release from all legal liability, regardless of whether the man likes what is written. The price for this arrangement is that the accused murderer would receive a share of the book's proceeds.

DECISION A

You are the journalist. Do you attend the trial? Do you accept the man's proposal and exchange a promise of book royalties for an exclusive? What preparation do you make to help you decide? On what premises do you base your decision?

ETHICAL PROBLEM B

Regardless of your decision in A, assume that you have decided to proceed. You become the confidant of the accused and his defence team. You never specifically say you don't believe everything they tell you, but you allow them to believe you are an ally. The accused man calls you his 'friend'. You are privy to many secrets concerning the man's family life and the defence team's strategy. As the trial progresses, you become convinced that the man is guilty of the murders. The man is convicted. He begins a correspondence with you, still calls you 'friend' and still thinks you believe in his innocence. When you publish a book describing the man's guilt, he is anguished and outraged at your 'betrayal'.

DECISION B

Does your decision about the man's guilt have any effect on your role as confidant/interviewer, your writing or your original agreement? Do you answer the man's letters? Do you use the correspondence as material for your book? Do you continue to allow him to believe you're his 'friend'? Do you let him know that your book will be less flattering than he assumes (or hopes)? When you do publish and he feels betrayed, what is your response (a) to him? (b) to the public? Where do your responsibilities lie ... and your lies serve truth? To whom do you owe loyalty? If the man were proven *not* guilty, or if you continued to believe in his innocence, would you apply a different set of ethical standards? Try to separate your *ethical* decisions from related legal concerns.

(Based on the case discussed in Janet Malcolm's book, *The Journalist and the Murderer*, 1990)

Further reading

Fallaci, Oriana (1976) *Interview with History*. Boston: Houghton Mifflin.
Malcolm, Janet (1990) *The Journalist and the Murderer*. London: Papermac.

Viewing

For details see the annotated filmography in Appendix B at the end of the book.

Absence of Malice
Ace in the Hole
All the President's Men
Antonia: A Portrait of the Woman
Libeled Lady
The Mean Season

9 Specialist media: entertaining and informing the public

A travel story in a regional newspaper featured several full-colour photographs and detailed description filled with the lavish use of the word 'blissful'. At the end of the story, where readers are accustomed to find factual details for the planning of trips was the name and website address of a single travel company. What's wrong with this picture? For a start, we might ask whether any holiday is totally blissful and trouble-free. More to the point, we might ask whether such a story is journalism. It looks like journalism. It's presented as journalism. But where are the critical elements and the interviews with people of differing perspectives?

When I discuss this, I ask students if they have ever had a 'holiday from hell'. Invariably, the stories come pouring out. A recent discussion included several tales of discomfort, disillusionment and even death. One student recalled an earlier experience with her family. They arrived at a mountain campsite prepared for 'total safety' by the sponsoring travel company, and lived through several days of increasing horror that culminated in death as one tent set too close to the edge of windswept cliffs slipped off the edge while its occupants were sleeping. Another spoke of visiting an idyllic Greek resort she chose after seeing gorgeous and detailed photographs in a travel brochure. When the group of travellers arrived, they found bare walls and concrete floors and the most rudimentary of unpicturesque facilities. To surprise my husband on a special birthday at a time when I was immersed in work, I chose a well-known travel company to organise a two-week holiday. I explained that this was a very special occasion – I was taking my husband back to his birthplace in Italy. I said we needed absolute rest. I was assured all of the details would be arranged by the company. We arrived in the middle of the night at a small, darkened airport with an empty lobby and no 'waiting driver' in sight. After an hour or so of waiting, we found our own (expensive) taxi to take us more than 30 miles up the coast. Each day brought new surprises. In short, nothing was as promised. The low point was our carefully planned overnight ferry from Genoa to Palermo. We were told to arrive at least an hour before departure time so we started out with several extra hours, to be sure. The travel company's driver showed up late. No one had bothered to mention that it was a national holiday, there was only one road, and traffic on such days moves at approximately an hour for each mile. When it became apparent we could not possibly make the ferry, we had the driver leave us at the nearest railway station, caught the train, found another taxi that got us to the ferry five minutes before departure as the doors were being shut. Luckily, we got on board.

Such stories are rampant. Everybody knows it. Yet when is the last time you read of such an experience on the travel pages of your local or national newspaper? When you do read stories of catastrophic travel, it is usually on the editorial pages. The only critical travel writing is generally by full-time members of the newspaper staff. The reason? Almost all travel writing is by freelance writers, and a double ethical standard applies: members of staff must observe the usual rules of practice; others have no constraints. Newspapers don't pay much for travel stories, nor do they pay the costs of freelance writers' travel. Few writers can afford the cruises and 'paradise' holidays they write about, so they take the lavish, company-sponsored junkets provided for their convenience. Travellers should be able to read about several possible ways of travelling, gain a comparative understanding of various options and make informed decisions. Instead, they read what is often scarcely more than a journalistic *version* of a travel brochure. We need travel *critics*, not just thinly disguised publicists.

The case of restaurant critics is altogether different. Newspapers pay the costs; they do their utmost to remain anonymous to avoid special treatment. The point is to experience the same kind of food and service as every other diner. The rule for arts and entertainment critics is generally the same – except for the more commercial end of the industry. To cover Hollywood movies these days, critics often must suspend the sharper of their critical judgements. If they don't they may get some things published, but they won't be invited back to the press screenings or given access to interviews with the 'stars'.

Thought for food

Journalists, actors and writers are notorious for using their own life experiences in their work. While convalescing from surgery (at a time when I lived alone) I found myself at the mercy of friends and deliveries from the local food catering shop. They made only one error in filling several weeks of orders – but it was a big one, and the consequences could have been far more serious. I decided not to name the shop, but to write an opinion column that might help educate those in the food industry and the public. I decided that humour would be more effective than the rant I had considered. The following piece was published in *The Globe and Mail*, Canada's national newspaper. It was reprinted and used (with permission) by a government agency to aid its programme of educating restaurant, home catering and other food service providers.

Confession of a serious nutcase

By Valerie Alia

If anybody had suggested I write about food, I would have laughed. But sometimes you just reach the last straw – or in this case, the last nut.

On the surface, this might seem like a health nut's petty complaining. Rest assured, it goes much deeper. It will give those of you who keep up with the trends one more in the ever-increasing line of 'PCs' – a cautionary tale for the palate-ically correct. I ask that you challenge your hearts, minds and taste buds …

I have never understood why otherwise respectable chefs thought walnuts and pecans were interchangeable. All you have to do is taste one of each to know the difference. And for people like me, that breach of culinary etiquette is a matter of life or death.

I am allergic to walnuts. Unlike some less fortunate people, I don't have an allergy to *all* nuts. And contrary to the insinuations of those who are offended by rejection of the food they have so carefully prepared, I do not *dislike* walnuts. Some of my best friends eat them. Some of my favourite furnishings and musical instruments are made of their wood. No bigoted 'nutist,' I.

Nevertheless, I'm here to tell you all nuts are not created equal. Their differences are celebrated the world over in fabulous cuisines, in delectable dishes that exploit their tastes and textures. An almond isn't a hazelnut isn't a macadamia isn't a pecan isn't … a walnut.

I promise you, I didn't ask for trouble. As on so many other occasions, my latest mishap started innocuously, with something many of us have done before: I bought a loaf of bread. To be precise, a fruit and pecan loaf from my favorite food shop, just like one I had enjoyed not long before. Wholesome, tasty, walnut-free.

Stuck at home during an illness, I had ordered several items, carefully explaining to the person in charge that walnuts were totally taboo. With a laugh, I said, 'Just be sure they haven't started adding walnuts to the pecan loaf.' She laughed, too.

The laugh was on me. I bit off a pungent chunk – and went running to the medicine cabinet. Luckily, the allergy medication kept the reaction down to a modest rash and a brief bout of wheezing.

I am sharing this private moment, not to air my dirty linen or oven in public, but as a call to action. For this walnut encounter was just one of many. I have had my health challenged by 'pecan' breads, stuffings, pies, vegetarian stews, meat dishes to which the cook found a last-minute need to add walnuts. The explanations ranged from 'I ran out of pecans' to 'any nuts taste fine' to 'walnuts and pecans are pretty much the same.'

This is a plea. To amateur cooks who unwittingly subject their families and friends to danger. To professional cooks who carelessly ignore rules of good cooking and good health. To labelers of foods sold to trusting shopkeepers and consumers. To salespeople who think it is ok to tell a customer an item's ingredients without really checking. To folks who think nobody will notice.

Please understand, you are not merely careless; you are threatening people's lives.

It happens everywhere, every day. People allergic to fish, or to substances used for colour or flavour, are told the processed fish euphemistically known as 'restaurant crab' is crabmeat. People allergic to peanuts are given baked goods or entrees topped with 'almonds' fashioned of shaved peanuts. People who can't eat preservative-laden fruits are told that fruit salads are 'absolutely fresh'.

Why does this happen? I have never met anyone who insisted on taking a non-swimmer into deep water. I have never asked for an apple and been given an orange.

To all of you who cook, package or sell food: It is time you took us seriously. For you, it is a matter of honour and reputation. For me, it is a matter of survival. (Alia, 1993: A23)

C'mon. Be a sport!

'There was a time when sports was a very comfortable place for journalists. The stories came easily, along with the perks: free tickets, free meals, access to the heroes of the day' (Law, 1996: 186). Now journalists must contend with sports as mega-business, and they are often entangled in the webs of their own and others' media organisations. Media barons such as Rupert Murdoch and Silvio Berlusconi own both media and sports empires (not to mention Berlusconi's position at the helm of a national government!) controlling the organisation and marketing of 'their' teams and the media coverage of the events. Finding the public and public information in this picture is not always easy. If travel is fraught with ethical dilemmas, it pales in comparison to sports. Sports writers and broadcasters must develop (at least professionally workable) relationships with the teams and players they cover. They may question the morality of accepting luxurious junkets, but refusing these 'gifts' may mean losing access to the very players and events they are hired to cover. In some ways it is a lose–lose scenario.

Like anywhere else in society, sports has its problems and scandals. How are they to be reported? And where? Take a look at the sports section in today's newspaper of your choice. See if you can find a story that is critical or investigative. Chances are, if these stories are reported it will be on the news pages, and the writer is not likely to be a regular sports writer. It can be argued that this is appropriate and fitting. But it should not be a product of corporate coercion or journalistic self-censorship. Somewhere in this picture is the reader. Remember that long-held journalistic objective of supporting the public's right to know?

The writer and broadcaster William Law says older sportswriters take few risks.

> The old guard is still dominant ... Sports reporting remains a conservative bastion which puts up obstacles for those who deviate from the path and ask tough questions ... With ... emphasis placed on camaraderie and well-oiled contacts, independent analysis and investigative questioning are not welcomed ... (Law, 1996: 195)

The problems are not just in areas of ownership and investigation, friendliness and freebies. Racism, sexism, homophobia and xenophobia are rampant. If a player is good enough, he will generally be accepted on the team, regardless of skin colour or ethnic origin. I say 'he' because sports is male-dominated in ways that are at least being challenged elsewhere in society. A man of exceptional skill will be hired by any major football club. A woman of exceptional skill will not. Sports teams remain gender-segregated, and except for tennis and Olympic sports figure skating, women's events are almost never given the news space, television or radio time of equivalent men's events.

When we discuss these issues in class, I am always stunned by the energy with which many male students reject even the vaguest possibility that women's sports might merit equal coverage and women's teams equal funding and promotion. The reactions to such suggestions are both irrational and emotional – which in itself is interesting, given the cliché that men are 'logical' and women 'emotional'. There have been some heavy confrontations, often along gender lines. One year there were several serious sportswomen in the seminar – some with career aspirations in sports and sports journalism. When we looked at the sports pages of even the more liberal papers, such as *The Independent* and *The Guardian*, women were seldom there. Unless Wimbledon was on, the women tended to show up, in sexy sports-inspired clothing, in ads for everything from cars to tennis balls. The journalists, too, were usually men – though female sports reporters and commentators do exist, especially on television. When the male students start saying things like, 'Women footballers will never get the money or the crowds or the coverage that men footballers do', I try to get them to think historically. Remember when they said no woman would ever cover 'men's' sport, let alone set foot in a locker room? There has been some progress, but it is pathetically slow.

When the media do challenge the status quo, it is seldom on the sports pages or the main television sportscasts. In June 2003, in the midst of the tennis season, *The Guardian* published a three-page spread critiquing media coverage of women players. Where did they run it? In the *G2* magazine – about as far from the sports pages as you can get (*The Guardian*, G2, 2003: 1–3). Included is Annabel Croft's reminiscence of women's tennis since her own years on the circuit. The media did not just discover women players, and women players did not just discover the media.

> From Guffy Moran with her frilly knickers to Chris Evert in her specially made ... creations, the appetite has always been there. The papers are suddenly full of photographs of skirts flying up ...

In the end, it is all about money. 'Anna Kournikova makes more money than anyone, without ever having won a tournament' (Croft, 2003: 2). The editors had a good time with this feature. They put the story on the *G2* cover, using a 'test of parallels' premise. Headlined 'A few stories you won't be reading about the tennis stars* at Wimbledon ... (*the male tennis stars, that is)'. The male model on the cover is in tennis black-and-whites, shirt 'flying up' to reveal a bare and hairy midriff. Linked by arrows to various parts of his body are notes such as: 'Not just a pretty face! But does the modelling contract mean he's taken his eye off the ball?' Some comments address his personal attributes, others his choice of costume. The raunchiest is pointed you-know-where and refers to 'balls' and perfect 'service' (*The Guardian*, G2, 2003: 1). It is broad satire, but it's no exaggeration. Unfortunately, such criticism would have far greater impact if it appeared on the sports pages.

William Law challenges the media to use more imagination and help change 'monolithic television coverage', media, sports industry and business practices, and attitudes. He proposes starting with a basic code of conduct requiring reporters to refuse free meals, rides and tickets. He calls for a financial commitment by media organisations to support these principles. He recommends rotating beat reporters so they are harder to 'cultivate'. 'This is the technological age, and it ought to send sports pack journalism the way of the dinosaurs … The game has changed. It doesn't run the way it used to. It never will again' (Law, 1996: 205).

Case study: covering the arts

> Reviewing has one advantage over suicide. In suicide you take it out [on] yourself; in reviewing you take it out [on] other people. (George Bernard Shaw, playwright and music critic)

> With the exception of Wodehouse's *Oh Lady, Lady!* where she deemed it politic to lay praise on thick, she proceeded to slice up the rest with a poison stiletto. Since it is always more fun to revile than extol … she made it her modus operandi. (Meade, 1988: 44–5)

The problematic metaphor notwithstanding (stilettos stick, not slice), the points about Dorothy Parker are familiar to arts journalists. In reviewing a bouquet of five musical comedies for her *Vanity Fair* column, she was uniquely kind to the work of P .G. Wodehouse, her predecessor as *Vanity Fair* drama critic and a member of the magazine's 'family'. Most of the time she was free to revile and skewer artists at will. Although she had a clear preference for the negative, Parker's personality and incisive (and witty) evaluation made her a best-selling critic. Despite the intensity of today's focus on consumer- and personality-driven media, it is not new to entertain readers or use the personalities of journalists to sell magazines and newspapers. The Canadian media critic Rick Salutin (1994) separates criticism into two categories: the 'tough-love division' in which reviews are 'a form of support for the arts' and 'exercises in cultural sadism'.

Adventures of a (female) critic

On the eve of my departure from a small town to the intimidating vast-ness of Boston, a kindly mentor warned, 'You'll never get to be a critic – there simply aren't any jobs. Unless, of course, you're willing to sleep with an editor'. The mentor was making two points. First, there were no jobs for critics (something Shaw said a long time ago). Second, if you were a woman, there were always mitigating circumstances. I am pleased to report that neither of his warnings turned out to be the case. The ever-changing news requires constant relearning, but reviewing is supposed to be different. A critic *knows* things. I knew things – but they were not always the things I was asked to cover. As a child, I scribbled critical notes on concert and theatre programmes, read my father's book reviews and treasured volumes of his favourite critics such as James Gibbons Huneker. From these, I absorbed the pre-specialist tradition of an earlier age, when a (well educated) critic might cover opera and painting at the same time or – as in the case of George Bernard Shaw – might be a playwright who wrote music reviews.

Unable to afford tickets, I discovered I could get the best seats in the house, five dollars (US) and a by-line, merely for giving my opinion in print. I don't think I hurt anyone. Some early judgements proved accurate. A couple of summer-theatre reviews hailed the promise of a wonky and precocious 18-year old actor named William Hurt. Reviewing was so much fun, I abandoned plans to become an academic and set off to seek my journalistic fortune. At the weekly *Boston Phoenix*, I wrote on music and theatre, subjects I knew fairly well, having had training in both. Cuttings in hand, I marched into the Boston *Herald Traveller* arts department and asked its editor for a job reviewing drama or music. No, he said, but he needed a dance critic – immediately. I had taken modern dance classes and bought a ballet book at age five. Did that count? Apparently, it did. They sent me to cover a major ballet company. I wrote possibly the most embarrassing review of my life, underwent the horror of seeing it in print and decided I'd better do some homework. I took class, watched rehearsals and attended the wonderful critics' training-ground at the American Dance Festival. Soon, I really did know something about dance.

I had no idea how lucky we were or how radically things would change. On any given night, half a dozen reviewers would show up representing several broadsheets, weekly and monthly magazines, radio and television. We could compare observations and test perceptions; if one of us missed a detail, another would catch it. No one person can ever recapture an event. 'It's partly the *Rashomon* thing,' said novelist and playwright Timothy Findley: 'Three people seeing the same event and they remember three separate versions ...' (Black, 1993: 5). None of us saw the brave new world of narrowing coverage that lay just ahead. Today, the typical city has a daily, perhaps a weekly, the occasional radio or television review. Most of them hire generalists who must serve as both reporters and reviewers – a far cry from the time-honoured ideal of the historian-critic.

That was the image in my mind when I landed my first job (based on education, cuttings from a student paper and something they optimistically called 'promise'). I soon learned that lots of women got hired to cover dance. When I was offered the music critic's job as well, there were grumblings. Dance was the stepchild of the arts – the poorest of the under-funded arts. 'Serious' music was another matter. I was young, female and faulted on both counts. Today, things have not changed all that much. The field remains stacked and unrepresentative – most critics are male, white, middle-aged and seldom sensitive about questions of gender and diversity, even when they think they are.

One critic bent over backwards to give credibility to the guest conductor of the Toronto Symphony Orchestra. He mentioned her awards and gender-barrier-breaking career path. What was wrong? He had never told an equivalent story about a male conductor, he had simply reviewed the performance. This review was full of paternalistic appreciation. The conductor, Catherine Comet, 'belonged' on the podium 'by virtue of sheer musicianship, rather than in response to a legitimate call for affirmative action'. The review begins with a cute story about her five-year old daughter. The day I read a comparable description of Simon Rattle's children, I will cease to protest. It is galling to see the reviewer flaunt his tolerance while telling a mummy–daughter story. The performance is not even mentioned until the seventh of thirteen paragraphs. The review serves neither music nor affirmative action. Such treatment is unethical because it has a different premise from a 'normal' review.

Principles and problems

Responsible reviewing is driven by respect for arts and artists. I cannot imagine covering music if, left to your own devices, you would not spend time in concert halls. The actor and director Charlie Tomlinson once told students in my arts criticism seminar: 'You are the enemy' (Tomlinson, 1992, 1994 – see note at the end of the chapter). The director Robert Brustein agrees that critics and artists are adversaries:

> For more years than I care to count, the critic and the artist have
> circled each other warily, staring into each other's eyes with coldness
> and suspicion, in a manner usually associated with the mongoose and
> the snake ... (Brustein, 1997: 9)

At one extreme are the tabula-rasa critics who claim to have no biases or
agendas; at the other extreme are those who say there are no impersonal
critics because there are no impersonal people. One school believes that
responsible criticism is an account of the critic's personal experiences.
The other school thinks the critic should never reveal her values, politics
or biases.

> In most cases objective criticism means that someone whom you have
> slammed wishes that you hadn't slammed them and says John [Simon]
> should be more objective ... the only thing that can be objective is a
> machine and we know now that even computers can't be objective.
> (Brustein, 1997: 9)

For Timothy Findley, art must be courageous and challenging:

> A book *should* be dangerous ... If a book isn't dangerous, it's worthless.
> Art must menace. It can be gentle menace, but it must make you feel
> quite uncomfortable. (Black, 1993: 5)

Under repressive regimes, courageous artists are often the first to be
imprisoned or killed (for example, the execution of musician and poet
Victor Jara in Chile). The film critic Jay Scott said that the 'difference
between criticism and straight reporting is that reporting *lies* about the
person who's writing and criticism doesn't' (Scott, 1991 – see note at the
end of the chapter).

Too much is made of the differences between 'reviewers' and 'critics'.
The scholar-critic, seldom a journalist, is usually confined to small
journals, magazines or books. I tend to use the terms interchangeably. All
responsible criticism is careful, thoughtful, educated – given restrictions
of time and space. I think the fuss over distinctions is more about class
than function. More important than how we label reviewing is the extent
to which it is available to the public. It used to be that most important
events were reviewed; when there was more than one important event,
we had 'stringers' (second-string reviewers) to help. Today, media cover
fewer events and rely on national and international news services more
than local reviewers. Even where arts pages are substantial, there are
often double standards.

Jazz gets small spaces on back pages. No theatre critic would cover
only one of a play's three acts; no music critic would hear two move-

ments of a concerto and run across town to catch the third movement of another – a critic covers the artist's shaping of a performance, not just a musical moment. Yet, in their effort to do too much in too little time, some jazz critics rush from performance to performance, covering fragments of each. I have heard the solo of the century in a third set, only to read that the player was bland (by implication, all evening).

Powerful … moi?

> Drama critics tend to regard playwrights, actors, directors and designers as thin-skinned egotists who respond only to ecstatic and unqualified praise, while theater people tend to think critics lack any understanding of their process, preferring to treat them as sacrificial animals … artists are so alienated from the critical process that they profess not to read reviews [and] … deny that criticism ever played any part in the development of their art. (Brustein, 1997: 37)

Some critics insist they are ordinary people whose ephemeral (re)views evaporate in the morning air. I think this is an irresponsible and groundless game. Consider the following example of the critic's power.

Art, sex and responsibility: artists and critics

In 1993, Toronto art critic Kate Taylor inadvertently caused a scandal. Reviewing an exhibition by a young artist whose intentionally shocking subject-matter (children and adults in sexual play) she found 'self-conscious' and 'juvenile' and the gallery's euphemistic commentary offensive, she wrote: 'Langer is young and he can paint marvellously well. Maybe when he grows up he'll be an artist' (Taylor, 1993a: C5). The drama that followed continued for months. Merely by covering the show, Taylor called attention to its existence. The day after the review was published two readers telephoned a complaint to the police. Within two days, the work was seized and charges laid against the artist and the gallery director for possessing child pornography and displaying obscene material. In this case, the critic's impact was unambiguous. Until she reviewed it, the show went unnoticed for three weeks.

> Had I not written about it, I believe it would have wrapped up quietly … as scheduled. Instead, Langer is the first artist to be charged under new child pornography provisions added to the [Canadian] Criminal Code last summer. (Taylor, 1993b: C5)

The story did not end there. Taylor was vilified at a press conference sponsored by free-speech activists, criticised for having ignored the history of 'sexual material in art' and misquoted as having said the paintings, rather than the acts they depicted, were illegal. In fact, she did not judge the work pornographic. She defended her position with eloquence and passion.

> Although I reviewed it very negatively ... it could be argued that I made a much stronger statement about its artistic merit than those Toronto media who chose not to review it at all. I am ... one of only two critics who wrote about the show ... I believe it is the [gallery's] right and responsibility to show art, Eli Langer's to make it and mine to write about it – without any of us being stifled by the police, the courts or the tyranny of public opinion. I believe in free speech for Eli Langer ... and for Kate Taylor. (Taylor, 1993b: C5)

The now prominent case was not just about free speech or definitions of pornography. Taylor made two choices which led directly to the artist's arrest: she decided to review the show (for a major newspaper), and she described the content of the work (such description being typical in a review). She believes that the artist would not have been charged had she not revealed the explicitness of the work. Whether Taylor performed a public service or a disservice, her small review for a large newspaper has had enormous impact on media consumers (the 'public'), artists, gallery directors and other players in the continuing drama. So much for the 'critics-have-no-power' school of thought. It can also be argued that while critics have power, they are not all-powerful. As Brian Brennan points out, many shows survive, even triumph over, bad reviews (Brennan, 1996a).

Conflicts of interest

When I became a critic in the 1970s, it was a time of specialisation. The newspapers wanted to project an image of expertise. They asked me not to write on other topics, saying it would harm my (read, the newspaper's) credibility. When I wanted to write on politics and other issues, I adopted pen names. I never saw it as conflict of interest; nobody questioned the quality of my reviews and the other work was unrelated to the events I reviewed.

The Globe and Mail Arts and Books Editor Katherine Ashenburg assigned one person to interview an artist and another to review the work, and praised film critic Pauline Kael's avoidance of industry press kits, directors' lunches and social events. For Kael, the responsible critic sits in dark houses, watching movies 'to minimize the possibility that a

critic will be charmed (or antagonized or distracted) by the artist ...'
(Ashenberg, 1993). Staff cutbacks and other institutional constraints
make it increasingly difficult for any news organisation to follow such
principles.

I define 'conflict of interest' rather broadly, referring not just to unethical financial gain but to conflicts of *loyalty*. While the consolidation of
arts coverage creates what some call conflict of interest, it is not the first
time accepted roles and practice have shifted. In the early days of newspapers, multiple roles were not only accepted, they were the norm.
People worked part-time as journalists and part-time as artists or politicians with little worry about overlapping loyalties. Rules and mores
change. Part-time and freelance journalism is again on the rise. If all
critics got the same services – theatre tickets, a press kit, excellent seats,
parking privileges – it can be argued that such 'gifts' have no effect on
the ethics of coverage. That was the view in my early years of writing; it
is not the argument currently in fashion. News organisations now prefer
to purchase reviewers' tickets. Although press kits are meant to influence
us, they are unlikely to bias a review. In the best instances, they are
educational tools that expand the critic's (and the public's) knowledge.
My all-time favourite publicist worked for a major ballet company. She
was not a 'flak' but a valued colleague who provided carefully researched
documents that enriched many a review.

Confessions of moral imperfection

1. Journalists, including arts journalists, still moonlight. Most journalists
   I know have worked 'on the side' as speech writers, publicists or
   trainers (coaching people they sometimes cover, on how to use the
   media).
2. As an editor for a weekly with double standards for the publishers'
   friends, I had to choose between printing copy so bad it would fail a
   school exam or 'editing' to the extent of virtually ghost-writing the
   columns of some of the by-lined critics.
3. At a major newspaper, arts staff took turns covering an annual society
   charity event. It was an inside joke and we all learned the rules:
   we were to 'review' the amateur performers 'seriously', yet avoid
   damaging their egos, their cause or their reputations. When my turn
   came, I did not uphold morality and risk my job, I took the assignment.
4. The musician spouse of a highly placed editor gave occasional
   concerts, distinguished by a consistent lack of musicality or pitch.

The staff rotated reviewing duty. If I recall correctly, I wriggled out of *my* ethical dilemma by passing the assignment off on a colleague.

As a rule, we should not apply different standards in different places. If I can't accept a gift in London or Edinburgh, neither can I accept an airline ticket and free 'northern adventure' in the Arctic. A moral absolute? Yet suppose there is a story of global importance, the fare is astronomical (as Arctic fares are) and my publisher won't pay the bill? For John Hulteng,

> the ethical rights and wrongs in this area are particularly difficult to sort out. Journalists cannot be expected to lead antiseptic lives ... a kind of double standard sometimes seems to be in effect. In small towns, particularly, the editor or reporter may indeed hold office on the city council ... (Hulteng, 1981: 29–31)

In some communities, there is nothing left to review and no one left to do the reviewing unless you allow conflicts of interest or hire visitors. As an outsider wintering in the small Yukon city of Whitehorse I was asked to review Yukon artists. A year later, I knew most of the artists and some were friends. The artists need reviews for professional credibility, funding and feedback; the public was also entitled to this service. Yukon artists wanted to be reviewed but complained the reviews were biased, a Catch 22 much lamented by the editor of the local newspaper. How do you review in a community in which nothing is conflict-free?

The public's view of a region, an art or an entertainer may be dictated by a single junket sponsored by a company promoting its own interests. The American Society of Professional Journalists takes the position that any gifts, favours, free travel or special treatment 'can compromise the integrity of journalists and their employers' and therefore, nothing 'of value should be accepted' (American Society of Professional Journalists, 1992: 38).

Framing the issues

The critic experiences a performance in illness or health, joy or depression, comfort or discomfort. She is open or closed to an artist because of these physical or mental states, the ambience of setting, the season, company, place and time. I try to see a performance more than once. Sometimes I change my mind, as in the case of the great American choreographer Paul Taylor's work *Runes*. When I first saw it, it seemed pretentious and cultish. The second time, I was profoundly moved. It is important to share that experience with audiences – to remind them of the validity of their own experience, the fallibility and changeability of ours. It is inaccurate and irresponsible to pretend that a single performance is the definitive work. It is also inaccurate and irresponsible to remove a work from its context. In 2002, Hollywood released a film version of an earlier musical, based on a still earlier stage play, based on an actual case.

Amid all the hype and noise about *Chicago*, nobody seems to have noticed that beneath the movie's speed, glamour, glitz and flash is a deeply cynical tale of corruption. As the world roars its protest against US war-hungry, greed-driven bullying tactics, Chicago's deeper messages are all too timely. It was presented and (judging from Catherine Zeta Jones' ill-deserved Oscar) received as a sound- and colourscape created as a vehicle for the stars to strut their stuff. The non-stop camera makes it impossible to see, let alone appreciate Bob Fosse's choreography (while attempting to disguise the fact that the stars can't dance). The perpetual-motion dialogue, brash and brusque musical direction and visual chicanery keep us from dwelling on the actual story.

An ugly little story seethes and simmers nastily just below the sequined surface. *Chicago* is a morality tale (or, more accurately, an amorality tale) of the evils embedded in the core of American life. Look again at this dazzlingly costumed melodrama of the urban American food-chain. Organised crime feeds on disorganised prisons. Scandalmongering media and opportunistic lawyers feed on ambitious, selfobsessed entertainers and each other. Government feeds on all of them. Some of the top feeders sink to the bottom; some of the bottom feeders rise to the top. The publicists would have us believe it's just about showbiz … 'and all that jazz'. Or is it? Bob Fosse based his original musical production on a stage play by Maurine Dallas Watkins. A reporter for *The Chicago Tribune*, Watkins drew on her experience of the various greedy interest groups in the eponymous city – a subject Lincoln Steffens examined in great detail in his series on municipal corruption republished in 1903 as *The Shame of the Cities*.

> … Chicago. First in violence, deepest in dirt; loud. Lawless, unlovely, ill-smelling, irreverent, new; an overgrown gawk of a village, the 'tough' among cities, a spectacle for the nation … [A police] force so insufficient (and inefficient) that it cannot protect itself, to say nothing of handling mobs … and the rest of that lawlessness which disgraces Chicago … For Chicago is reformed only in spots … a settlement of individuals and groups and interests with no common city sense and no political conscience … There were political parties … controlled by rings … which in turn were backed and used by

leading business interests through which this corrupt and corrupting system reached with its ramifications far and high and low into the social organization. (Steffens, 1903/1957: 164–5)

Sound familiar? The Chicago of Maureen Watkins owed much to the Chicago of Lincoln Steffens. It is the same Chicago that features in news reports of the E2 club disaster exactly 100 years after Steffens' report, in 2003. E2 sprawls across the second floor of a restaurant called Epitome; it had been cited for eleven safety violations and ordered to close in July 2002. Six months later, in February 2003, it was still open. Twenty-one people died and many more were injured in an apparently preventable stampede. The club stayed open and the violations unrepaired thanks to the help of corrupt officials.

Social commentary is not unknown in musical theatre and is more often highlighted than hidden. Consider the anti-racism themes of *South Pacific*, the pro-union themes of *The Pajama Game*, the portrait of Russian poverty, pogroms and a budding revolution in *Fiddler on the Roof. Chicago* is costumed to look nostalgically backwards, but the tangled, frenzied feeding is still with us. It is all too timely, this tale of incessantly replaceable, greedy, manipulative and vulnerable female 'stars', two-timed by their legal, political and media guardians. *Chicago* may be a charming musical period piece, but it has more to say about today than anyone seems prepared to admit. So why, I wonder, has Hollywood treated it like a cutesie, jazzy, girlie show? And why did so many critics parrot the publicists' version? We must beware of such discrepancies.

We must also beware of making class or cultural distinctions in the guise of evaluating quality. I have tried to give 'classical', 'popular', 'folk' and other art equal credibility. I do not consider 'popular' dance or music inherently less important, less serious, less skilfully performed than so-called 'high' art. It is not enough to find folk roots in classical works (folk themes in Tchaikowsky or Beethoven, folk dances in the ballets of the great choreographer, Petipa). Western critics too often call Danish or Russian ballet 'classical' but label classical Indian or Cambodian dance 'ethnic', along with the *folk* arts of India or Cambodia. The dilemmas are endless. The best we can do is acknowledge and address them, struggle with temporary solutions, search for codes and continuities.

Some issues are clear and unarguable. I remember my shock upon reading a colleague's review of an entire performance, having seen him leave at the interval. And consider the experience of singer Frances Somerville:

> … I was often engaged as a recitalist on [CBC Radio]. On one occasion my programme had to be cancelled at the last moment

because I was ill. But it had been advertised earlier with a list of the songs … One was a Bach aria, 'My Heart Ever Faithful'; it would have been my first time to sing Bach on the air. Imagine my surprise when … [the national magazine] *Saturday Night's* music critic acclaimed me as 'an accomplished Bach interpreter.' This would have thrilled me if I had sung the recital. (Somerville, 1991: 9)

I think we can agree that here is a moral absolute: no one should review a performance he or she has not attended! In a symposium organised by the drama historian and director, Robert Brustein, critics and artists alike skewered the critical profession. The film critic John Simon said:

… two critics … have come in for the most praise … Bernard Shaw and Kenneth Tynan. If you ask yourself what do these two critics have in common, the obvious thing is that they're both dead … Bernard Shaw was a much hated person in his day. All kinds of venomous and vituperative things were written and said about him and this was simply because he was sharp and a tough critic. (Brustein, 1992: 36–7)

Still-living critics should be able to write and broadcast responsibly and incisively. Respect is the foundation; adulation is not. Actor Alisa Palmer told one of my seminars: 'Good critics are like family – they give you unconditional love and also criticism' (1994 – see note at the end of the chapter). I also think that the love is partly unrequited – that the critic's job is to be always a little unloved. Maybe that is the job of all media practitioners.

Note

Jay Scott (1991), Charlie Tomlinson (1992, 1994) and Alisa Palmer (1994) presented guest lectures to my arts criticism seminar at the University of Western Ontario Graduate School of Journalism.

Exercises

9.1 Art, pornography and responsibility

Read the case of Kate Taylor (above) and discuss it. Consider the following questions:

1. Was she right to review the exhibition in the first place?
2. When she discovered its subject matter, should she have published the review? Why or why not?
3. Do you agree with her position on free speech for the reviewer and a public forum for the artist?

4. She did not anticipate the effects of her decision to review the show. What do you think she should have done?
5. What are the proper roles of critic, editor or station manager, artist, gallery director, lawmakers and police, with regard to the public interest in such a case?

9.2 Conflicts of interest and double standards

Consider the case of reviewing in Whitehorse, Yukon.

1. What choices do writers, broadcasters, editors and artists have in small communities?
2. If I am the only reviewer in town and the performer is a friend, do I refuse to cover the performance?
3. If I occasionally perform, am I disqualified from reviewing in the same field?
4. Do the rules change if I perform frequently?
5. Is it ethical to set the same standards for an amateur company as for a company of professionals?
6. Is it ethical to set different standards?
7. What principles apply if I write under different names?

Discuss some possible ways to approach reviewing and other specialist stories in these conditions.

9.3 Women in sports

Bring cuttings of recent newspaper and magazine sports coverage. Discuss the differences in treatment of male and female athletes and the participation (or non-participation) of women as sports journalists. Which sports are male- or female-dominated? Is attention ever paid to the costumes, hair, weight, body types and love lives of sports*men*? If so, when? Who? In what context(s)?

Further reading

Arts and entertainment

Alia, Valerie (1996) 'Better than suicide?', in Valerie Alia, Brian Brennan and Barry Hoffmaster (eds), *Deadlines and Diversity: Journalism Ethics in a Changing World*. Halifax, NS: Fernwood, pp. 207–18.
Brennan, Brian (1996) 'Confessions of an unlettered critic', in Valerie Alia, Brian Brennan and Barry Hoffmaster (eds), *Deadlines and*

Diversity: Journalism Ethics in a Changing World. Halifax, NS: Fernwood, pp. 218–27.

Environmental issues

Frome, Michael (1998) *Green Ink: An Introduction to Environmental Journalism.* Salt Lake City: University of Utah Press.
Roy, Arundhati (1999) *The Cost of Living.* London: Flamingo.

Sport

Canadian Woman Studies (2002) Special Issue on Women and Sport.
Law, William (1996) 'More than a game: the business and ethics of sports journalism', in Valerie Alia, Brian Brennan and Barry Hoffmaster (eds), *Deadlines and Diversity: Journalism Ethics in a Changing World.* Halifax, NS: Fernwood, pp. 186–206.

Film

For details see the annotated filmography in Appendix B at the end of the book.

Chicago
Between the Lines

10 Changing technologies: prospects and problems

> The printing press changed the course of human history. It produced an information revolution. It changed what human beings know, and how we think. (Spender, 1995: 1)

Before the printing press, exchange of information was the province of religious and political elites. When the presses started rolling, there was no stopping the spread of public information and news. Today, we hear about unprecedented and earth-shaking technological changes. In truth, there is nothing new except the nature and scale of the technologies. The speed of Net-surfing relative to the earlier speed of, say, typing and sending a letter is roughly equivalent to the speed of a rotary press relative to the speed of a scribe-written, hand-delivered letter or manuscript. Nothing changes; everything changes. The idea of linking speed and access to the democratisation of information-sharing dates back to the fifteenth century. It is probably more accurate to think of waves of restriction and access than to imagine a smoothly linear progression.

> More and more of the world is becoming 'wired'. We are entering a generation marked by globalization and ubiquitous computing. … The stakes are much higher, and consequently considerations and applications of social responsibility must be broader, more profound and above all effective in helping to realize a democratic and empowering technology rather than an enslaving or debilitating one. (Rogerson and Fairweather, 2003: S4)

Despite the claims of salespeople and advertising campaigns, new technologies do not automatically empower people or improve communications. However complicated and sophisticated, they are still designed and run by people, and are only as effective as the people involved. Many of the patterns and ethical problems encountered in earlier versions of the media persist in higher-tech versions.

Ownership, censorship and control

As the discussion in Chapter 5 indicated, the old 'press barons' became 'media barons', and in today's ever-changing technological climate I have called media barons such as Microsoft owner Bill Gates cyber barons. Efforts to limit Bill Gates's monopoly have been largely unsuccessful, and the Microsoft empire continues to grow as the world grows increasingly dependent on computer-related technologies. The impact of technology is clearly related to who owns it and who is able to use it. Governments and businesses work separately and together to influence the nature and scope of public information.

You might think that the kind of government censorship that occurred during the Second World War, discussed in Chapter 5, is no longer considered acceptable. Think again. Government and corporate censorship, surveillance and control are with us still. They escalated during the Gulf War, after the destruction of New York's twin towers, and most recently during the so-called 'war' on Iraq in 2003. Today, the United States and Britain have expanded their collaborative international surveillance efforts and extended the US presence in Britain. While this is often blamed on the recent wars and crises, the recent activities began in 1999 with approval by the US Patent Office of a new telephone-monitoring technology to be used by the government-run National Security Agency (NSA).

The NSA was already able to use computers to transcribe voice conversations and conduct mass electronic eavesdropping on e-mail, faxes and other written communications. The new system includes telephone calls and can analyse speech in any language. It is being developed not only in the United States but in Britain. The NSA has a satellite listening station at Menwith Hill in Yorkshire, which is part of an ever-expanding surveillance and security complex in the region. Yaman Akdeniz, director of Cyber-Rights and Cyber-Liberties UK, is concerned that a US–UK joint telephone venture and the new technology will allow US law enforcement agencies to invade British communications. In the worst instance, all British communications would be monitored by the US-run organisation (Dreyfus, 1999: 12).

The NSA already listens in on private communications worldwide, using Echelon – an international web of eavesdropping stations which began after the Second World War with a secret agreement signed by Britain, Canada, Australia, New Zealand and the US. Dr Brian Gladman, former MoD director of Strategic Electronic Communications, says 'widespread interception is a fact of life' (Dreyfus, 1999: 12). In 2003, the Office of the Information Commissioner published a code of practice preventing employers from monitoring employees without serious cause. Techniques used by employers include using 'filters' to check the addresses and content of employees' e-mails, monitoring employees' Internet use, and recording employees' conversations and the telephone numbers they use (Verkaik, 2003: 9). Although employers have been told to restrict these activities, the penalties vary, and while the new code may inhibit some employers, it is unlikely to stop all of their surveillance activities.

Transparency and public trust

According to the Canadian television journalist, Pierre Mignault, public trust in journalism is based on an assumption that the journalist is a direct witness to events. The journalist 'has been granted the authority ... to decide what should be printed or broadcast so [citizens] will be well enough informed to make up their minds about important issues' (Mignault, 1996: 132). But the days of direct reporting – while not over – are waning. Fewer and fewer news organisations can afford to send their own reporters into the field. 'Even if journalists are still the next best thing to being there, there has been a significant change in news-gathering with the coming of videotape, satellites and live broadcasts. Is the journalist still a first-hand witness of events?' (Mignault, 1996: 133). Mignault says there are now more cameras than reporters, many of them are government controlled, and in today's financial climate US television networks dominate the industry.

Increasingly, TV news reports rely on a technique called a 'melt-down', in which media are allowed to use each other's images, recorded interviews and news reports and 'melt them down' into a unified report narrated by their own reporter. 'The overwhelming presence' of US networks allows them 'to operate as international news agencies ...' There is 'room for monumental fraud ...' (Mignault, 1996: 134). The television viewer watches a report by a familiar journalist from her or his home country, compiled from several sources unknown to the viewer (and often, to the reporter). Broadcasts are more powerful than govern-ments – they are able to cross politically defined, geographic boundaries. US and other powerful media control public access to information in their own countries and around the world. In many instances (e.g. CNN in the Gulf War and 'embedded journalists' in the Iraq conflict) some media outlets are given unique access to the 'official' (and sometimes the only) sources of information about a current and continuing crisis.

Once the attacks began, CNN became the anchor of our lives. Although all reporting from Israel was subject to military censorship,

CNN gave us a broader view of what was happening elsewhere in the region. When it reported that Iraq had launched an attack on Saudi Arabia, we know that we had thirty minutes in which to get organized … (Ben Artzi-Pelossof, 1996: 65–6)

However beneficent CNN's broadcasts may have been for Israelis lucky enough to have satellite dishes, such immense media power merits very serious discussion.

In the new world of international communications, a single news organisation is capable of transcending geographic, ideological and ethical boundaries and transmitting 'melted-down information' for which no recognisable reporter is responsible. The frightening message is that a single news organisation could theoretically run the world, or serve as the pipeline for others who run it. Mignault and others say media need to make their methods more transparent to viewers. One way to do this is to indicate what sources have been used for a broadcast story. Another way is to speak or print a note to viewers explaining the melt-down technique. This is cumbersome, because it affects so many television news programmes. During the Iraq conflict, some BBC television reports were prefaced by an explanation that they were produced by 'embedded' or non-embedded journalists. There is no perfect solution. What is clear is that melt-down techniques are not going away, they are expanding; the public must be informed; and someone has to take responsibility for presenting a clear and honest picture of the news.

New technologies offer empowerment and disempowerment in nearly equal measure. The public has two main forms of access: the material derived from known and unknown sources, available on television, and the wider array of sources available on the Internet. At the same time that melt-downs are confusing and obscuring information sources and narrowing television perspectives, people and media organisations are using the Internet to expand public access to information. There is one major limitation – access to this new information universe is limited to those with access to computers. Canada has a strong record of providing media services to its citizens. The following case study describes how this has empowered people in the tiniest, most remote communities, as well as in the more media-privileged cities.

Case study: technology and the circumpolar village

The most effective technology is not always the most sophisticated. People in Arctic and sub-Arctic countries and communities are using an inventive mix of complex and simple technologies to communicate among themselves and with what in the northern regions is often called 'Outside'.

In the Arctic, a breakdown in transportation or communication is not just an inconvenience; it is often a matter of life or death. Transportation, radio and television outlets, mobile and land-line telephones, and computers link people with survival as well as with each other. People who spend much of their time in remote locations on the land carry low-cost, technologically simple radios (and, where accessible, mobile telephones). Small-scale radio stations are everywhere, and 'talk radio forges the communication links in ethnic neighbourhoods, small towns and aboriginal communities from the farthest Arctic coasts to the outskirts of major Canadian cities, sending hundreds of languages through the air'. A former talk-show host in the Mohawk community of Kahnawake, Conway Jocks is especially interested in the connectedness and intimacy this medium brings to people who live in small and remote communities (Jocks, 1996). In 1960, the first indigenous language radio programme was broadcast in Inuktitut (the Inuit language) via shortwave that was rebroadcast to the North out of CBC's studios in Montreal. In northern Ontario, a radio station for Ojibway and Cree people started in a van that travelled from community to community. For minority communities, radio is a medium of linguistic and cultural continuity, and survival.

More than any other country, Canada has supported the development and distribution of innovative communication technologies, by and for minority communities. Other northern nations have joined its efforts to provide media outlets for the inhabitants of its northernmost regions. A series of satellites made it possible to develop Television Northern Canada, produced by indigenous leaders across the Canadian Arctic and sub-Arctic. As indigenous broadcasting was emerging in the Canadian North, Greenland was enjoying its own communications revolution. Kalaallit Nunaata Radioa (KNR), Greenland's public national broadcaster, joined the European Broadcasting Union in 1978. In Alaska, KYUK radio and television broadcast in the Yup'ik language.

We now find ourselves in the middle of the age of communication … the millennium is upon us and it seems at times we're more isolated than ever before. TV and computers are taking us further and further away from human contact. Yet, we yearn for human interaction …

Seventy-five years ago, we were all we had except for Saturday night radio. A hundred and fifty years ago, we were all we had. We must have been a hell of a lot more fascinating. We had to have been great storytellers. We certainly had a lot more time for each other …

No TV to keep us amused, or e-mail love to find a relationship. Yet, the amount of information we have at our finger tips is astounding. Access such as we have never had before ...

I wonder about our existence in the future and what communication skills will be required to survive ... Can we live off our creativity and our ability to communicate? ... (Farmer, 1998: 6)

Gary Farmer's words of caution, question, and inspiration infuse every aspect of the publication he founded, *Aboriginal Voices*. The print version of the magazine has ceased publication, but the project continues as a website and an on-air magazine on APTN (Aboriginal People's Television Network – the nationwide service that evolved from TVNC). Farmer's concerns about the limitations of technology are heard widely in Aboriginal communities everywhere. However, especially in northern and remote communities, few people advocate avoiding the Internet or ignoring its potential power. Instead, the trend is toward using that power to communicate the messages and languages of the senders, clearly and carefully, from community to community and from Aboriginal communities to the Outside world. By the time this information reaches you, I expect the list of web pages, e-mail addresses and websites included in Appendix C at the end of the book will have doubled.

While Gary Farmer struggles to find the proper balance between human and electronic contact from his informationally advantaged, urban home base in Toronto, the founders of Nunavut – Canada's newest, Inuit-majority territory – are embracing new telecommunications technologies without hesitation. In 1996 the Nunavut Implementation Commission released a report about the role they hoped telecommunications would play in the new territory. 'The road to Nunavut is along the information highway,' they wrote (Bell, 1996: 16–17). The new digital network is creating jobs for Nunavut citizens (a technician for each community, regional technologists and systems engineers), developing and linking libraries and databases, and establishing a sophisticated videoconferencing system that – in a region in which climate and distance make physical travel costly and difficult – amounts to an arm of government.

The unique conditions of northern life are ideally suited to such experimentation. While teleconferences cannot replace direct human contact, they can certainly replace a good deal of the very difficult travel which stalls government processes and absorbs northern budgets. In Nunavut, futuristic communications systems will help maintain the Inuit way of governing, with power widely distributed and structures decentralised. The widely scattered, remote communities are able to stay in touch without the dangers and delays experienced in the past. The system allows members of the Legislative Assembly to attend meetings in their home communities, without having to leave Iqaluit (the capital), and to attend caucus meetings in Iqaluit without having to leave their home communities.

Nunavut's citizens have greater access to each other and to government. And a videoconferencing system is helping to reduce the enormous travel budget. Thanks to the well developed, Inuit-directed broadcast industry, people in Nunavut are already comfortable with adapting television to their own needs. They were among the first Canadians (and the first Aboriginal Canadians) to take television and radio into their own hands.

> At exactly 8:30 p.m., an Inuktitut voice signals the start of the world's largest aboriginal television network. Elder Akeeshoo Joamie of Iqaluit asks Jesus to guide *TVNC* to success. An English translation rolls slowly across the screen ...
>
> The vision of *TVNC* became a reality with a montage of Inuit, Dene, Metis, Gwich'in, Kaska, Tuchone, Tlingit and non-aboriginal faces beamed to 22,000 households from Northern Labrador to the Yukon-Alaska border ...
>
> *TVNC* is a non-profit consortium which aims to use television for social change. (Thomas, 1992: 14)

TVNC served 100,000 viewers north of 55 degrees latitude, covering a third of Canada (Television Northern Canada, 1993). In its new incarnation as APTN, it broadcasts nationwide.

Technology for people

In many ways the Arctic is a huge 'small town'. Its sparse population is distributed across an enormous region, yet its position as the globe's smallest populated circle makes the interconnectedness of separate countries, cultures and communities exceptionally transparent. It is one reason Inuit have one of the world's most successful minority organisations, the Inuit Circumpolar Conference (ICC). The Arctic's small-town qualities persist in the computer age. In many ways the Internet and satellite technology have picked up where town meetings left off. In some cases, they have *become* the town meetings. Satellites carry community-to-community meetings, enabling people to convene in weather which would prohibit air travel or to bridge distances beyond the capabilities of travel budgets.

The Internet carries interpersonal, intergroup, inter-regional and international dialogue. It helps bring indigenous people and indigenous media to each other, and to non-indigenous people. It helps to 'mainstream' marginalised media – which is a mixed blessing, since 'alternative' and 'minority' media have in the past both lost and gained from privacy and smallness. As Gary Farmer says, there is a need for caution and for careful education about the beneficial and the damaging uses of new and emerging technologies.

In 1990, the Internet was the province of a few 'techies'. Today, it is rapidly becoming the primary medium of expression for the voices of many individuals and peoples. Of the earlier communication media, only radio continues to relay grassroots information frequently, freely and rapidly throughout the North. In terms of North–South communication, the Internet is far more effective. Thus, what may have begun as carefree local expressions are becoming increasingly conscious media for sending out carefully chosen and constructed messages. The same concerns indigenous journalists are expressing about who controls their newspapers affect the Internet communications (which are often linked directly to the newspapers, and therefore are subject to the same struggles for power, expression and control). The one unarguable truth is that these sites are expanding and increasing and are likely to continue to do so in the foreseeable future.

In 1998, all 58 of the communities in the Northwest Territories (including the portion which in 1999 became Nunavut) were connected to the World Wide Web. The two-year project was undertaken by a consortium of predominantly indigenous-owned northern businesses, Ardicom (Zellen, 1998: 50). Jim Bell, editor of *Nunatsiaq News*, sees great potential for Aboriginal communities in CD-Rom, digital video discs and other multimedia technologies, which can provide storage for important audio and visual material (Zellen, 1998: 52). These technologies offer an effective way to store and transmit oral histories, materials from community and regional archives, music and visual art – resources which are currently available or are being developed. Bell thinks the Internet offers a way of 'fighting back' – a chance to 'send the information the other way' (Zellen, 1998: 52) and an antidote to the cultural demolition that has occurred in some other media. Zellen contrasts the new technologies' culture-preserving potential with the negative effects of television described in the Inuit leader Rosemarie Kuptana's famous speech.

> We might liken the onslaught of southern television and the absence of native television to the neutron bomb … Neutron bomb television

.. *I'VE MISSED OUT FORWARD SLASH!*

Indigenous communications progress from space to cyberspace. (Ron Walton)

... destroys the soul of a people but leaves the shell of a people walking around. (Kuptana, in Brisebois, 1983: 107)

The uses of teleconferencing are still being explored. In Nunavik (Inuit northern Quebec), students at Ulluriaq School in the village of Kangiqsualujjuaq are studying the violin. They played their first concert in 2003. The lessons and rehearsals were carried between Kangiqsualujjuaq and their teacher's home in Buckingham, Quebec – thousands of kilometres to the south – by satellite.

The satellite connection ... uses protected bandwidth ... because this connection is separate from the Internet, it allows for high-quality videoconferencing ...

> Every week, [the school principal and the teacher] begin the violin class by linking the two schools' computers using their broadband satellite connections ... (Nelson, 2003: 20–1)

Students and teacher can watch each other, and work together individually and in groups, on high-quality computer monitors. The plan is to extend the technology to carry Inuit cultural traditions of throat singing, drum dancing and carving from community to community, as well as to carry non-Inuit cultural instruction from south to north.

Elsewhere in the circumpolar region, Sámi (sometimes called Lapps by outsiders and colonial governments) have well-established websites in Finland, Sweden and Norway. They communicate in Swedish, Norwegian and Finnish, and also in Sámi languages, using type fonts developed by Apple. Apple also developed an Inuktitut program for use by Canadian Inuit in Nunavut and Nunavik, and Dene fonts for Windows and Mac, in several Athabaskan languages. In the United States, the American Indian Radio on Satellite network distribution system (AIROS) has a 24-hour a day distribution system using the Internet and public radio, run by Native American Public Telecommunications. It has a website and a video distribution service with an archive of Native American videos and public television programmes, available to tribal communities.

In the polar countries, northerners are often more familiar with high-tech communications than southerners. Sophisticated computers have been commonplace in adult education and other centres for years. Satellite dishes sit on ancient rocks in tiny settlements whose inhabitants still spend much of their lives on the land (see Figure 10.1).

In the new North, fax is a fact of life. Phone lines are the most reliable and least fallible means of reaching other communities and Outside. Fax is an alternative to costly air freight and slow postal service. But every technology has its limitations, and facsimile is no exception. Despite the promises of its promoters, facsimile technology is not problem-free. Some communities have only a single telephone, which means adding fax to already overused facilities. And fax machines cannot be installed in communities which have only radio telephones.

Here we return to Gary Farmer's cautionary words about the limits to technology. The particular conditions in which northern communications are placed make every technological breakthrough a welcome event. Thoughtful northerners are aware of the pitfalls in assuming that technology will replace human-to-human contact. Even in the Utopian vision of the Nunavut founding parents, caution will have to be exercised.

Figure 10.1 Satellite dish at Pangnirtung, Nunavut (Canadian Arctic). Photograph by Valerie Alia.

Interactive computers provide a new medium for print and are swiftly evolving into media which transmit visual and auditory material as well. Interactive radio carries voices across great and small distances. Interactive television goes a step farther, allowing body language and facial expressions to be carried. Soon, virtual media will produce facsimiles of 'real' experience, including tactile experience. None of these can replace the joys and stresses of communicating in person. But then, news media haven't been face-to-face since the days when troubadours and town criers roamed the streets. Their closest descendants are probably the storytellers who still inhabit longhouses and tents, snow houses, friendship centres and public libraries.

The limits of technology

These dreams were dreams of delight. But dreams can be nightmares, and the sinister aspects or capabilities of new technologies have coloured many dreams as multimedia have advanced, making it possible to 'track' people as well as record them ... (Briggs and Burke, 2002: 326)

It is unfortunate that most of today's public discussion of new information technologies is focused on technological change, as if it were occurring in a human-free vacuum. Such discussion relies on the pretence that information somehow emerges on its own, rather than being generated, created and selected by people with different experiences, biases and agendas.

That is a dangerous pretence for any group or region, and for the communication universe as a whole. We must pay close attention to the impact of new technologies on questions of ethics and human rights, and on *people*. No matter how sophisticated the technology, nothing can replace the responsible work of responsible media practitioners. No technology can provide universal access to all people, without prejudice to where they live or how much they earn. These are the real challenges for the innovators, techno-experts and communicators of the future. The well-being and perhaps the very survival of humanity – and the planet – will depend on our ability to abandon the obsession with how to send the information, and to carefully consider what messages are sent, how they are processed and controlled, and by whom.

Exercises

10.1 Information control

Select video clips from the television series *The Prisoner* and the scene in the James Bond film *Tomorrow Never Dies* in which the evil, megalomaniac media baron goes mad. Discuss the clips in relation to government and media collusion and information control, and the idea of Microsoft's Bill Gates as a media 'cyber-baron'.

DISCUSSION POINTS
Consider how Bill Gates controls information:

- Limiting access to the Internet – the forced use of Microsoft products.
- Gateway access to his (and/or your Internet server's) choice of businesses and information services – costlier and more time-consuming to reach a wider array of choices.
- Intimidating competitors – limiting or killing off the competition (much as the early press barons squeezed out the competition when production costs went up).
- Irony: *The Guardian* newspaper's coverage of the November 1999 US Microsoft trial was offered in expanded form on the *The Guardian Unlimited* website and a website with the judge's findings. But despite the outcome (prohibiting Microsoft monopoly) many people have to use Microsoft's Internet Explorer to access these websites!

10.2 The surveillance society

Outline a plan for (a) private citizens, (b) media organisations and (c) individual journalists to cope with increasing surveillance and eavesdropping, and loss of privacy, considering how these groups should work with (or against) governments.

Further reading

AIROS (American Indian Radio on Satellite network distribution system) website: http://airos.org/

Alia, Valerie (1996) *Un/Covering the North: News, Media and Aboriginal People.* Vancouver: UBC Press.

Alia, Valerie (1989) 'Closing the Circle', *Up Here Magazine*, September/October.

Girard, Bruce (1992) *A Passion for Radio: Radio Waves and Community.* Montreal: Black Rose.

Inuit Circumpolar Conference website, especially materials on Arctic communications policy and programmes, including international news network: http://www.inuitcircumpolar.com/

Jocks, Conway (1996) 'Talk of the Town', in Valerie Alia, Brian Brennan and Barry Hoffmaster (eds), *Deadlines and Diversity: Journalism Ethics in a Changing World.* Halifax, NS: Fernwood.

Maori Radio Network website: http://www.ruimai.co.nz

Media Link, Inc. website. Journalists' research service: http://www.medialin.com/

Roth, Lorna (1996) 'The politics and ethics of inclusion: cultural and racial diversity in Canadian broadcast journalism', in Valerie Alia, Brian Brennan and Barry Hoffmaster (eds), *Deadlines and Diversity: Journalism Ethics in a Changing World.* Halifax, NS: Fernwood.

Viewing

For details see the annotated filmography in Appendix B at the end of the book.

The Insider
Switching Channels
Tomorrow Never Dies
The Truman Show
Wag the Dog
The Prisoner (TV series on videotape or DVD)

11 Codes and principles: what (and where) are they, and are they useful?

Take a look at the advertisements in any current magazine. Consider what you know about the actual products or services. How well is that reality reflected in the following principles, set out in the code of the American Advertising Federation and Association of Better Business Bureaus International?

1. *Truth.* Advertising shall tell the truth, and reveal significant facts, the concealment of which would mislead the public.
2. *Responsibility.* [...]
8. *Unprovable Claims.* Advertising shall avoid the use of exaggerated or unprovable claims.
9. *Testimonials.* Advertising containing testimonials shall be limited to those of competent witnesses who are reflecting a real and honest choice.

A look at some of the codes developed by different media organisations worldwide provides a window on the range of thinking – and seriousness of purpose – of various media owners, directors, editors and practitioners. Consider, for example, the following excerpts:

Associated Press – Managing Editors' Code of Ethics

Adopted by the ... Board of Directors [in] 1975, [the code] is meant to apply to news and editorial staff members and others who are involved in, or who influence, news coverage and editorial policy. It has been formulated in the belief that newspapers and the people who produce them should adhere to the highest standards of ethical and professional conduct.

Responsibility

A good newspaper is fair, accurate, honest, responsible, independent and decent. Truth is its guiding principle ...

The newspaper should serve as a constructive critic of all segments of society. It should vigorously expose wrongdoing or misuse of power, public or private. Editorially, it should advocate needed reform or innovations in the public interest.

News sources should be disclosed unless there is clear reason not to do so. When it is necessary to protect the confidentiality of a source, the reason should be explained ...

Code of Ethics of the Australian Journalists' Association

Respect for truth and the public's right to information are overriding principles for all journalists ...

1. They shall report and interpret the news with scrupulous honesty by striving to disclose all essential facts and by not suppressing relevant, available facts or distorting by wrong or improper emphasis.
2. They shall not place unnecessary emphasis on gender, race, sexual preference, religious belief, marital status or physical or mental disability. [...]
8. They shall identify themselves and their employers before obtaining any interview for publication or broadcast.
9. They shall respect private grief and personal privacy and shall have the right to resist compulsion to intrude on them.

British Newspaper Code

We, the editors of all Britain's national newspapers, declare our determination to defend the democratic right of the people to a Press free from government interference.

... While supporting the Press Council, each individual national newspaper now accepts the need to improve its own methods of self-regulation, including procedures for dealing promptly and fairly with complaints ...

If a dispute cannot be settled in this way the right to appeal to the Press Council, of course, remains.

Code of Practice
Respect for privacy: Intrusion into private lives should always have a public interest justification.
Opportunity for reply: Mistakes will be corrected promptly and with appropriate prominence.
Conduct of journalists: Subject only to the existence of an overriding public interest, information for publication will be obtained by straightforward means. Similarly, newspapers will not authorize payment to criminals or their families and associates to enable them to profit from crime.

Race, colour: Irrelevant reference to race, colour and religion will be avoided.

Detroit Free Press Guidelines (Michigan, USA)
December 13, 1984

Attribution, unnamed sources:
Our readers usually are best served when we can identify news sources by name. We should work hard to identify the source(s) although there will be instances when the pursuit of truth will best be served by not naming a source. Sources will be named unless the reason not to do so is an overriding consideration ...

Misrepresentation:
Staff members generally should identify themselves as Free Press staff members. In those justifiable circumstances when we may be unable to report a story without concealing our identity, approval of a managing editor is required. The story's value should justify the decision to conceal our identity. Whenever we have not disclosed our identity in reporting a story, the story needs to say so ...

Paying for news:
When money is paid for information, serious questions can be raised about the credibility of that information and the motives of the buyer and seller. We generally avoid paying for information. Exceptions must be approved in advance by a managing editor.

Race, ethnic origin:
The race of a person in the news won't be reported unless it is clearly relevant to the story or is part of a detailed physical description. If a strong case cannot be made for mentioning race, it should be omitted. Racially and ethnically derogatory terms are to be treated as obscenities; such a term should be spelled as an initial followed by hyphens, and be used only in quoted material, when it is essential to a story, and with approval of a managing editor. Photos or art work which foster racial stereotypes are to be avoided unless there is justifiable news value. In such cases, a supervising editor should be consulted ...

Recording interviews and phone conversations:
Except in rare and justifiable instances, we do not tape anyone without that person's knowledge. To do otherwise violates a general policy of treating people as we would want to be treated. An exception may be made only if we are convinced the recording is necessary to protect

us in a legal action or for some other compelling reason, and if other approaches won't work. Such instances require a managing editor's approval in advance.

Respect for privacy:
The public's right to know often needs to be weighed vis-à-vis the privacy rights of people in the news. We need to respect not only their legal rights, but also their own and our readers' sensibilities about what is reasonable coverage and what is unfair or intrusive coverage.

Generally, we do not identify living victims of sex crimes or persons whose safety would be jeopardized by publishing their names or addresses. Exceptions must be approved by a managing editor ...

Sexism:
Women and men should not be treated differently. Physical description and familial connections of a woman are appropriate only if a man would be described comparably in similar circumstances. We generally avoid terms that specify gender, e.g. police officer rather than policeman, although such uses as actor/actress and waiter/waitress are acceptable. Phrases that suggest there is something unusual about the gender of someone holding a job (woman lawyer, male nurse) should be avoided. When referring to members of a group, a construction correctly using THEIR is generally preferable to one requiring HIS or HER. Photos should have justifiable news value to be used ...

Political activity:
Journalists should avoid work for pay or as a volunteer in a political campaign or organization. If a staff member has a close relative – spouse, parent, child, brother or sister – or a person with whom the staff member has a close and continuing personal relationship, who is involved in a political campaign or organization, the staff member should not cover or make news judgments about the campaign or organization; if the individual circumstances are felt to justify another course of action, a managing editor needs to be consulted. If a staff member feels compelled to seek public office, the executive editor's permission is required.

Wilson Daily Times (North Carolina, USA)
Many newspapers have long, detailed and complex ethics policies that outline what is and is not acceptable conduct by reporters and editors. The *Wilson Daily Times* has no separate, formal ethics statement, but it does adhere to a strict code of ethics.

Reporters may accept free meals or transportation, when offered, in connection with coverage of news stories. Many civic clubs and other organisations will invite reporters to be their guests in order to accommodate news coverage. If accepting the invitation will make coverage more convenient, it may be acceptable. Invitations should not be accepted simply because a reporter wants a free meal ...

Reporters should not make a habit of accepting gifts from news sources. Acceptance of such gifts can leave the impression, correctly or not, in the eyes of the giver or of the public, that something is being 'bought' with these gifts. Small gifts tendered for purely altruistic reasons or because a person genuinely likes a reporter may be accepted. A reporter should avoid offending genuinely benevolent persons by refusing a gracious offer ...

Reporters may hold down part-time jobs, so long as they do not interfere with the primary job. Reporters may not work for advertising agencies, other news organizations or for employers the reporter is likely to encounter as a news source. Reporters may not endorse products ...

The use of 'off the record' assurances should be avoided. Such promises are seldom worth the dilemmas they can create. If a reporter gives a promise that   information will be 'off the record,' however, he must not violate that trust. This does not preclude using that knowledge to obtain the same information from another source, if that is possible.

The *Wilson Daily Times* has no formal dress code, but reporters are expected to dress in a manner appropriate to the event they are covering. Dress at the office should be appropriate to the highly educated, professional role reporters and editors are performing. Chewing gum is permitted in the newsroom; however, blowing bubbles adds no distinction to the news staff. You may chew, but do not blow.

From truth, accuracy and the public interest to the etiquette of chewing gum – the makers of codes and guidelines have expressed the gamut of preferences and priorities. A review of these and other statements, such as those included in Appendix D, makes it easy to understand such observations as those of Arthur Kent and Lincoln Steffens:

> We work in a craft governed more by instinct than by rules ... (Kent, in Alia, Brennan and Hoffmaster, 1996: 1)

> General reporting in New York in my day was a series of daily adventures, interesting, sometimes thrilling, but, on the *Evening Post*, rarely perilous ...

The news department of the *Post* had, theoretically, nothing to do with the editorial policy. Reporters were to report the news as it happened, like machines, without prejudice, color, and without style; all alike. Humor or any sign of personality in our reports was caught, rebuked, and, in time, suppressed. (Steffens, 1931: 179)

... 'the *Evening Post* will not take sides. A fair paper, it will be just and true to the facts ... You will seek the truth, and the truth you will report, as you find it'. (Steffens, 1931: 200)

Although there was no specific, spelled-out code of ethics, the *Evening Post* of Lincoln Steffens' early newspaper years had a sharply defined set of principles underscoring daily practice: the news was to be presented with neutrality and objectivity and without bias, in a cool and humourless fashion. The story of Steffens' career is the story of his break from those principles and his struggle to present news and information in a passionate and potentially life-changing way. As we have seen, he was a reporter and a reformer, in equal measure. He did not just want to *notice* poverty, inequality, injustice, government and corporate collusion and corruption. Nor did he just want to *communicate* those conditions and inform the public. He wanted his journalism to reveal and communicate in a way that could help people to *change* things for the better. He learned that one of the ways to do this was to abandon the cool, humourless and passionless reportorial style for a more literary and involved style of writing. In the following case, he uses humour to illuminate some of the principles implicit in appropriate and inappropriate media practice.

I Make a Crime Wave

Every now and then there occurs the phenomenon called a crime wave ...

I enjoy crime waves. I made one once. Jake Riis helped; many reporters joined in the uplift of the rising tide of crime; and T.R. [President Theodore Roosevelt] stopped it ...

The basement of the old police headquarters was a cool place in summer and detectives, prisoners, and we reporters used to sit together down there and gossip or doze or play cards. Good stories of the underworld were told there, better than are ever printed as news. They were true stories, and true detective stories are more fascinating than the fiction even of the masters. Sometimes a prisoner would give his version of his crime and his capture after the detective who had caught him told his. Sometimes the stories were dull, technical ... interesting enough to the participants ...

[One day I heard about a burglary] done with police aid and protection ... In my office across the street I wrote a news story of that robbery, but only because the victim was the well-known family of a popular Wall Street [stock] broker. I could not give away the source of my information; it might exclude me from the basement ... That afternoon Riis reported a burglary which I knew nothing about ... My editor wanted to know why I was beaten.

'I thought you didn't want crimes in the *Post* ...'

'No, but a big burglary like that – '

All right. I called on my assistant, Robert, and told him we must get some crimes ... Robert saved the day. He learned, and I wrote, of the robbery of a fifth Avenue club. That was a beat, but Riis had two robberies that were beats on me. By that time the other evening papers were having some thefts of their own. The poker club reporters ... could get the news when they had to, and being awakened by the scrap between Riis and me, they broke up their game and went to work ... and they were soon beating me, as Riis was. I was sorry I had started it. Robert or I had to sleep in turns in the basement, and we picked up some crimes, but Riis had two or three a day ... The morning newspapers not only rewrote [our stories]; they had crimes of their own, which they grouped to show that there was a crime wave.

It was indeed one of the worst crime waves I ever witnessed, and the explanations were embarrassing to the reform police board, which my paper and my friends were supporting, in their difficult reform work. The old system was built upon the understood relations of the crooks and the detective bureau. Certain selected criminals in each class, pickpockets, sneak thieves, burglars, etc., were allowed to operate within reason; the field was divided among them by groups, each of which had a monopoly. In return for the paid-for privilege the groups were to defend their monopoly from outsiders, report the arrival in town of strangers from other cities, and upon demand furnish information (not evidence) to the detectives and return stolen goods. This was called regulation and control, and it worked pretty well; more to the glory of the police, who could perform 'miracles of efficiency' when the victim of a robbery was worth serving, but of course it did not stop stealing; it protected only citizens with pull, power, or privilege ...

[New Yorkers had learned] to report their losses to the police, never to the press ... If citizens would ... report both to the press and the police they would ... soon find out how many crimes are committed ... how few are 'detected,' and force the police to detect many more ... these wise men know that ... detectives work hardest on a case that is in the papers.

[At a secret meeting of the police board, the Commissioner said to Roosevelt:]

'Mr. President, you can stop this crime wave whenever you want to.'

'I! How?'

'Call off your friends Riis and Steffens. They started it, and – they're sick of it. They'll be glad to quit if you'll ask them to.' ...

They explained [that] the morning newspapers got their crimes from the courts where only arrested prisoners are tried or held for trial ... the evening papers got their stories by hard detective work, which they hate to have to do. But they must continue as long as your friends, Mr. President, keep up their fight ... T.R. adjourned the meeting, sent for Riis and me, and bang!

'What's this I hear? You two and this crime wave? Getting us into trouble? ...'

'and you laugh!' he blazed at me. I couldn't help it. But Riis saved us. He was contrite; he looked ashamed ... And Riis, the honest, told us how the reports of all crimes of high degree against property were sent in by the precincts to the heads of inspection districts and then were all compiled in a completed list ... filed in a certain pigeon-hole in the outer office of the chief inspector ...

'And you?' T.R. whirled upon me.

I had to tell him about my naps in the basement among the gossiping detectives. I did not want to give up hearing the gossip, and I asked, and T.R. and Riis agreed to grant me, leave to go there on condition that I would use it only to collect local color for fiction or data for the scientific purposes of my studies in sociology and ethics.

Thus the crime wave was ended to the satisfaction of all ... When Riis and I ceased reporting robberies the poker [group] resumed their game, and the morning newspapers discovered that the fickle public were 'sick of crime' and wanted something else. The monthly magazines and the scientific quarterlies had some belated, heavy, incorrect analyses of the periodicity of lawlessness; they had no way to account for it then. The criminals could work o' nights, honest citizens could sleep, and judges could afford to be more just. (Steffens, 1931: 285–91)

Steffens's 'crime wave' might today be called a 'moral panic'. His approach combines the techniques discussed in Chapter 2, of ethnographic description and participant observation. By revealing the social strata, strategies and structures that are usually hidden from the public, his account has the potential to alter public perceptions. If you think his story may be dated, consider the massive 'Special Investigation' published over several days in 2003 by *The Guardian*. According to journalist Nick Davies, Britain's criminal justice system 'succeeds in bringing to justice only 3% of the offences that are committed ... frequently fails to enforce its sentences against those it does catch, and ... routinely fails to prevent them offending again' (Davies, 2003: 1).

The article reports that fiddling of crime statistics is 'part of the everyday reality of British policing' and that chief constables who insist on 'ethical crime recording' suffer politically for their honesty. There are 'people who know a lot about crime but who are running a criminal justice system which does not deliver results.' Government figures showing a decrease in crime have been 'fiddled'. In case the main point has been missed, we are told that the criminal justice system is mired in 'engulfing bureaucracy,' and Britain is in the midst of a 'crimewave'. (Davies, 2003: 4–6). Sound familiar? Perhaps *The Guardian* editors should reread Lincoln Steffens before committing so much time and newspaper space to what one of the several headlines labels 'The war on crime' (Davies, 2003: 6). The larger agenda is the newspaper's challenge to the government of Tony Blair.

On the 'Opinion' page, Polly Toynbee criticises both the tabloids and the news pages of her own newspaper (*The Guardian*) for misleading the public.

> Crime Wave UK! shrieked this week's *News of the World* ... before the release of tomorrow's annual crime figures. Nothing but lies, damned lies, can be expected from most of the press and all the Tories ... The real figures most newspaper readers may never get to see ... are likely to show a slight decrease in overall crime ... Violence is only around 2% of crime and last year it fell, but you would never have guessed it ... If tomorrow's media blast yet again warps public opinion on crime, it will do damage again to the home secretary's sense of proportion. He may know the real figures ... but headlines too often intimidate him ... So pause by the newsstand tomorrow morning, peruse the press and consider how much the culture and contentment of the country is harmed by this daily distortion of the way we live now. (Toynbee, 2003: 20)

However important that challenge, it is worth asking whether this particular story merits such extensive coverage, and whether the manner of reporting it gives the public much-needed information or merely escalates a moral panic. These are important questions to ask, especially since crime and policing comprise a central arena in which xenophobic and racist problems and agendas emerge. Here is an example of media decision-making that can help to escalate, or alleviate, violence.

In another 'world', a 2003 case raises questions about the nature, extent and potential regulation of plagiarism. Like all of his albums, Bob Dylan's 2001 CD, *Love and Theft*, featured original songs by the singer-songwriter 'who has inspired generations with his free-wheeling language'. While browsing in a shop, a Dylan fan who teaches English in Japan chanced upon an English translation by John Bester of a 1991 book, *Confessions of a Yakuza*, by Junichi Saga. Having 'probably listened to that album at least 100 times', the fan, Chris Johnson, saw phrases that 'jumped right out at me' – phrases suggesting that Dylan may have 'borrowed' many of the lyrics on the CD from Saga's book. Two examples:

> If it bothers you so much, she'd say, 'Why don't you just shove off' [Saga's book, p. 9]
>
> Juliet said … 'Why don't you just shove off if it bothers you so much' [Dylan's song, 'Floater']
>
> My mother … was the daughter of a wealthy farmer … died when I was 11 … my father was a traveling salesman … I never met him. [My uncle] was a nice man, I won't forget him. [Saga, pp. 57–8]
>
> My mother was a daughter of a wealthy farmer, / My father was a travelin' salesman, I never met him. / When my mother died, my uncle took me … He did a lot of nice things for me and I won't forget him' [Dylan's song, 'Po' Boy'] (Campbell, 2003: 2)

Anti-plagiarism rules figure importantly in most codes. Even where plagiarism is not spelled out, it is unlikely to be acceptable; it is safe to say that no media organisation would go on record as supporting it. What complicates the Dylan–Saga saga is the author's response to learning of Dylan's alleged plagiarism. Saga had not heard of Dylan, but bought the CD after hearing of the accusations posted on Chris Johnson's website, dylanchords.com. Saga told the *The Wall Street Journal* 'he was flattered someone he had never heard of should possibly have found his words inspiring'. 'I like this album … His lines flow from one image to the next and don't always make sense, but they have a great atmosphere.' Although he said he would not 'make a fuss about the lyrics', Saga said it would be 'honourable' if he received credit.

He also hopes it will help the sales of the book, which has jumped more than 20,000 places on the Amazon.com list since the first whispers about the similarities started to appear on the internet. (Campbell, 2003: 2)

The case raises some interesting questions. Is the ironically titled *Love and Theft* CD unethical, even if the source of the alleged plagiarism likes the album and is flattered by the attention? If book sales increase, does that constitute reparation for the alleged textual theft? Japan is a less litigious society than the United States, with a strong culture of honour, politeness and respect. How do Japanese codes of behaviour figure in the ethical equation? Might Saga be understating his objection, in culturally relativistic terms? If so, how does this 'translate' into appropriate action by an American songwriter? Can we devise cross-culturally relevant and enforceable codes of media practice? This brings us to the central question of the present chapter: Can codes of ethics or statements of principles make a difference?

Taking the moral high ground ... or is it quicksand?

There is no guarantee that setting out a statement of guidelines or principles, or a more formal code of ethics, will cause or produce responsible media practice. Nor is there a guarantee that those who struggle to create such statements are in good and honourable company. As Brian Brennan points out:

British pirates had a code of ethics. In 1640 they loosely banded themselves into a democratic fraternity and adopted a set of vows collectively titled 'The Custom of the Brothers of the Coast, or the Pirates' Creed of Ethics'. It was signed by the whole ship's company before every departure and served as the social contract of the expedition. (Brennan, 1996: 112)

As someone living on Britain's Barbary Coast (whose local pub is called Smuggler's) I am frequently reminded of the questionable company we keep. 'A very mixed bag' is how ethicist John L. Hulteng describes media codes. He traces the history from the 1920s:

... the early statements of principle or codes of conduct ... tended to be couched in general terms, leaving the specific application ... to the individual judgments of the men and women who had to make the decisions ... (Hulteng, 1985: 13)

In the United States, interest in codifying ethical media practice escalated sharply in the mid-1970s following the Vietnam War and the Watergate scandal.

> [Media] coverage of the war ... helped to bring about a national repudiation of [US] involvement in Southeast Asia and the earlier-than-expected retirement from public life of President Lyndon Johnson. And in Watergate, media efforts contributed importantly to the exposure of a cancerous corruption and to the first instance in American history of a president resigning in disgrace. (Hulteng, 1985: 15)

Although the public was generally supportive of media interventions in these events, 'public disaffection with the press grew more widespread and more pronounced' during the late 1970s and early 1980s. 'News media leaders quickly became aware of the changing public mood' (Hulteng, 1985: 15). In the 1981 film *Absence of Malice*, Megan – the reporter played by Sally Field – reflects: 'A lot of damage has been done, and I'm responsible for a lot of it. I keep thinking there must be rules to tell me what I'm supposed to do now' (screenplay by Karl Luedtke). Increasingly, employers began to set out rules and guidelines. A glance at almost any newspaper or television programme of today (not to mention radio, Internet and other media) reveals that the proliferation of rules and guidelines in the past thirty years has not created problem-free journalism or reduced the quantity of bad media practice. It is no co-incidence that *Absence of Malice* was based on a play by Kurt Luedtke, a former newspaper executive editor. Given the writer's background, it is probably also no coincidence that it features an extremely kindly and thoughtful editor who provides caring, if imperfect, guidance to the reporter.

John Pilger recalls a code of ethics developed during his early days at *The Daily Mirror*, in the 1960s. It 'left the staff in no doubt that if they knowingly submitted false or distorted stories, they would be dismissed' (Pilger, 1998: 375). Tolerance 'was part of the paper's character' and was extended to both staff and readers.

> Every letter, every phone call, no matter how cranky, was taken seriously. During the Second World War the Daily Mirror Readers' Service was set up to help families ... Guiding people through the bureaucracy was a speciality ... it was entirely free of charge and what the *Mirror* got in return was good will, loyalty and affection. The *Mirror* was the first popular paper to encourage working-class people to express themselves ... to *their* newspaper. (Pilger, 1998: 375)

Without detracting from Pilger's point about responsibility to readers, it should be noted that his claim is exaggerated. In 1802, William Cobbett created a forum for working-class people in the form of the *Weekly Political Register*. In 1830, Henry Hetherington founded *The Poor Man's Guardian*, affiliated to the National Union of Working Classes and based on the premise that 'knowledge is power'. Three years later, *The Northern Star* was founded as a voice of the Chartists – Britain's first working-class political movement.

Pilger implies that the *The Mirror*'s code protected both staff and readers, and had a positive impact on the quality, responsibility and ethics of the newspaper's output. Brennan thinks codes have little value, and journalists

> must still find a way of showing the public that words like 'account-ability' and 'sacred trust' are more than just the clichés of the pro-fession. In practical terms, ethical codes may be structurally flawed as devices for producing accountability, especially when they contain no enforcement provisions and are seen ... as mantles of arrogance, self-protection and status quoism. They may also promote weak and inadequate journalism because of their traditional emphasis on 'don'ts' rather than 'dos' ... (Brennan, 1996: 120)

Tim Gopsill, editor of the National Union of Journalists (NUJ) maga-zine *The Journalist*, is equally suspicious of codes, and more generally of media self-regulation as exemplified by the Press Complaints Commission (see Appendix D).

> It is not real. It is the fable of the emperor's new clothes, and over the last 20 years the emperor has been through several wardrobes. He used to wear the uniform of the Press Council ... set up in 1954, in the face of fierce resistance from the publishers, as a serious attempt to institute self-regulation. It was a cross-industry body, with represen-tatives of the unions as well as the publishers and editors. But journalists began to see it as an apologist for the editors who domi-nated it ... and in 1981 the NUJ pulled out. (Gopsill, 1999: 6)

The flaws of self-regulation are underscored by a 2003 case in which two judges criticised a newspaper for undermining the work of the justice system. In one case, drugs charges against singer Brian Harvey

> were dropped after the prosecution said the main witness had been paid £15,000 by the *News of the World*. Judge Gareth Hawkesworth told Mr Harvey: 'You leave this court without a stain on your character. May this be a salutary lesson to the proprietors of that newspaper.' (Kirby, 2003: 1)

Harvey's lawyer said he was arrested 'solely because of an article in *The News of the World*' and called on the Crown Prosecution Service to conduct an investigation. In a second case, Nadine Milroy-Sloan – jailed 'for fabricating allegations against' former Tory minister Neil Hamilton and his wife Christine – was paid £50,000 for telling her story to *The News of the World*. Judge Simon Smith said: 'It is becoming all too easy for people to sell allegations about well-known people to the press and the courts have got to deal with it' (Kirby, 2003: 1). Her claim of sexual assault was thrown out when (among other things) it was learned she had never met the Hamiltons. Despite the court's dismissal of her case, the newspaper's generosity made sure she was rewarded for inventing the story. What is most pertinent for our discussion of media codes, principles and self-regulation is the defence which the newspaper presented to the public. A statement issued by the newspaper said:

> *The News of the World* is bewildered to have been blamed for the collapse of [the Harvey] trial ... Our informant was paid prior to any arrests fully within the PCC code. (Kirby, 2003: 1)

Where do we go from here?

Tim Gopsill thinks that far more radical changes are required before a useful self-regulatory system can emerge. 'To bring in a system of regulation independent of both government and the press barons requires, firstly, changes to the pattern of ownership ... Secondly, it requires the establishment of an independent body' (Gopsill, 1999: 7).

As we seek understanding of today's unique or particular problems, it helps to remember yesterday's struggles, mentors and heroes. Describing a proud moment in journalistic history, Pete Steffens notes Benjamin Franklin's pamphlet protesting the killing of '20 peaceable Indians ... who had long liv'd quietly among us'. 'Franklin's tract headed off a feared further massacre' (Steffens, 1978: 8). Conway Jocks, a Mohawk broadcaster in Canada, was on the air during the 1990 crisis at Kanehsatake and Oka, Quebec. His radio station, CKRK-FM, is situated in the community of Kahnawake, a few miles from Kanehsatake – cut off during the crisis by an army blockade. 'Kahnawake was the sole connection with the outside and was an important link between the communities' (Jocks, 1996: 173). It provided an important forum for public debate that helped to defuse the crisis.

In such a case, the ability to defuse rather than inflame a crisis depends almost entirely on the judgement of the individual broadcaster. Jocks is concerned that too much is left to individual conscience and judgement.

Media malpractice can be as much a matter of life or death as medical malpractice. Yet there are extensive safeguards against malpractice in medicine and other fields, and virtually none against media malpractice. In fact, in the professional world, those who manage and produce communications are uniquely unaccountable for their actions. I believe that it is our obligation to clarify and codify standards and make media practitioners accountable to the public.

In the interest of media accountability, Raphael Cohen-Almagor proposes a system in which the media regulate themselves (Cohen-Almagor, 2000). His view follows the position that is overwhelmingly preferred in Canada, the United States, Britain and other countries. I share his concerns about the dangers of state intervention in the media practices of liberal democracies. I am equally concerned about the dangers of media self-regulation. We live in an age of media monopoly. One of the most blatant examples of media–government collusion is in Italy, where Sylvio Berlusconi is Prime Minister and owns nearly all of the media. In the countries in which governments do not control the major media, massive private corporations often do. I have no greater faith in the ability of a mega-corporate-controlled media to regulate itself than in the ability of a state-controlled media to do so. In 2000 I proposed creating a media tribunal with two decision-making bodies – a press council and a public forum – two levels of accountability, each with decision-making power and guided by an enforceable code of ethics. Another approach would be to create a single body with equal representation from inside and outside the media community, but managed and mediated entirely from the outside. Although existing press councils sometimes include 'citizen' members, I think they are too close to the media insiders, in terms of both administration and the decision-making process. We need a more neutral, agenda-free review process. Claude-Jean Bertrand has considered such questions in greater detail in his work on 'Media Accountability Systems' (Bertrand, 2001a, 2001b).

The media can help to escalate, or alleviate, structural, personal and state violence (Alia, 2000: 289–90). The role of codes, principles, regulation and self-regulation is open to discussion and debate. What is less open to question is the need to lower the level of all kinds of violence, and to make mass media constructive and humane contributors to the cause.

Exercises

11.1 Class discussion

Reread Lincoln Steffens's account of how he started a 'crime wave' (above). Each person should write a list of the ethical problems and principles that can be found 'between the lines' of the story. Then hold a class discussion: What are the problems? How should they be addressed? What principles would be useful in setting guidelines for responsible coverage of crime, criminals, law enforcement and the social context?

11.2 Futuremaking: creating a code of ethics

This is a consensus-building exercise the objective of which is to discover whether the class can agree on a set of principles or guidelines. Other relevant questions include: Should there be a formal code? Informal guidelines? Separate guidelines for each employer? Print? Broadcast? New media? What would a code be? How can we help assure ethical journalism throughout one's career?

SUGGESTED SEQUENCE
At the next to last class, students are asked to prepare for the final class session.

There is widespread disagreement as to whether there should – or can – be a single Code of Ethics for Canadian journalists. Regardless of your position on whether there should be a formal code, identify the principles you consider essential to a working journalist's professional life. Write a brief, rough draft statement and bring it to class. (This can also be done in a single class session of 2–4 hours.)

FINAL CLASS SESSION
A. *Small-group work (30 minutes)*
Divide into groups of four or six students (if possible, it should be an even number). Each group gets an acetate sheet and an overhead projector pen – if possible, a different colour for each group. Ideally, there should be break-out rooms to enable the small groups to work independently. If these are unavailable, the groups can meet within the classroom.

1. Each person should write down three essential principles they think media practitioners should live by.
2. Each person reads their three principles to the group.

3. Break into pairs. Each pair tries to find three principles they can agree on.

4. For the full group meeting, appoint a reporter to take notes, with the overhead projector pen, on the acetate sheet. Each pair presents the principles it has agreed. The group now attempts to find three or more principles everyone can agree on. The reporter writes them on acetate for presentation to the class.

B. *Class work: building consensus, setting ethical standards and objectives (30 minutes or more)*

1. The class reconvenes. Each group reports its findings, using the acetates and overhead projector

2. The tutor records the results of the following discussion on a new acetate

   Class discussion:
   − Should there be formal statements of principles?
   − Should there be an enforceable code of ethics?
   − Can we agree on at least three principles that are acceptable to everyone?

Further reading

Brennan, Brian (1996) 'Codes of ethics: who needs them?', in Valerie Alia, Brian Brennan and Barry Hoffmaster (eds), *Deadlines and Diversity: Journalism Ethics in a Changing World.* Halifax, NS: Fernwood, pp. 112–20.

Steffens, Lincoln (1931) *The Autobiography of Lincoln Steffens.* New York: Harcourt Brace.

Viewing

For details see the annotated filmography in Appendix B at the end of the book.

Absence of Malice
Citizen Kane
Mad City
Shock Corridor
Washington Story

Appendix A
Notes on case analysis

There are many 'case methods' of study and some confusion about them. The method suggested in this book is my own, developed over many years of teaching and workshop facilitation. As they are used in business, medical and other programmes, case studies often require small groups for discussion only rather than for actual decision-making exercises. Rather than develop 'expert' solutions or leave the issues dangling, the method in this book emphasises the need for journalists to work together. Although it is seldom analysed, 'real-life' decision-making in journalism involves an intricate interplay of personalities and principles. Advertisers affect publishers who affect editors who affect reporters who affect headline-writers who affect readers ... Although they are seldom labelled 'ethical', ethical decisions are made daily, by teams, hierarchies, individual journalists.

I have therefore focused the case method in this book on consensus-building and problem-solving. You may never again have the luxury of playing a decision out in this way, but perhaps the skills will prove useful in your daily work lives. It is important to remember that there are no 'right' or 'wrong' answers. The students are assessed on the integrity of their *participation*, not on their particular ethical perspective or the solutions they propose. Each case can be solved in a number of ways, but each case must be solved in *some* way. Every day is a news day; every news day presents problems journalists must solve to keep on working. The goal of each case study is to:

1. identify the problems;
2. consider the options;
3. reflect on the options in relation to the resources at hand (time, personnel, media policies, information available, sources available, etc.);
4. devise a plan of action – not the only available plan, but a *workable* plan, with the best possible outcomes.

Appendix B
Journalists and journalism on film: an ethics-based filmography and videography – and a CD

The history of cinema contains a surprising number of landmark films in which journalists play a central role – or in which journalism as a profession is the central subject. Several films mark landmark events in the history and ethics of journalism (e.g. *Reds* – John Reed and Louise Bryant's coverage of the Russian Revolution; *All the President's Men* – Bob Woodward and Carl Bernstein's coverage of Watergate; *Citizen Kane* – Orson Welles' study of the rise and fall of a media magnate modelled on William Randolph Hearst). The filmed portrayals encompass a number of basic themes (e.g. the journalist as pariah, life-risking hero or saviour, conscience or voice of the people, feminist, human rights advocate, muckraker, self-promoter, Quixote, press baron, fanatic).

Films

Abandoned (1949) Joe Newman (USA) Raymond Burr, Jeff Chandler, Gale Storm.

Newspaperman helps a woman find her sister's 'illegitimate' baby and finds himself involved in an illegal adoption ring.

A Bell for Adano (1945) Henry King (USA) Gene Tierney, William Bendix.

Based on the book on Italy in the Second World War by American journalist John Hersey.

Absence of Malice (1981) Sydney Pollack (USA) Sally Field, Paul Newman.

Reporting unsubstantiated information; leaked documents and the relationship between politicians and the press; ethics of interviewing; journalist–subject relations.

Ace in the Hole – retitled *The Big Carnival* (1951) Billy Wilder (USA) Kirk Douglas, Jan Sterling.

Opportunistic and careerist journalist exploits his accidental discovery of a man trapped underground and turns the story into a media circus.

All the President's Men (1976) Allan J. Pakula (USA) Dustin Hoffman, Robert Redford.
Thoughtful and well researched depiction of the process by which Carl Bernstein and Bob Woodward uncovered the Watergate scandal in the pages of their newspaper, *The Washington* Post, which led to the downfall of US President Richard M. Nixon.

Antonia: A Portrait of the Woman (1974) Judy Collins and Jill Godmilow (USA).
Documentary about orchestra conductor Antonia Brico's battle against sexism in the world of classical music – a world in which women remain marginalised and must usually serve as guest conductors rather than leaders of their own organisations. Moving and informative.

Before the Rain (1994) Milcho Manchevski (Macedonia/Britain/France) Katrin Cartlidge, Rade Serbedzija.
Experiences of a photojournalist in the postwar Republic of Macedonia (formerly in Yugoslavia).

Berlin Correspondent (1942) Eugene Forde (USA) Virginia Gilmore, Dana Andrews.
American journalist becomes personally involved in helping his girl-friend and her father escape Nazi Germany.

Between the Lines (1977) Joan Micklin Silver (USA) John Heard, Lindsay Crouse, Jeff Goldblum, Joe Morton.
Portrait of a Boston underground newspaper (modelled on real-life events in the history of *Boston After Dark*, *The Phoenix* and *The Real Paper*) on the eve of its takeover by a press baron.

Black Like Me (1964) Carl Lerner (USA) Roscoe Lee Browne, James Whitmore, Will Geer, Al Freeman, Jr.
Based on the book by journalist John Howard Griffin, in which he (a white journalist) artificially coloured his skin to experience the life of a black man in 1960s racist America.

Bowling for Columbine (2003) Michael Moore and Michael Donovan (USA).
Incisive, Cannes Film Festival and US Academy Award-winning feature-length documentary about gun culture and violence in the US. Further information, suggestions for activist projects and film clips are

available on Michael Moore's website (see Appendix C).

Broadcast News (1987) James L. Brooks (USA) William Hurt, Holly Hunter.

Amusing and instructive comedy about a team of ambitious television journalists; deals with international coverage, a pretty-faced empty-headed (male) news anchor and other aspects of the daily life of a US TV station.

Bulworth (1998) Warren Beatty (USA) Warren Beatty, Halle Berry, Paul Sorvino, Amiri Baraka.

Delightful political satire – good choice as an aid to discussion relations between politicians, government, media and public information.

The China Syndrome (1979) James Bridges (USA) Jane Fonda, Jack Lemmon, Michael Douglas.

Members of a television news team uncover life-threatening flaws in a nuclear power plant and have to decide how to reveal the information to the public; relations between journalists and whistle-blowers; science and environment reporting; assessing information from public relations/promotion sources.

Citizen Kane (1941) Orson Welles (USA) Orson Welles, Joseph Cotten, Agnes Moorehead.

Some consider this the greatest film ever made. Strongly acted, directed and photographed. Close-to-reality portrayal of the life, work and death of 'Charles Foster Kane', a character modelled so sharply on William Randolph Hearst that Hearst tried to prevent the film from being shown. Media ownership; press barons and politics.

Cry Freedom (1987) Richard Attenborough (Britain) Kevin Kline, Penelope Wilson, Denzel Washington.

Account of the relationship between the newspaper editor Donald Woods and the South African political activist Steven Biko, who was killed while in prison under the apartheid regime. Deals with life-threatening, campaigning journalism.

A Cry in the Dark (1988) Fred Schepisi (Australia) Meryl Streep, Sam Neil.

True story of a family whose newborn daughter was taken from their tent while they holidayed at Ayers Rock. The mother said a dingo (wild dog) took the baby; the police arrested her for murder. This is a powerful, well acted story of justice done, undone and redone with the help – and hindrance – of a sensation-hungry media.

Dave (1993) Ivan Reitman (USA) Kevin Kline, Sigourney Weaver, Ben Kingsley.
Political comedy with cameo appearances by real-life journalists and politicians.

The Day the Earth Caught Fire (1961) Val Guest (Britain) Edward Judd, Janet Munro.
Excellent science fiction drama about the dilemma facing a journalist who learns of the potentially impending destruction of the earth.

Death Watch (1980) Bertrand Tavernier (France/Germany) Romy Schneider, Harvey Keitel, Harry Dean Stanton, Max von Sydow.
Science fiction drama challenging hidden-camera and other techniques in a story of a journalist secretly photographing a dying man.

Each Dawn I Die (1939) William Keighley (USA) James Cagney, George Raft, Victor Jory.
A journalist is framed and sent to prison.

Ed TV (1999) Ron Howard (USA, based on Canadian film, *Louis XIX: Roi des Ondes*) Woody Harrelson, Sally Kirkland, Martin Landau, Ellen DeGeneres, Rob Reiner.
Pre-reality-TV science fiction about secret televising and control-by-media of ordinary people's lives. Interesting film.

Foreign Correspondent (1940) Alfred Hitchcock (USA) Joel McCrea, Laraine Day.
Journalists involved in a spy ring.

The Front Page (1931) Lewis Milestone (USA) Adolphe Menjou, Pat O'Brien.
Film version of the Charles MacArthur–Ben Hecht play about Chicago journalists in the 1920s. Focuses on tensions between editor and reporter.

The Front Page (1974) Billy Wilder (USA) Jack Lemmon, Walter Matthau, Susan Sarandon.
Remake/update (see also *Switching Channels*).

Front Page Story (1954) G. Parry (Britain) Jack Hawkins, Elizabeth Allan.
Newspaper editor's relationships with staff; ethical and personal problems.

Front Page Woman (1935) M. Curtiz (USA) Bette Davis.
Competition between two journalists covering a murder trial.

Gandhi (1982) Richard Attenborough (Britain/India) Ben Kingsley, Candice Bergen.

Life of Gandhi with portrait of his relationship with the media, and the impact of journalists' roles and decisions on his rise and eventual assassination.

Gentleman's Agreement (1947) Elia Kazan (USA) Gregory Peck, Dorothy McGuire.

Precursor to *Black Like Me* – reporter masquerades as Jewish to uncover and understand the effects of anti-Semitism in American society. Based on novel by Laura Z. Hobson.

Good Morning, Vietnam (1987) Barry Levinson (USA) Robin Williams, Forest Whitaker.

Portrait of real-life radio broadcaster Adrian Cronauer's experiences in the Vietnam War.

Hearts and Minds (1974) Peter Davis (USA).

Award-winning documentary about US promotion of and involvement in the Vietnam War. Controversial at the time, timely in the wake of recent efforts to promote a 'war on terrorism' and war on Iraq.

Hiroshima (1995) Roger Spottiswoode and Koreyoshi Kurahara (Canada–Japan) Kenneth Welsh, Hisashi Igawa.

Extensive documentary footage interspersed with US and Japanese perspectives (developed as two separate strands) on the bombing of Hiroshima; complements journalist John Hersey's landmark portrait of the human effects of political decision-making and war.

His Girl Friday (based on *The Front Page*) (1940) Howard Hawks (USA) Cary Grant, Rosalind Russell.

Yet another remake of *The Front Page*, this time delightfully funny and scripted by Ben Hecht, who co-authored the original play.

The Insider (1999) Michael Mann (USA) Al Pacino, Russell Crowe, Christopher Plummer, Diane Venora, Lindsay Crouse.

Excellent and gripping film based on an actual case involving a producer for the US current affairs television programme, *60 Minutes*, and a tobacco company whistleblower. The screenplay by Michael Mann and Eric Roth is based on a magazine story by Marie Brenner (Maltin, 2003: 675).

Keeper of the Flame (1943) George Cukor (USA) Spencer Tracy, Katharine Hepburn, Howard da Silva.

Journalist discovers truths behind the myth of a leading citizen he is assigned to write about. Challenges journalism's reliance on 'spin', emphasising the need for accurate research and reporting. Script by Academy award-winning writer Donald Ogden Stewart.

Lakota Woman: Siege at Wounded Knee (1994) Frank Pierson (USA) Irene Bedard, Floyd Red Crow Westerman, Tantoo Cardinal.
Based on true story of conflict between Native Americans and government. Includes important role of radio broadcasts in maintaining community morale and solidarity.

Libeled Lady (1936) Jack Conway (USA) Jean Harlow, Spencer Tracy.
Well acted comedy about a dishonest newspaper editor.

Mad City (1997) Constantin Costa-Gavras (USA) John Travolta, Dustin Hoffman, Alan Alda, Mia Kirshner, Blythe Danner.
A tale of political, journalistic and police corruption in which every character (male and female) gets a mix of good-guy and bad-guy lines and the only total villains are the folks at the top of the news, government and policing organisations. Much of it reads like a media ethics training manual – a bit too pat, but powerfully acted and conceived, with a rich array of issues for discussion.

The Mean Season (1985) Phillip Borsos (USA) Kurt Russell, Mariel Hemingway.
Reporter caught in a situation that has him the only contact of a killer; the film asks questions which may be useful in discussing Janet Malcolm's book, *The Journalist and the Murderer*.

Missing (1982) Constantin Costa-Gavras (USA). Jack Lemmon, Sissy Spacek, Melanie Mayron, John Shea, Charles Cioffi, David Clennon, Joe Regalbuto, Richard Venture, Janice Rule.
Fictionalised and set in an unknown Latin American country, the film is based on the true story of Ed Horman, a journalist 'lost' in the last days of Allende's Chile.

Network (1976) Sidney Lumet (USA) William Holden, Faye Dunaway.
Award-winning, well acted satire of ratings-hungry television, scripted by Paddy Chayevsky.

Newsfront (1978) Philip Noyce (Australia) Bill Hunter, Angela Punch.
Fictionalised study of the 1940s and 1950s newsreel industry (news and current affairs short films shown weekly in cinemas that were replaced by television).

Newsies or *Howard the Paperboy* (1992) Kenny Ortega (USA) Christian Bale, Ann-Margret.

Musical about the early days of press empires, focused on the real-life events of the 1899 paper carriers' strike

The Paper (1994) Ron Howard (USA) Michael Keaton, Glenn Close.
Deadlines and ethics in the (satirised) daily life of a newspaper; cameos by several New York journalists.

Park Row (1952) Samuel Fuller (USA) Gene Evans, Mary Welch.
New York journalist takes on a press baron by starting his own newspaper; set in the 1880s.

The Pelican Brief (1993) Alan J. Pakula (USA) Julia Roberts, Denzel Washington, Sam Shepard.
An investigative reporter helps a law student prove her hunch about the assassinations of US Supreme Court justices; absorbing drama based on the John Grisham novel.

Pump Up the Volume (1990) Allan Moyle (USA) Ellen Greene, Annie Ross, Christian Slater.
Pirate radio station appeals to young listeners and upsets some of the community; timely look at the world of talk radio.

Reds (1981) Warren Beatty (USA) Warren Beatty, Diane Keaton.
Portrait of journalists John Reed and Louise Bryant, their love affair and great adventure covering the Russian Revolution, with secondary portraits of Emma Goldman and other luminaries.

Rashomon (1950) Akira Kurosawa (Japan).
The landmark film about different perspectives; each of several characters tells 'the same' story as she or he perceives it 'really happened'. Kurosawa questions the nature of truth and objectivity.

Salvador (1986) Oliver Stone (USA) James Woods, James Belushi.
Based on the journalist Richard Boyle's experiences covering El Salvador; Boyle wrote the screenplay.

Scandal Sheet (1952) Phil Karlson (USA) Broderick Crawford, Donna Reed.
Newspaper reporters end up investigating a killing committed by their editor; based on a Samuel Fuller novel (no connection to the 1931 film of the same name).

The Scoundrel (1935) Ben Hecht (USA) Noel Coward, Julie Hayden.
Manipulative New York publisher gets caught in his own game; performances by award-winning script writers Charles MacArthur and Ben Hecht, and Alexander Woollcott.

The Sellout (1952) Gerald Mayer (USA) Walter Pidgeon, Paula Raymond, Karl Malden.
Editor of a small-town newspaper tries to expose corruption.

Shock Corridor (1963) Samuel Fuller (USA) Peter Breck, Constance Towers.
Journalist goes undercover in a mental institution.

Skokie (1981) Herbert Wise (USA) Danny Kaye, Carl Reiner, Eli Wallach, Ruth Nelson.
Ernest Kinoy's dramatisation of the infamous Skokie case involving demonstrations by neo-Nazis. An excellent parallel to study of Raphael Cohen-Almagor's discussions (in his articles and books) of Skokie in relation to hate speech and journalistic ethics.

Switching Channels (1988) T. Kotcheff (USA) Kathleen Turner, Burt Reynolds.
Good performances in yet another remake of *The Front Page* this time set in the context of satellite television.

Tomorrow Never Dies (1997) Roger Spottiswoode (Britain).
James Bond takes on media ethics – and (as usual) the world. At the heart of this nasty little number is a gem of an only slightly exaggerated portrait of a megalomaniac media baron with all of the latest technical gadgets at his disposal.

The Truman Show (1998) Peter Weir (USA) Jim Carrey.
Like *Ed TV*, a surrealistic, comic and chilling pre-reality TV science fiction portrait of what happens to a young man whose life is secretly appropriated for 24-hour television coverage.

Wag the Dog (1997) Barry Levinson (USA) Al Pacino, Dustin Hoffman, Anne Heche.
Chilling political satire (written by David Mamet) about the ethics of political spin, media complicity and sinister manipulation by a presidency somewhere between Bill Clinton and George W. Bush.

Washington Story (1952) Robert Pirosh (USA) Patricia Neal.
Female journalist covering the Washington political scene and experiencing some conflicts of interest.

Welcome to Sarajevo (1997) Michael Winterbottom. (Britain/USA) Stephen Dillane, Woody Harrelson, Emira Nusevic.
Excellent film for media ethics discussions. True story of a television war correspondent who crosses the personal/professional line, helping to bring a convoy of children out of Sarajevo and eventually adopting

one of them and bringing her to live in England.

Woman of the Year (1942) George Stevens (USA) Kathryn Hepburn, Spencer Tracy.

Comic sparring colours this tale of an internationally famous political journalist and her encounter with a sports writer.

The Year of Living Dangerously (1983) Peter Weir (Australia) Mel Gibson, Sigourney Weaver, Linda Hunt.

Experiences and ethical dilemmas of journalists in Indonesia in the 1960s.

Television programmes/videography

The Prisoner 1967–68 (UK), 17 episodes

Original concept by Patrick McGoohan, who performs in the starring role of the man called 'Number Two'. A science fiction account of people imprisoned in 'The Village', a falsely idyllic setting in an undisclosed location. (When the series ended, it was revealed that it was filmed at Portmeirion, Wales.) There are two particularly relevant episodes: Episode 4, 'Free for All', written by Paddy Fitz and directed by Patrick McGoohan, concerns a manipulated election and the role of the newspaper in covering it. Episode 6, 'The General', written by Joshua Adam (the pen name of Lewis Greifer) and directed by Peter Graham Scott, is a brilliantly caustic – and depressingly timely – satire of new ways of educating and controlling the population. Available on video and DVD.

The West Wing (2001–04, continuing) (USA)

Aaron Sorkin and Thomas Schlamme developed the (deservedly) award-winning series and wrote or co-authored many episodes, with the help of Dee Dee Myers and other former White House staff. The first three seasons are available on DVD. Consistently fine performances by Martin Sheen (as the 'President'), John Spencer, Allison Janney, Rob Lowe, Moira Kelly, Dulé Hill, Richard Schiff, Bradley Whitford and others; fast-paced direction. The role of the President's press secretary, C.J. (Allison Janney), provides a continuing examination of the relationship between politicians (and their spin doctors) and the media. All of the episodes are relevant for a media ethics discussion.

CD

Manifiesto. Victor Jara: Chile September 1973, reissued on CD in 1998, with the supervision of Joan Jara, England: Castle Communications.

Appendix C
Media ethics resources on the Internet

AIROS
http://airos.org/
The American Indian Radio on Satellite network, based in Lincoln, Nebraska (USA). Radio distribution and video and public television programmes; can be reached by e-mail through its assistant manager, John Gregg: jgregg@unlinfo.unl.edu.

ASNE Ethics Codes Collection
http://www.asne.org/ideas/codes/codes.htm
American Society of Newspaper Editors website.

Brasscheck.com
http://www.brasscheck.com/
US site featuring pro bono, human rights oriented Internet projects

The Centre for Public Services
   Resources for social change – publications include: *Mortgaging Our Children's Future: The Privatisation of Secondary Education* and *The Investigator's Handbook: The Handbook for Democracy – How to Find Out About Companies, Organisations, Government and Individuals.*
Address: 1 Sidney Street, Sheffield S1 4RH
Tel: (0114) 272 6683
Fax: (0114) 272 7066
E-mail: mail@centre-public.org.uk

Cyber-Rights & Cyber-Liberties (UK)
A non-profit civil liberties organisation.
http://www.cyber-rights.org

Ethical Space
http://www.ethicalspace.org
Online version of the international journal of communication ethics

EthicNet
http://www.uta.fi/ethicnet/
Databank of mainly European media ethics codes compiled by the University of Tampere Department of Journalism and Mass Communications, Finland.

Ethics Connection
http://www.scu.edu/SCU/Centers/Ethics/
Website for the Markkula Center for Applied Ethics, Santa Clara University.

Ethics in Journalism
http://www.spj.org/ethics.asp
Society of Professional Journalists website.

Ethics on the World Wide Web
http://commfaculty.fullerton.edu lester/ethics/ethics_list.html
Web page compiled by photojournalist and ethicist Paul Lester.

FAIR: Fairness and Accuracy in Reporting
http://www.fair.org
US media watch organisation.

The Institute of Communication Ethics (ICE)
http://www.communication-ethics.org.uk
UK-based international institute founded in 2002. Publishes *Ethical Space* (journal). Individuals and institutions may join, and there are special student memberships as well. In addition to the material posted on the website, further information can be obtained by e-mailing Robert Beckett: Robert@communication-ethics.co.uk, Karen Sanders: k.sanders@sheffield.ac.uk or Valerie Alia: valerie.alia@sunderland.ac.uk

Inuit Circumpolar Conference (ICC)
http//www.inuitcircumpolar.com/

Journal of Mass Media Ethics
http://jmme.byu.edu/
Journal website.

Journalism Ethics Cases Online
http://www.journalism.indiana.edu/Ethics/
Indiana University School of Journalism website.

Media Ethics Resources on the World Wide Web
http://www.ethics.ubc.ca/resources/media/
Site maintained by the University of British Columbia Centre for Applied Ethics.

Media Link
http.//medialine.com/
Resources for journalists.

Media Watch
http://www.pbs.org/newshour/media/
Website for US public television media criticism programme.

Mediabeat
mediabeat@lgc.apc.org
Weekly analysis of US news media by media critic, Norman Solomon.

Mediaethics.ca
http://www.mediaethics.ca/
Canadian media ethics web page.

Mediaethics.org
http://www.mediaethics.org
Provides links to online resources on media ethics.

Michael Moore
http://www.michaelmoore.com/
Website of the contemporary media critic, muckraker and documentary film-maker, Michael Moore.

National Union of Journalists (NUJ)
http://www.nuj.org.uk
Site provides ethics- and industry-related information. Membership information (including student memberships) from:
membership@nuj.org.uk

Online Journalism Review – Ethics section
http://www.ojr.org/ojr/ethics/
Site produced by the University of Southern California Annenberg School for Communication.

Organization of News Ombudsmen
http://www.newsombudsmen.org/
Information-sharing website designed primarily for news ombudsmen.

Poynter online
http://www.poynter.org
Poynter Institute website. *See also* Poynter online ethics journal, resources and ethics tip sheets.

PR Watch Archives
http://www.prwatch.org/prwissues
Site run by the Center for Media and Democracy, devoted to the ethics of public relations and spin.

Press Complaints Commission
www.pcc.org.uk
Website of the British media self-regulation body.

Radio-Television News Directors Association (RTNDA) Code of Ethics
http://www.rtnda.org/ethics/coe.shtml
National US association; *see also* ethics project and coverage guidelines.

Rui-Mai – Maori Radio
http://www.ruimai.co.nz
One of a number of websites of Maori radio outlets, this is New Zealand's major Maori language broadcaster.

Silha Center for the Study of Media Ethics and Law
http://www.silha.umn.edu/
Academic media ethics centre, located in the University of Minnesota School of Journalism and Mass Communication.

Web Resources for Studying Journalism Ethics
http://www2.hawaii.edu/~tbrislin/jethics.html
Resources compiled by Professor Tom Brislin of the University of Hawaii Department of Journalism.

World-Wide Codes of Journalism Ethics
http://www.presswise.org.uk/ethics.htm
International codes compiled by the British media criticism and ethics organisation, PressWise.

Yamada Language Center (online)
http://babel.uoregon.edu/yamada/guides/Inuit.html
Site maintained by the University of Oregon's Yamada Language Center, with information on a multitude of international languages. The address given here is for the Inuit language guide, but the site is an excellent resource for checking usage in many other languages.

Appendix D
Codes of practice and statements of principles

United Kingdom

National Union of Journalists Code of Conduct
Adopted on 29 June 1994 by British National Union of Journalists (NUJ).

1. A journalist has a duty to maintain the highest professional and ethical standards.
2. A journalist shall at all times defend the principle of the freedom of the press and other media in relation to the collection of information and the expression of comment and criticism. He/she shall strive to eliminate distortion, news suppression and censorship.
3. A journalist shall strive to ensure that the information he/she disseminates is fair and accurate, avoid the expression of comment and conjecture as established fact and falsification by distortion, selection or misrepresentation.
4. A journalist shall rectify promptly any harmful inaccuracies, ensure that correction and apologies receive due prominence and afford the right of reply to persons criticised when the issue is of sufficient importance.
5. A journalist shall obtain information, photographs and illustrations only by straightforward means. The use of other means can be justified only by overriding considerations of the public interest. The journalist is entitled to exercise a personal conscientious objection to the use of such means.
6. Subject to the justification by overriding considerations of the public interest, a journalist shall do nothing which entails intrusion into private grief and distress.
7. A journalist shall protect confidential sources of information.
8. A journalist shall not accept bribes nor shall he/she allow other inducements to influence the performance of his/her professional duties.

9. A journalist shall not lend himself/herself to the distortion or suppression of the truth because of advertising or other considerations.

10. A journalist shall only mention a person's age, race, colour, creed, illegitimacy, disability, marital status (or lack of it), gender or sexual orientation if this information is strictly relevant. A journalist shall neither originate nor process material which encourages discrimination, ridicule, prejudice or hatred on any of the above-mentioned grounds.

11. A journalist shall not take private advantage of information gained in the course of his/her duties, before the information is public knowledge.

12. A journalist shall not by way of statement, voice or appearance endorse by advertisement any commercial product or service save for the promotion of of his/her own work or of the medium by which he/she is employed.

Press Complaints Commission Code of Practice

The Press Complaints Commission is charged with enforcing the Code of Practice (which appears here in slightly abbreviated form), framed by the newspaper and periodical industry and ratified by the Press Complaints Commission in 1997.

All members of the press have a duty to maintain the highest professional and ethical standards. This Code sets the benchmarks for those standards ... protects the rights of the individual and upholds the public's right to know.

1 *Accuracy*
(i) Newspapers and periodicals must take care not to publish inaccurate, misleading or distorted material including pictures.
(ii) ... [inaccuracies and errors] must be corrected promptly and with due prominence.
(iii) An apology must be published whenever appropriate.
(iv) Newspapers, whilst free to be partisan, must distinguish clearly between comment, conjecture and fact.
(v) A newspaper or periodical must report fairly and accurately the outcome of an action for defamation to which it has been a party.

2 *Opportunity to reply*
A fair opportunity to reply to inaccuracies must be given ...

*3 *Privacy*
(i)   Everyone is entitled to [privacy]. A publication will be expected to justify intrusions into any individual's private life without consent.
(ii) The use of long lens photography to take pictures of people in private places without their consent is unacceptable ...

*4 *Harassment*
(i)   Journalists and photographers must [not] ... obtain information or pictures through intimidation, harassment or persistent pursuit.
(ii) They must not photograph individuals in private places ... without their consent, persist ... after having been asked to desist ...
(iii) Editors must ensure that those working for them comply with these requirements and must not publish material from other sources which does not meet these requirements.

5 *Intrusion into grief or shock*
... enquiries must be carried out and approaches made with sympathy and discretion. Publication must be handled sensitively ... but ... should not ... [restrict] the right to report judicial proceedings.

*6 *Children*
(i)   Young people should be free to complete their time at school without unnecessary intrusion.
(ii) Journalists must not interview or photograph children under the age of 16 on subjects involving the welfare of the child or of any other child, in the absence of or without the consent of a parent or other adult who is responsible for the children.
(iii) Pupils must not be approached or photographed while at school without the permission of the school authorities.
(iv) There must be no payment to minors for material involving the welfare of children ... [or] to parents or guardians ... unless it is demonstrably in the child's interest.
(v)   Where material about the private life of a child is published, there must be justification ... other than the fame, notoriety or position of his or her parents or guardian.

7 *Children in sex cases*
1. The press must not, even where the law does not prohibit it, identify children under the age of 16 who are involved in cases concerning sexual offences, whether as victims or as witnesses.
2. In any press report of a case involving a sexual offence against a child –
   (i) The child must not be identified.
   (ii) The adult may be identified.

(iii) The word 'incest' must not be used where a child victim might be identified.

(iv) Care must be taken that nothing in the report implies the relationship between the accused and the child.

*8 *Listening devices*

Journalists must not ... [use] clandestine listening devices or ... [intercept] private telephone conversations.

*9 *Hospitals*

(i) Journalists or photographers ... must identify themselves to a responsible executive and obtain permission before entering non-public areas ...

*10 *Innocent relatives and friends*

The press must avoid identifying relatives or friends of persons convicted or accused of crime without their consent.

*11 *Misrepresentation*

(i) Journalists must not generally obtain ... information or pictures through misrepresentation or subterfuge.

(ii) Documents or photographs should be removed only with the consent of the owner.

(iii) Subterfuge can be justified only in the public interest and only when material cannot be obtained by any other means.

12 *Victims of sexual assault*

The press must not identify victims ... or publish material likely to contribute to such identification unless there is adequate justification and, by law, they are free to do so.

13 *Discrimination*

(i) The press must avoid prejudicial or pejorative reference to a person's race, colour, religion, sex or sexual orientation or to any physical or mental illness or disability.

(ii) It must avoid publishing [such] details ... unless these are directly relevant to the story.

14 *Financial journalism*

(i) Even where the law does not prohibit it, journalists must not use for their own profit financial information they receive in advance of ... publication, [or] ... pass such information to others ...

15 *Confidential sources*

Journalists have a moral obligation to protect confidential sources of information.

*16 *Payment for articles*
(i)   Payment or offers of payment for stories or information must not be made ... to witnesses or potential witnesses in current criminal proceedings except where the material ... ought to be published in the public interest [and information can only be obtained in this way].

The Public Interest
There may be exceptions to the clauses marked * where they can be demonstrated to be in the public interest ...

Canada

Native News Network of Canada (NNNC) Statement of Principles

Journalists can change or influence the thinking of those who are mere bystanders or news followers ... How can the public judge, if they never have a chance to read? First of all, you need to hire Native writers. Let them write the stories they feel are important and let readers decide if this is what they've been looking for all these years.
– Bud White Eye, founder of NNNC

The human being has been given the gift to make choices, and ... guidelines, or what we call original instructions. This does not represent an advantage for the human being but rather a responsibility.
– Oren Lyons, 'Spirituality, Equality and Natural Law', in L. Little Bear, M. Boldt and J. A. Long (eds), *Pathways to Self-Determination: Canadian Indians and the Canadian State*. University of Toronto.

Native News Network of Canada (NNNC) is dedicated to the gathering and distributing of print and broadcast news, features, reviews, and opinion by, about and for First Peoples. Its purpose is to inform all people and enable them to make judgments on the issues of the day, and to this end, to give expression to the interests of people who are underrepresented in 'mainstream' news media.

The ethical practice of journalism is paramount. An ethical journalism is a journalism of courage and conscience. It must reflect the diversity of the society, in terms of both hiring of journalists and representing people in news media. To carry out its purpose, NNNC has adopted the following principles:

1. Journalism should be fair, accurate, honest, conscientious and responsible.

2. Journalists and media outlets should be free from government or other outside interference; journalists must be free to discuss, question, or challenge private or public actions, positions or statements.
3. Journalism should
   - encourage creativity in writing and broadcasting, and foster the different, authentic voices of Aboriginal people;
   - promote the public's right to know;
   - critically examine the conduct of those in the public and private sectors;
   - expose any abuse of the public trust, evidence of wrongdoing or misuse of power;
   - advocate reform or innovation whenever needed, in the public interest;
   - avoid unfair bias, distortion, or sensationalism in written and broadcast text and in printed or broadcast images;
   - clearly distinguish editorials and opinion from reporting;
   - present information in context;
   - present information without irrelevant reference to gender, culture, color, 'race,' sexual preference, religious belief, marital status, physical or mental disability;
   - treat racial, ethnic or other derogatory terms as obscenities, used in quoted material only when essential to a story;
   - avoid photography or art work which fosters racial, ethnic, gender or other stereotypes;
   - respect individuals' dignity and right to privacy; avoid unnecessary intrusion into private grief;
   - except in extreme cases in which information vital to the public interest cannot be obtained in any other way, obtain information in a straightforward manner, without misrepresenting the journalist's identity;
   - except in rare cases in which information vital to the public interest cannot be obtained in any other way, tape-record, videotape, or photograph an interview only with the interviewee's knowledge and permission;
   - avoid identifying the names or addresses of individuals whose safety might be jeopardized;
   - preserve NNNC's independence from the vested interests of any particular individual, organization, institution or community;
   - encourage thoughtful criticism of the news media as well as the society at large.
4. We recognize that journalists are citizens. An NNNC journalist should

- be free to be active in the community, perform work for religious, cultural, social or civic organizations and pursue other activities of commitment or conscience, provided these activities do not distort the quality of his or her coverage;
- disclose any involvement in outside organizations, political or other activities, to the NNNC editors and the public;
- avoid covering stories in which he or she has a conflict of interest (for example, most stories concerning close relatives or friends);
- disclose to sources, if he or she is doing freelance work for a media outlet other than NNNC (for example, if an interview will be used for a story submitted to another news organization);
- avoid plagiarizing, by carefully quoting from or attributing information to other sources, and by assuring that his or her name is only used to identify the journalist's own work;
- honour pledges of confidentiality, which should be made with great care, and only when necessary to serve the public's need for information;
- make respect the watchword of journalistic practice – respect for subjects and sources, for other journalists, for the public we serve, and especially for the First Nations which are the backbone and the raison d'être of NNNC.

Dan Smoke
President, Native News Network of Canada
Treasurer, Native Journalists' Association

Valerie Alia, PhD

April 1997

International media ethics codes – selected excerpts

Author's note. I have selected the codes included here to demonstrate the commonalities, differences and range of principles and codes worldwide. Unfortunately, the English translations provided by the news organisations are inconsistent. Where possible, I have provided correction and clarification, but most of the codes appear as they are provided on the Internet (grammatical and other errors included). This situation points to a need for improving the accuracy of these translations. Perhaps one of the international organisations, such as the Institute of Communication Ethics, will take on the project of re-translation and correction.

Code of Ethics of the Country Press Association of New South Wales (Australia)

We believe –

That journalism is an honourable profession, essential to the welfare of society.

That the success of domestic government depends upon sound public opinion, and that the newspapers should aim at creating and maintaining sound public opinion by publishing significant news and editorial interpretation of news ...

That a newspaper that goes into the home should publish nothing which cannot be read in the family circle.

That news of crime, scandal and vice should be presented in such a manner as to deter readers from imitating the criminal and the vicious.

That all persons and organisations are entitled to fair play in the columns of the newspaper.

That privacy of the individual in all matters not of public concern is a right to be respected.

That no propaganda or publicity matter should be published unless it contains information to which readers are entitled, and that whenever such matter is printed its source should be indicated..

That neither the business interest of a newspaper nor any outside influence should interfere with the publication of truth in news or in editorials ...

That advertisements should be clean and wholesome as news and editorials ...

Society of American Travel Writers – Ethics Code

... The Society of American Travel Writers has the responsibility of accenting the need for truth and accuracy in all aspects of travel journalism, while setting standards which leave no room for dishonest or distorted stories.

... SATW recognizes the need for annual and ongoing scrutiny of its membership, eliminating those dilettantes who merely engage in travel journalism as a hobby, and at the same time demanding very high professional standards for admission to membership.

... SATW will maintain liaison with segments of the travel industry which sponsor familiarization trips, while at the same time underscoring the complete independence of the travel journalist in reporting on the negative as well as the positive results of such trips, or to decide that the material justifies no report of any kind ...

... professional travel journalists are expected to be thoroughly professional, exercising common courtesy and respect for fellow members and for the customs and cultures of other countries.

... Members shall not accept payment or courtesies for producing favorable materials about travel destinations against their own professional appraisal.

... Members shall deal with only those destinations of which they have first-hand knowledge or have utilized reliable sources of information ...

National Victim Center (Fort Worth, Texas, USA)

Never feel that because you have unwillingly been involved in an incident of public interest that you must personally share the details and/or your feelings with the general public. If you decide that you want the public to be aware of how traumatic and unfair your victimization was, you do not automatically give up your right to privacy ...

You have the right to select the spokesperson or advocate of your choice ...

You have the right to select the time and location for media interviews ...

You have the right to request a specific reporter ...

You have the right to refuse an interview with a specific reporter even though you have granted interviews to other reporters. You may feel that certain reporters are callous, insensitive, uncaring or judgmental. It is your right to avoid these journalists at all costs. ... However, recognize that the reporter may write the story regardless of your participation ...

... victims often ride an 'emotional roller coaster.' You may be able one day to talk with a reporter, and be physically or emotionally unable to do so the next. Victims should never feel 'obliged' to grant interviews ...

You have the right to release a written statement through a spokesperson in lieu of an interview ...

You have the right to exclude children from interviews ...

You have the right to refrain from answering any questions with which you are uncomfortable or that you feel are inappropriate ...

You have the right to ask for review of your quotations in a storyline prior to publication ...

You have the right to avoid a press conference atmosphere and speak to only one reporter at a time ...

You have the right to demand a retraction when inaccurate information is reported.

You have the right to ask that offensive photographs or visuals be omitted from airing or publication ...

You have the right to conduct a television interview using a silhouette or a newspaper interview without having your photograph taken ...

There are many ways for reporters to project your physical image without using your photograph or film footage of you, therefore protecting your identity.

You have the right to completely give your side of the story related to your victimization ...

You have the right to grieve in privacy ...

You have the right to suggest training about media and victims for print and electronic media in your community ...

You have the right at all times to be treated with dignity and respect by the media.

WISH-TV, Indianapolis (Indiana, USA)

... PRODUCTION STANDARD

MEMO#2

Coverage of Terrorists

Because the facts and circumstances of each case vary, there can be no specific self-executing rules for the handling of terrorist/hostage stories. CBS News will continue to apply the normal tests of news judgment and if, as so often they are, these stories are newsworthy, we must continue to give them coverage despite the dangers of 'contagion.' The disadvantages of suppression are, among things, (1) adversely affecting our credibility; (2) giving free rein to sensationalized and erroneous word of mouth rumors; and (3) distorting our news judgments for some extraneous judgmental purpose. These disadvantages compel us to continue to provide coverage.

Nevertheless in providing for such coverage there must be thoughtful, conscientious care and restraint ... We should exercise particular care in how we treat the terrorist/kidnapper.

More specifically:

(1) ... we must report [the terrorist/kidnapper's] demands. But we should avoid providing an excessive platform for the terrorist/kidnapper ... unless such demands are succinctly stated and free of rhetoric and propaganda, it may be better to paraphrase the demands instead of presenting them directly through the voice or picture of the terrorist/kidnapper.

(2) Except in the most compelling circumstances, and then only

with the approval of the President of CBS News, or in his absence, the Senior Vice President of News, there should be no live coverage of the terrorist/kidnapper since we may fall into the trap of providing an unedited platform for him …

(6) Guidelines affecting our coverage of civil disturbances are also applicable here, especially those which relate to avoiding the use of inflammatory catchwords or phrases, the reporting of rumors, etc. …

(7) Coverage of this kind of story should be in such overall balance as to length, that it does not unduly crowd out other important news of the hour/day.

MEMO #3

… We don't automatically go LIVE with such stories. A decision is made after consideration of what's happening at the scene, including whether it is a news story; whether LIVE EYE coverage is warranted; and what potential impact such LIVE coverage may have on the situation.

… We do not report rumors, second-hand 'gossip,' statements, charges, etc., without verification from authorities that ascertain the facts.

… We carefully choose our words, avoiding emotional and/or inflammatory comments and interviews …

Sweden: Code of Ethics for the Press, Radio and Television (updated 1995)

Translated from Swedish to English by Tina Laitila

The press, radio and television shall have the greatest possible degree of freedom, within the framework of the Freedom of the Press Act and the constitutional right of freedom of speech, in order to be able to serve as disseminators of news and as scrutinizers of public affairs. In this connection, however, it is important that the individual is protected from unwarranted suffering as a result of publicity …

… Be critical of news sources. Check facts as carefully as possible in the light of the circumstances even if they have been published earlier. Allow the reader/listener/viewer the possibility of distinguishing between statements of fact and comments.

… Make sure of the authenticity of pictures. See to it that pictures and graphical illustrations are correct and are not used in a misleading way …

… Exercise great caution in publishing notices concerning suicide and attempted suicide, particularly out of consideration for the feelings of relatives and in view of what has been said above concerning the privacy of the individual.

… Always show the greatest possible consideration for victims of crime and accidents. Carefully check names and pictures for publication out of consideration for the victims and their relatives.

… Do not emphasize race, sex, nationality, occupation, political affiliation or religious persuasion in the case of the persons concerned if such particulars are not important in the context or are disparaging.

… Making a montage, retouching a picture by an electronic method, or formulating a picture caption should not be performed in such a way as to mislead or deceive the reader. Always state, close to the picture, whether it has been altered by montage or retouching. This also applies to such material when it is filed …

… Give careful thought to the harmful consequences that might follow for persons if their names are published. Refrain from publishing names unless it is obviously in the public interest.

… If a person's name is not to be stated, refrain from publishing a picture or particulars of occupation, title, age, nationality, sex, etc., which would enable the person in question to be identified.

American Society of Newspaper Editors – Statement of Principles (updated 2002)

ARTICLE I – Responsibility. The primary purpose of gathering and distributing news and opinion is to serve the general welfare by informing the people and enabling them to make judgments on the issues of the time. Newspapermen and women who abuse the power of their professional role for selfish motives or unworthy purposes are faithless to that public trust. The American press was made free not just to inform or just to serve as a forum for debate but also to bring an independent scrutiny to bear on the forces of power in the society, including the conduct of official power at all levels of government …

ARTICLE VI – Fair Play. Journalists should respect the rights of people involved in the news, observe the common standards of decency and stand accountable to the public for the fairness and accuracy of their news reports. Persons publicly accused should be given the earliest opportunity to respond. Pledges of confidentiality to news sources must be honored at all costs, and therefore should not be given lightly. Unless there is clear and pressing need to maintain confidences, sources of information should be identified .... .

The Washington Post Standards and Ethics (updated 1999) (USA)

The Washington Post is pledged to an aggressive, responsible and fair pursuit of the truth without fear of any special interest, and with favor to none ...

Washington Post reporters and editors are pledged to approach every assignment with the fairness of open minds and without prior judgment. The search for opposing views must be routine. Comment from persons accused or challenged in stories must be included. The motives of those who press their views upon us must routinely be examined, and it must be recognized that those motives can be noble or ignoble, obvious or ulterior.

We fully recognize that the power we have inherited as the dominant morning newspaper in the capital of the free world carries with it special responsibilities:

to listen to the voiceless
to avoid any and all acts of arrogance
to face the public politely and candidly ...

... Although it has become increasingly difficult for this newspaper and for the press generally to do so since Watergate, reporters should make every effort to remain in the audience, to stay off the stage, to report the news, not to make the news.

In gathering news, reporters will not misrepresent their identity. They will not identify themselves as police officers, physicians or anything other than journalists.

... The Washington Post is pledged to disclose the source of all information when at all possible. When we agree to protect a source's identity, that identity will not be made known to anyone outside The Post.

Before any information is accepted without full attribution, reporters must make every reasonable effort to get it on the record. If that is not possible, reporters should consider seeking the information elsewhere. If that in turn is not possible, reporters should request an on-the-record reason for concealing the source's identity and should include the reason in the story ...

No pseudonyms are to be used.

However, The Washington Post will not knowingly disclose the identities of U.S. intelligence agents, except under highly unusual circumstances which must be weighed by the senior editors.

... After Eugene Meyer bought The Washington Post in 1933 and began the family ownership that continues today, he published 'These Principles':

> The first mission of a newspaper is to tell the truth as nearly as the truth may be ascertained.
>
> The newspaper shall tell ALL the truth so far as it can learn it, concerning the important affairs of America and the world.
>
> As a disseminator of the news, the paper shall observe the decencies that are obligatory upon a private gentleman.
>
> What it prints shall be fit reading for the young as well as for the old.
>
> The newspaper's duty is to its readers and to the public at large, and not to the private interests of the owner.
>
> In the pursuit of truth, the newspaper shall be prepared to make sacrifices of its material fortunes, if such course be necessary for the public good. The newspaper shall not be the ally of any special interest, but shall be fair and free and wholesome in its outlook on public affairs and public men.

'These Principles' are re-endorsed herewith.

Finland: Guidelines for Good Journalistic Practice (1992)

... The basis of good journalistic practice is a citizen's right to correct and essential information by which he can form a realistic picture of the world and society around him.

The professional ethics of a journalist involves the respecting of basic human values, like human rights, democracy, peace and international understanding.

A journalist must recognize his responsibility for the environment and be aware of the environmental effects related to the questions he deals with.

Good journalistic practice does not limit either the journalist's own or the public's freedom of expression. It aims at promoting discussion and information flow, and involves responsibility for the principles and policies of communication ...

... Decisions concerning the content of communications must be made on journalistic grounds. In no way must this authority be relinquished outside the editorial office.

... A journalist is primarily responsible to his readers, listeners and viewers. He should not deal with subjects which might involve personal gain.

... A journalist has the right and obligation to reject pressure or inducement with which someone might try to direct, prevent or limit communications.

... Information must be acquired openly and by using honest means. Exceptional methods can only be resorted to if information of general public importance cannot be obtained by normal means

... The human dignity and reputation of every individual must be protected. Skin colour, nationality, origins, religious or political convictions, sex or other personal characteristics must not be published if they are not related to the matter or in a derogatory way.

Ireland: Code of Conduct (1994)

... A journalist shall at all times defend the principle of the freedom of the press and other media in relation to the collection of information and the expression of comment and criticism. He/she shall strive to eliminate distortion, news suppression and censorship.

... A journalist shall obtain information, photographs and illustrations only by straightforward means. The use of other means can be justified only by overriding considerations of the public interest. The journalist is entitled to exercise a personal conscientious objection to the use of such means ...

... A journalist shall only mention a person's age, race, colour, creed, illegitimacy, disability, marital status (or lack of it), gender or sexual orientation if this information is strictly relevant. A journalist shall neither originate nor process material which encourages discrimination, ridicule, prejudice or hatred on any of the above-mentioned grounds.

France: Charter of the Professional Duties of French Journalists (updated 1938, revised from 1918)

A journalist worthy of the name:

* assumes responsibility of all that he writes;
* considers the slander, unfounded accusations, alteration of documents, distortion of facts, and lying to be the most serious professional misconduct;
* recognizes the jurisdiction of his colleagues as the only one which is sovereign in matters of professional honour;
* accepts only such assignments that are compatible with his professional dignity;
  ...

- does not receive money in a public service or a private enterprise where his status of journalist, his influence and his relations may be made use of;
- does not sign articles of commercial or financial advertising;
- does not commit any plagiarism;
- does not claim the position held by another colleague nor ... cause him to be dismissed by offering to work under inferior conditions;
- keeps the professional secrecy;
- does not make use of the freedom of the press with profit-seeking intentions;
- demands the freedom to honestly publish his information;
- respects justice and gives it top priority;
- does not confuse his role with a policeman's.

Spain: Deontological Code for the Journalistic Profession (Federation of the Spanish Press, 1993)

... In the framework of the civil rights, which are established in the Constitution and which form the basis of the wholly democratic society, journalism is an important social tool which puts into effect the free and efficient development of the fundamental rights of all citizens to freedom of information and the freedom to express one's opinions.

As a subject and an instrument of the freedom of expression, journalists acknowledge and guarantee that journalism is the basis from which the public opinion manifests itself freely in the pluralism of a democratic state governed by law.

However, journalists also take into consideration that when in their profession [they] use their constitutional rights to the freedom of the expression and the right to information, their conduct is subject to limitations, which prevent the violation of other fundamental rights.

Therefore, when taking on these obligations, and as a true guarantee which a journalist offers to the Spanish society, which he/she serves, journalists understand that they must maintain, collectively or individually, uncensurable conduct when it comes to the ethics and deontology of the information ...

... The first obligation of a journalist is to respect the truth.

... In agreement with this principle a journalist shall always defend the principle of the freedom to investigate and honestly disseminate information as well as the freedom to comment and to criticise ...

... A journalist scrupulously sees that the public administration fulfils its duty to the transparency of information. In particular, he/she always shall defend the free access to information which comes from or is produced by public administration, and the free access to public archives and administrative registers ...

Catalonia: Deontological Code. Statement on the Principles of the Catalan Journalism Profession (1992)

This code is an initiative of the 'Col.legi de Periodistes de Catalunya' (Catalan Journalists Association) ... [it] has been elaborated ... by an ad hoc Commission constituted in the bosom of it. In this process a relevant participation has been assumed by the Consultative Council of the Col.legi, where are represented all Catalan media, press, radio and television.

... A sheer difference between facts and opinions or interpretations has always to be observed avoiding any deliberated confusion or distortion of both ...

... To use correct methods to obtain information or images without recurring to unlawful procedures ...

... To respect the rights of persons to their own privacy and image, principally in those cases or events which originate feelings of sadness or pain ...

... To deal with special care with all kind of news concerning children ...

To behave with a definite sense of responsability (*sic*) and harshness when it deals with informations (*sic*) or opinions with a content which may provoke sex, race, beliefs, social class or cultural discriminations ...

Greece: Principles of Deontology (1988)

Approved on 31 October 1988 by five Greek journalists' unions: the Union of Journalists of Daily Newspapers of Athens, the Union of Journalists of Daily Newspapers of Macedonia-Thrace, the Union of Journalists of Daily Newspapers of Peloponissos, Epirus and Islands, the Union of Journalists of Daily Newspapers of Thessaly, Sterea, Evia and the Union of Journalists of Periodical Press.

... The journalist defends everywhere and always ... freedom of press, the free and undisturbed propagation of ideas and news, as well as the right to opposition ...

... The religious convictions, the institutions, the manners and customs of nations, peoples and races, as well as citizens' private and family life are respected and inviolable.

... [The] Primary task of the journalist is the defence of people's liberties and of the democratic regime, as well as the advancement of social and state institutions.

... Respect for national and popular values and the defence of people's interests should inspire the journalist in the practice of his function.

... access to sources of news is free and undisturbed for the journalist, who is not obliged to reveal his information sources.

... The function of journalism may not be practised for self-seeking purposes.

Bulgaria: Rules of Journalistic Ethics (1994)

Adopted by the Tenth Congress of the Union of Bulgarian Journalists on 6 March 1994.

The indestructible right for information, freedom of expression and criticism, the indestructible right of man to be informed about facts and opinions constitute the bases of the rights and duties of journalists.

As the journalist takes on the great civic responsibility of his/her profession, he/she defends freedom of expression, maintains true independence of his/her political views, beliefs and biases. The journalist bears the entire responsibility for his/her works – signed or not, published or broadcast. In his/her work the journalist observes the norms of journalistic ethics, limited by the following rules:

1. The journalist does not let his/her work contribute to conflicts due to racial, ethnic, religious, or class differences; does not use words violating human dignity; does not oppose, but helps, people who feel they have been treated unfairly by his/her work and news organisation to answer and show their side of the story on the same page or in the same news program; does not allow his/her work to appear distorted; does not permit comments to slant the truth; does not present only part of the facts, which are known to achieve one-sided coverage of an event or a process.

2. The journalist does not abuse freedom of expression and the opportunities provided by the profession for his/her own profit ...

3. The journalist does not use dishonest means for gathering information; does not violate the right of privacy; except in cases when this would benefit society in an extraordinary way; does not plagiarize ... does not take advantage of the honesty and suffering of people covered by his/her stories; does not reveal the identity of criminals under age or victims of crime.

4. The journalist does not accept tasks incompatible with his/her professional dignity, does not hamper his/her colleagues from gathering information ...

5. The journalist does not put him/herself in service of intelligence services.

Bibliography

Abrams, Janet (1995) 'Little photoshop of horrors: the ethics of manipulating journalistic imagery', *Print*, November/December, 43.

Adams, Sally with Wynford Hicks (2001) *Interviewing for Journalists*. London: Routledge.

Adler, Leonore Loeb (ed.) (1977) *Issues in Cross Cultural Research*, vol. 285. New York: New York Academy of Sciences.

Alia, Valerie (1989a) 'Closing the Circle', *Up Here Magazine*, September/October, 18–20.

Alia, Valerie (1989b) 'Female conductor unequally reviewed', *Toronto Star*, 18 January, Editorial Page.

Alia, Valerie (1991a) *Communicating Equality* (manual). Whitehorse: Government of the Yukon.

Alia, Valerie (1991b) 'The powwow is more than just a carnival of color'. *The London Free Press*, 16 July, A7.

Alia, Valerie (1991c) 'Aboriginal perestroika', *Arctic Circle Magazine*, vol. 2, no. 3, November/December, 23–31.

Alia, Valerie (1993) 'Confession of a serious nutcase', *The Globe and Mail*, 19 February, A23.

Alia, Valerie (1994) *Names, Numbers and Northern Policy: Inuit, Project Surname and the Politics of Identity*. Halifax, NS: Fernwood.

Alia, Valerie (1995) 'A restaurant with a franchise on kindness', *The Globe and Mail*, 18 January, A20.

Alia, Valerie (1996) 'Better than suicide', in Alia, Valerie, Brennan, Brian and Hoffmaster, Barry (eds), *Deadlines and Diversity: Journalism Ethics in a Changing World*. Halifax, NS: Fernwood, 207–18.

Alia, Valerie (1997) 'A conflict of interest', *Media Ethics*, vol. 9, no.1, Fall, 1, 12.

Alia, Valerie (1999) *Un/Covering the North: News, Media, and Aboriginal People*. Vancouver: UBC Press.

Alia, Valerie (2000) 'The boundaries of liberty and tolerance in the Canadian North: media, ethics, and the emergence of the Inuit homeland of Nunavut', in Cohen-Almagor, Raphael (ed.), *Challenges to Democracy: Essays in Honour and Memory of Professor Sir Isaiah Berlin*. Aldershot: Ashgate, 275–93.

Alia, Valerie (2003) 'Indigenous radio in Canada', in Crisell, Andrew (ed.), *More*

Than a Music Box. Oxford: Berghahn.

Alia, Valerie (2003) 'Scattered voices, global vision: *indigenous peoples and the New Media Nation*', in Karim, Karim (ed.), *The Media of Diaspora.* London: Routledge, 36–50.

Alia, Valerie, Brennan, Brian and Hoffmaster, Barry (eds.) (1996) *Deadlines and Diversity: Journalism Ethics in a Changing World.* Halifax, NS: Fernwood.

Allman, T. D. (1993) 'Serbia's blood war', *Vanity Fair,* March, 95–118.

Anderson, Peter J. and Weymouth, Anthony (1999), *Insulting the Public? The British Press and the European Union.* London: Longman.

Arant, David (ed.) (1999) *Perspectives: Ethics, Issues and Controversies in Mass Media.* St Paul, MN: Coursewise Publishing.

Arnett, Peter (1998) *Flash! The Associated Press Covers the World.* New York: Abrams.

Ashenburg, Katherine (1993) 'Paper making', *The Globe and Mail,* 28 August [no page number available].

Associated Press (2003) 'Blair's office acknowledges copying work for Iraq file', *International Herald Tribune,* 8–9 February, 3.

Association of British Editors, Guild of Editors and International Press Institute (1994) *Media Freedom and Media Regulation: An Alternative White Paper.* London: Association of British Editors.

Atkins, Joseph B. (ed.) (2002) *The Mission: Journalism, Ethics, and the World.* Ames, IA: Iowa State University Press.

Barber, Lynn (1999) 'The art of the interview', in Glover, S. (ed.), *The Penguin Book of Journalism,.* London: Penguin, 196–205.

Barendt, E. (1985) *Freedom of Speech.* Oxford: Oxford University Press.

Barker, Hannah (2000) *Newspapers, Politics and English Society 1695–1855.* London: Longman.

Barron, Arthur (1999) 'The interview: ethical issues', *Media Ethics,* vol. 10, no. 2, Spring, 10–11.

Barry, Dave (2002) 'Down the newspaper tube', *International Herald Tribune,* 4–5 May, 20.

BBC News Online (2001) *Inside Afghanistan: Behind the Veil,* Wednesday, 27 June.

Beard, Matthew (2003) 'Children who set up art studio win £200,000 Lottery grant', *The Independent,* 2 June, 8.

Bell, Jim (1996) 'Footprints 2: road to Nunavut paved with electrons', *Nunatsiaq News,* 22 November [no page number available].

Bell, Jim (1997) 'New communication tools for Nunavut'. *Working in Nunavut,* special supplement to *Nunatsiaq News,* E7, 23.

Belsey, J. and Chadwick, Ruth (1992) *Ethical Issues in Journalism and the Media.* London: Routledge.

Ben Artzi-Pelossof, Noa (1996) *In the Name of Sorrow and Hope.* New York: Alfred A. Knopf.

Bentley, Eric (1969) *Shaw on Music.* New York: Doubleday Anchor.

Berger, John (1972) *Ways of Seeing.* London: Penguin Books.

Berger, John (1980) *About Looking.* New York: Pantheon Books.

Berry, David (ed.) (2000) *Ethics and Media Culture: Practices and Representations.* Oxford: Focal Press.

Bertrand, Claude-Jean (2000) *Media Ethics and Accountability Systems.* New Brunswick, NJ and London: Transaction.

Bertrand, Claude-Jean (2001a) *Why Not Listen?* Posted on website: cjbertrand@noos.fr.

Bertrand, Claude-Jean (2001b) *An Arsenal for Democracy: Media Accountability Systems.* Cresskill, NJ: Hampton Press.

Black, Patricia (1993) 'Writer Timothy Findley', *Scene*, 7 April.

Blumer, Herbert (1969) *Symbolic Interactionism.* Englewood Cliffs, NJ: Prentice-Hall.

Bok, Sissela (1978) *Lying: Moral Choices in Public and Private Life.* New York: Pantheon.

Bourdieu, Pierre (1990) *Photography.* Oxford: Blackwell.

Bourdieu, Pierre (1991) *Language and Symbolic Power.* Cambridge, MA: Harvard University Press.

Bourdieu, Pierre (1996) *On Television and Journalism.* London: Pluto Press.

Boyd, William (1992) Media Ethics seminar. St Petersburg, FL: Poynter Institute for Media Studies.

Brennan, Brian (1996a) 'Confessions of an unlettered critic', in Alia, Valerie, Brennan, Brian and Hoffmaster, Barry (eds), *Deadlines and Diversity: Journalism Ethics in a Changing World.* Halifax, NS: Fernwood, 207–18.

Brennan, Brian (1996b) 'Codes of ethics: who needs them?', in Alia, Valerie, Brennan, Brian and Hoffmaster, Barry (eds), *Deadlines and Diversity: Journalism Ethics in a Changing World.* Halifax, NS: Fernwood, 112–20.

Briggs, Asa and Burke, Peter (2002) *A Social History of the Media.* Cambridge: Polity.

Brisebois, Debbie (1983) 'The Inuit Broadcasting Corporation', *Anthropologica*, vol. 25, no. 1, 107.

Bristow, Gary, Kuptana, Robert and Condon, Richard (1992) Unpublished letter to the editor of *The Daily Telegraph*, 27 September.

Brooks, Libby (2003) 'Asylum: a special investigation – 5 tough questions about asylum', *The Guardian*, G2, 1–9.

Brustein, Robert (1992) 'Critics and the arts', Cambridge, MA: Special issue of *Nieman Reports*, Fall.

Bryant, Garry (1987) 'Ten-fifty P.I.: emotion and the photographer's role', *Journal of Mass Media Ethics*, vol. 2, no. 2, Spring/Summer, 32–9.

Bugeja, Michael J. (1995) *Living Ethics.* Needham Heights, MA: Allyn & Bacon.

Burchill, Julie (2003) 'Game, sex and match', *The Guardian*, G2, 18 June, 2–3.

Burne, Jerome (2003) 'The hidden power to heal', *The Independent Review*, 23 April, 8.

Calcutt, Sir David (1993) *Review of Press Self-Regulation*, CM 22135. London: Stationery Office.

Campbell, Duncan (2003) 'How Dylan's lyrics struck a chord', *The Guardian*, 10 July, 2.

Canadian Centre for Social Justice (1995) *Fact or Fantasy? Diversity and Employment Equity Handbook for Journalism Schools.* North Bay, Ont.: Canadian Centre for Social Justice.

Carter, Cynthia, Branston, Gill and Allan, Stuart (eds) (1998) *News, Gender and Power.* London: Routledge.

Centre for Public Services (2003) *The Investigator's Handbook.* Sheffield: Centre for Public Services.

Christians, Clifford G. (2001) *Social Justice and Internet Technology.* New York: Longman.

Christians, Clifford G., Ferré, John and Fackler, Mark (1993) *Good News: Social Ethics and the Press.* Oxford: Oxford University Press.

Clarke, Pat (2003) 'Tamil beat man to death through "sheer cruelty"', *The Independent*, 7 June, 8.

Clifford, James (1983) 'On ethnographic authority', *Representations*, vol. 1, no. 12, Spring, 118–46.

Code, Lorraine, Mullett, Sheila and Overall, Christine (eds) (1988) *Feminist Perspectives: Philosophical Essays on Method and Morals.* Toronto and London: University of Toronto Press.

Cohen, J. and Solomon, Norman (1995) *Through the Media Looking Glass: Decoding Bias and Blather in the News.* Monroe, ME: Common Courage.

Cohen-Almagor, Raphael (1994) *The Boundaries of Liberty and Tolerance: The Struggle against Kahanism in Israel.* Gainesville, FL: University Press of Florida.

Cohen-Almagor, Raphael (2001) *Speech, Media, and Ethics: The Limits of Free Expression.* London: Palgrave.

Coles, Robert (1989) *The Call of Stories: Teaching and the Moral Imagination.* Boston: Houghton Mifflin.

Colling, Linda (2003) 'Celebrating the difference', *Sunderland Echo*, 22 July, Lifestyle section, 6, 7.

Collins, Randall (1985) *Three Sociological Traditions.* New York: Oxford University Press.

Condon, Richard (1992) Personal communication, 6 November.

Cooper, Thomas W. with Christians, Clifford G., Plude, Frances Forde and White, Robert A. (1989) *Communication Ethics and Global Change.* London: Longman.

Coté, William and Simpson, Roger (2000) *Covering Violence: A Guide to Ethical Reporting about Victims and Trauma.* New York: Columbia University Press.

Coward, Ros (2002) 'Tourism as "casual imperialism"', *Ecologist*, December–January, reprinted in *The Guardian*, 'The Editor', 2 December, 15.

Crean, Susan (1985) *Newsworthy: The Lives of Media Women.* Toronto: Stoddart.

Croft, Annabel (2003) 'I didn't like the way I looked – like a brick', *The Guardian*, G2, 18 June, 2.

Crouse, Timothy (1973) *The Boys on the Bus.* New York: Ballantine.

Cudlipp, H. (1980) *The Prerogative of the Harlot: Press Barons and Power.* London: The Bodley Head.

Curran, James and Seaton, Jean (1981) *Power without Responsibility: The Press and*

Broadcasting in Britain. London: Routledge.

Daily Express (2002) 'Luxury life of asylum seekers', 17 December, 1.

Dao, James and Schmitt, Eric (2002) 'Pentagon is arming with words', *International Herald Tribune*, 20 February, 1, 7.

Davies, Nick (2003) 'Special Investigation. How politics put policing in the dock' (series of linked articles), *The Guardian*, 11 July, 1, 4, 5, 6.

Day, Louis A. (2003) *Ethics in Media Communications*, 4th edn. Belmont, CA: Wadsworth.

Denzin, Norman K (1992) *Symbolic Interactionism and Cultural Studies: The Politics of Interpretation.* Oxford: Blackwell.

Deverell, Rita Shelton (1996) 'On subjectivity: what you can see depends on where you stand and how "short" you are', in Alia, Valerie, Brennan, Brian and Hoffmaster, Barry (eds), *Deadlines and Diversity: Journalism Ethics in a Changing World.* Halifax, NS: Fernwood, 259–71.

di Leonardo, Micaela (1998) *Exotics at Home: Anthropologies, Others, American Modernity.* Chicago: University of Chicago Press.

Dines, G. and Humez, G. H. (eds) (1995) *Gender, Race, Class and Media.* London: Sage.

Dior, Christian (2001) Photograph from 2001 collection, *The Guardian*, 26 January, 11.

Dorril, Stephen (2003) 'Intelligence failure: no weapons of mass destruction', *Free Press*, Special Issue: Iraq and the Media War, June, 1.

Downing, J., Mohammadi, A. and Sreberny-Mohammadi, A. (1990) *Questioning the Media: A Critical Introduction.* Newbury Park, CA: Sage.

Dreyfus, Suelette (1999) 'This is just between us (and the spies)', *The Independent*, 15 November, 12.

Elliott, Deni (1990) 'As life passes by: A journalist's role: watch and wait'. *FineLine*, October, 2.

Englehardt, Elaine E. and Barney, Ralph D. (2002) *Media and Ethics: Principles for Moral   Decisions.* Belmont, CA: Wadsworth.

Étienne, Mona and Eleanor Leacock (eds) (1980) *Women and Colonization: Anthropological Perspectives.* New York: Praeger.

Fallaci, Oriana (1976) *Interview with History.* Boston: Houghton Mifflin.

Farmer, Gary (1998) 'Letter from the editor: time in a computer chip ...', *Aboriginal Voices*, July/August, 6.

Fienup-Riordan, Ann (1995) *Freeze Frame: Alaska Eskimos in the Movies.* Seattle, WA and London: University of Washington Press.

Fletcher, Frederick J. (1996) 'Journalism in a fish bowl: ethical dilemmas in campaign coverage', in Alia, Valerie, Brennan, Brian and Hoffmaster, Barry (eds), *Deadlines and Diversity: Journalism Ethics in a Changing World.* Halifax, NS: Fernwood, 140–50.

Foucault, Michel (1980) *Power/Knowledge.* New York: Pantheon.

Franklin, B. (1994) *Packaging Politics: Political Communications in Britain's Media Democracy.* London: Edward Arnold.

Franklin, Bob (1997) *Newszak and New Media.* London: Arnold.

Franklin, Bob (ed.) (1999) *Social Policy, the Media and Misrepresentation*. London: Routledge.

Frome, Michael (1998) *Green Ink: An Introduction to Environmental Journalism*. Salt Lake City, UT: University of Utah Press.

Garfinkel, Harold (1967) *Studies in Ethnomethodology*. Englewood Cliffs, NJ: Prentice-Hall.

Garfinkel, Harold (1982) *A Manual for the Study of Naturally Organized Ordinary Activities*. London: Routledge & Kegan Paul.

Giles, Robert and Snyder, Robert W. (eds) (2000) *What's Fair? The Problem of Equity in Journalism*. New Brunswick, NJ: Transaction Publishers.

Gilligan, Carol, Ward, J. V. and Taylor, J. M. (1988) *Mapping the Moral Domain*. Cambridge, MA: Harvard University Graduate School of Education.

Gilligan, Carol (1982) *In a Different Voice: Psychological Theory and Women's Development*. Cambridge, MA: Harvard University Press.

Girard, Bruce (1992) *A Passion for Radio: Radio Waves and Community*. Montreal: Black Rose.

Glover, S. (ed.) (1999) *The Penguin Book of Journalism: Secrets of the Press*. London: Penguin.

Goffman, Erving (1959) *The Presentation of Self in Everyday Life*. New York: Anchor.

Goffman, Erving (1963) *Behavior in Public Places*. New York and London: Collier/Macmillan.

Goffman, Erving (1974) *Frame Analysis*. Philadelphia: University of Pennsylvania Press.

Goodwin, H. Eugene and Smith, Ron F. (1999) *Groping for Ethics in Journalism*. Ames, IA: Iowa State University Press.

Gopsill, Tim (1999) 'Lord Wakeham's new clothes', *Free Press*, No. 112, September–October, 6–7.

Grindal, B. T. and Rhodes, R. (1987) 'Journalism and anthropology share several similarities', *Journalism Educator*, 41, 11–13.

Haan, N., Bellah, R. N., Rabinow, P. and Sullivan, W. M. (eds) (1985) *Social Science as Moral Inquiry*. New York: Columbia University Press.

Hall, Edward T. ([1981] 1990) *The Silent Language*. New York: Doubleday Anchor.

Hall, Edward T. ([1982] 1990) *The Hidden Dimension*. New York: Doubleday Anchor.

Hall, Edward T. (1990/83) *The Dance of Life: The Other Dimension of Time*. New York: Doubleday Anchor.

Hall, Stuart (1980) 'Race, articulation and societies structured in dominance', *Sociological Theories: Race and Colonialism*. Paris: UNESCO, 305–45.

Hall, Stuart (ed.) (1997) *Representation: Cultural Representations and Signifying Practices*. London: Sage.

Harper, Kenn (1986) *Give Me My Father's Body: The Life of Minik, the New York Eskimo*. Frobisher Bay (Iqaluit): Blacklead Books.

Harris, Christopher R. (1991) 'Digitization and manipulation of news photographs', *Journal of Mass Media Ethics*, vol. 6, no. 3, 164–74.

Hart, Carolyn G. (1989) *A Little Class on Murder*. New York and London: Bantam (and any others of the Henry O. detective novels).

Hartford Courant (1973) 12 November, 6–7.

Hartley, John (1992) *Understanding News*. London: Routledge & Kegan Paul.

Hechter, Michael (1975) *Internal Colonialism: The Celtic Fringe in British National Development, 1536–1966*. Berkeley, CA: University of California Press.

Hechter, Michael (1986) 'Rational choice theory and the study of race and ethnic relations', in Rex, John and Mason, David (eds), *Theory of Race and Ethnic Relations*. Cambridge: Cambridge University Press.

Herbert, John (2002) *Journalism and Broadcast Ethics*. Woburn, MA: Focal Press.

Herman, Edward S. and Chomsky, Noam (1994) *Manufacturing Consent*. New York: Vintage.

Hernandez, Debra Gersh (1995) 'J-school faculties get F in diversity', *Editor & Publisher*, 9 September, 7,13.

Hiassen, Carl (1991) *Native Tongue*. London: Macmillan.

Higgins, George V. (1999) in 'George V. Higgins, novelist of underworld, dies at 59', *The Boston Globe*, November, 10.

Hillerman, Tony (1971) *The Fly on the Wall*. New York: HarperCollins.

Hobson, Dorothy (1997) 'Housewives and the mass media', in Marris, Paul and Thornham, Sue (eds), *Media Studies: A Reader*. Edinburgh: Edinburgh University Press, 307–12.

Hoffmaster, Barry (1992) 'Can ethnography save the life of medical ethics?', *Journal of Social Science and Medicine*, vol. 35, no. 12, 1421–31.

Hollingsworth, Mark (1987) *The Press and Political Dissent: A Question of Censorship*. London: Pluto.

Howard, Frank (1996) 'Conflicts of interest and codes of ethics in the parliamentary press gallery', in Alia, Valerie, Brennan, Brian and Hoffmaster, Barry (eds), *Deadlines and Diversity: Journalism Ethics in a Changing World*. Halifax, NS: Fernwood, 121–31.

Huang, Edgar Shaohua (1999) *Perception of Digital Alteration and Truth-Value in Documentary Photographs*. PhD dissertation, Indiana University, School of Journalism.

Hulteng, John (1981) *Playing It Straight*. Chester, CT: The Globe Pequot Press.

Hulteng, John (1985) *The Messenger's Motives: Ethical Problems of the News Media*, 2nd edn. Englewood Cliffs, NJ: Prentice-Hall.

Hutchison, David (1990) 'Broadcasting policy in Canada and the United Kingdom: politics, technology and ideology', *Canadian Journal of Communications*, vol. 15, no. 2, May, 76–95.

Independent, The (2003) 'One death, five versions. Now it is for Lord Hutton to judge', 26 September, 1.

Isaacs, Harold R. (1989) *Idols of the Tribe: Group Identity and Political Change*. Cambridge, MA: Harvard University Press.

Ivins, Molly and Dubose, Lou (2000) *Shrub: The Short but Happy Political Life of George W. Bush*. New York: Random House.

Iyengar, S. and Reeves, R. (eds) (1997) *Do the Media Govern?* London: Sage.

Jaubert, Alain (1986) *Making People Disappear: An Amazing Chronicle of Photographic Deception.* Washington, DC: Pergamon-Brassy's International Defense Publishers.

Jensen, Carl (2000) *Stories that Changed America: Muckrakers of the 20th Century.* New York, Toronto, London and Sydney: Seven Stories Press.

Jocks, Conway (1996) 'Talk of the town: talk radio', in Alia, Valerie, Brennan, Brian and Hoffmaster, Barry (eds), *Deadlines and Diversity: Journalism Ethics in a Changing World.* Halifax, NS: Fernwood, 173–85.

Jones, N. (1995) *Soundbites and Spin Doctors: How Politicians Manipulate the Media andVice Versa.* London: Cassell.

Kasoma, Francis P. (ed.) (1994) *Journalism Ethics in Africa.* Nairobi, Kenya: African Council for Communication Education.

Keeble, Richard (2001) *Ethics for Journalists.* London: Routledge.

Keeshig-Tobias, Lenore (1990) 'White lies?', *Saturday Night*, October, 67–8.

Keneally, Thomas (1977) *A Victim of the Aurora.* London and Sydney: Collins.

Kieran, Matthew (ed.) (1998) *Media Ethics.* London: Routledge.

Killick, Adam (1996) 'Surfing the Net in Whitehorse', *The Globe and Mail,* 18 January, A20.

King, David (1997) *The Commisar Vanishes: The Falsification of Photographs and Art in Stalin's Russia.* New York: Metropolitan/Henry Holt.

Kirby, Terry (2003) 'Judges hit out at tabloid stings', *The Independent,* 14 June, 1.

Knightley, Phillip (1975) *The First Casualty: The War Correspondent as Hero, Propagandist and Myth Maker from the Crimea to Vietnam.* London: André Deutsch.

Kramarae, Cheris (ed.) (1988) *Technology and Women's Voices.* New York: Routledge & Kegan Paul.

Krugman, Paul (2003a) 'The great trans-Atlantic media divide', *International Herald Tribune,* 19 February, 7.

Krugman, Paul (2003b) 'Denial and deception', *International Herald Tribune,* 25 June, 9.

Kuptana, Rosemarie, in Brisebois, Debbie (1983), 'The Inuit Broadcasting Corporation', *Anthropologica*, vol. 25, no. 1, 107.

Kurosawa, Akira (1950) *Rashomon* (film), Japan.

LaDuke, Winona (1998) 'Power is in the Earth', in South End Press Collective (eds), *Talking About a Revolution.* Boston: South End Press, 67–80.

Lambeth, Edmund (1986) *Committed Journalism: An Ethic for the Profession.* Bloomington, IN: Indiana University Press.

Lasn, Kalle (1999) *Culture Jam: How to Reverse America's Suicidal Consumer Binge – and Why We Must.* New York: HarperCollins.

Latour, Bruno and Woolgar, Steve (1986) *Laboratory Life: The Construction of Scientific Facts.* Princeton, NJ: Princeton University Press.

Law, William (1990) *There is No Death Here.* Edmonton, Alta: CBC Radio (IDEAS), June.

Law, William (1996) 'More than a game: the business and ethics of sports journalism', in Alia, Valerie, Brennan, Brian and Hoffmaster, Barry (eds),

Deadlines and Diversity: Journalism Ethics in a Changing World. Halifax, NS: Fernwood, 186–206.

Lee, M. A. and Solomon, Norman (1991) *Unreliable Sources: A Guide to Detecting Bias in News Media*. New York: Lyle Stuart.

Leslie, Larry Z. (2000) *Mass Communication Ethics: Decision Making in Postmodern Culture*. Boston: Houghton Mifflin.

Lester, Paul (1996) *Images that Injure: Pictorial Stereotypes in the Media*. Westport, CT: Praeger.

Lester, Paul (1991) *Photojournalism: An Ethical Approach*. Hillsdale, NJ: Lawrence Erlbaum.

Levy, H. P. (1967) *The Press Council*. London: Macmillan.

McBride, Gordon (1994) 'Spelling mistake embarrassing', *Nunatsiaq News*, 16 December, 7.

Macdonald, Myra (1995) *Representing Women: Myths of Femininity in the Media*. London: Hodder Arnold.

MacDougall, Curtis (1964) *The Press and Its Problems*. New York: Macmillan.

McEwan, Ian (1998) *Amsterdam*. London: Random House.

MacLeod, Catherine (2003) 'Dinosaurs in the gallery', *The Guardian*, G2, 26 May, 8.

McLeish, Kenneth (ed.) (1993) *Key Ideas in Human Thought*. New York: Facts on File.

McLuhan, Marshall (1964) *Understanding Media*. London: Routledge & Kegan Paul.

McNair, Brian (1998) *The Sociology of Journalism*. London: Arnold.

McPhee, John (1968) *A Roomful of Hovings*. New York: Farrar, Straus & Giroux.

Malcolm, Janet (1990) *The Journalist and the Murderer*. New York: Random House Vintage.

Malcolm, Janet (1999) *The Crime of Sheila McGough*. New York: A. Knopf.

Maltin, Leonard (ed.) (2003) *Leonard Maltin's Movie and Video Guide, 2003 Edition*. New York: Signet.

Marris, Paul and Thornham, Sue (eds) (1997) *Media Studies: A Reader*. Edinburgh: Edinburgh University Press.

Martinez, Nadia and Engler, Mark (2002) 'Enron: A toxic export', *Red Pepper*, August, 28–9.

Mayer, Paul A. (2002) *Computer Media and Communication: A Reader*. Oxford University Press.

Meade, Marion (1988) *Dorothy Parker: What Fresh Hell is This?* New York: Modern Library

Merrill, John C. (1991) *Global Journalism*, 2nd edn. New York and London: Longman.

Mignault, Pierre (1996) 'Pictures, packages and public trust: the seamless byline and instant TV', in Alia, Valerie, Brennan, Brian and Hoffmaster, Barry (eds), *Deadlines and Diversity: Journalism Ethics in a Changing World*. Halifax, NS: Fernwood, 132–9.

Milgram, Stanley (1975) *Obedience to Authority*. New York: Harper Paperback.

Miller, Casey and Swift, Kate (1988) *The Handbook of Nonsexist Writing,* 2nd edn. New York: Harper & Row.

Miller, David (1994) *Don't Mention the War: Northern Ireland, Propaganda and the Media.* London: Pluto.

Miller, David (2003) 'Embedding propaganda', *Free Press,* Special issue: Iraq and the Media War, June, 3–4.

Mills, Merope (2003) 'Jackson exacts revenge on Bashir in two-hour TV rebuttal', *The Guardian,* 22 February, 7.

Moore, Michael (2001) *Stupid White Men.* New York: HarperCollins.

Mowlana, Hamid (1989) 'Communication, ethics, and the Islamic tradition', in Cooper, Thomas W. with Christians, Clifford G., Plude, Frances Forde and White, Robert A. (eds), *Communication Ethics and Global Change.* London: Longman, 137–46.

Mullett, Sheila (1988) 'Shifting perspective: a new approach to ethics' in Code, Lorraine, Mullett, Sheila and Overall, Christine (eds), *Feminist Perspectives: Philosophical Essays on Method and Morals.* Toronto and London: University of Toronto Press, 109–26.

Nelson, Odile (2003) 'Let the music flow: Kangiqsualujuaq students learn via satellite', *Nunatsiaq News,* 6 June, 20–1.

Nicholson, Michael (1993) *Welcome to Sarajevo (Natasha's Story).* London: Macmillan.

Over, David (2000) Personal communication.

Patterson, Philip and Wilkins, Lee (2002) *Media Ethics: Issues and Cases,* 4th edn. Boston: McGraw Hill.

Pearsall, Judy and Trumble, Bill (eds) (1996) *The Oxford English Reference Dictionary,* 2nd edn. Oxford: Oxford Univesity Press, 739.

Pickard, Nancy (2002) *The Truth Hurts.* New York and London: Pocket Books.

Pilger, John (1996) *Heroes.* London: Jonathan Cape.

Pilger, John (1998) *Hidden Agendas.* London: Vintage.

Pilger, John (2002) *The New Rulers of the World.* London: Verso.

Reitz, Jeffrey G. (1980) *The Survival of Ethnic Groups.* Toronto: McGraw-Hill Ryerson.

Reuters (2004) '36 journalists killed in line of duty in 2003', *International Herald Tribune,* 3–4 January.

Rhode, Eric (1976) *A History of the Cinema.* New York: Da Capo.

Richie, Donald (ed.) (1972) *Focus on Rashomon.* Englewood Cliffs, NJ: Prentice-Hall.

Ritchin, Fred (1999) *In Our Own Image: The Coming Revolution in Photography: How Computer Technology is Changing our View of the World (Writers and Artists on Photography).* New York: Aperture.

Ritter, R. M. (ed., compiler) (2000) *The Oxford Dictionary for Writers and Editors,* 2nd edn. Oxford: Oxford University Press, 172.

Rivers, Caryl (1996) *Slick Spins and Fractured Facts: How Cultural Myths Distort the News.* New York: Columbia University Press.

Robbins, Tim (2003) *Tim Robbins at the National Press Club April 15, 2003,* text of speech distributed on the Internet.

Robins, Natalie (1992) *Alien Ink: The FBI's War on Freedom of Expression.* New Brunswick, NJ: Rutgers University Press.

Robertson, G. (1993) *Freedom, the Individual and the Law.* London: Penguin.

Rogerson, Simon and Fairweather, Ben (2003) 'Information society – the reality', *Journal of Information, Communication and Ethics in Society*, vol. 1, supplement, 3–4.

Rohmann, Chris (2000) *The Dictionary of Important Ideas and Thinkers.* London; Random House/Arrow.

Roth, Lorna (1995) '(De)romancing the North', *Border/Lines*, 36, 36–43.

Roth, Lorna (1996) 'Cultural and racial diversity in Canadian broadcast Journalism', in Alia, Valerie, Brennan, Brian and Hoffmaster, Barry (eds), *Deadlines and Diversity: Journalism Ethics in a Changing World.* Halifax, NS: Fernwood, 72–91.

Roth, Lorna and Valaskakis, Gail Guthrie (1989) 'Aboriginal broadcasting in Canada: a case study in democratization', in Raboy, Marc and Bruck, Peter A. (eds), *Communication: For and Against Democracy.* Montreal: Black Rose.

Roy, Arundhati (1999) *The Cost of Living.* London: Flamingo.

Russell, Nicholas (1996) 'Lies, Damned Lies and Journalism', in Alia, Valerie, Brennan, Brian and Hoffmaster, Barry (eds), *Deadlines and Diversity: Journalism Ethics in a Changing World.* Halifax, NS: Fernwood, 30–9.

Said, Edward (1994) *Culture and Imperialism.* London: Vintage.

Salutin, Rick (1993) 'Profiles have two sides – good and bad', *The Globe and Mail*, 2 April.

Salutin, Rick (1994) 'Suing and reviewing: a critical issue', *The Globe and Mail*, 28 July.

Sampson, Anthony (1973) *The Sovereign State: The Secret History of ITT.* London: Hodder Fawcett.

Sampson, Anthony ([1975] (1991) *The Seven Sisters: The Great Oil Companies and the World they Made.* New York: Bantam.

Sampson, Anthony (1999) *Mandela: The Authorised Biography.* London: HarperCollins.

Sampson, Anthony (2000) 'Whatever happened to the first draft?' *British Journalism Review*, vol. 11, no. 2, 52–62.

Schaner, Michelle and Hussain, Nadia (2003) 'Newspaper bans racist mascots', *Cultural Survival Quarterly*, vol. 27, no. 1, Spring, 11.

Schrank (2003) 'Weapons of Mass Deception' (cartoon), Editorial & Opinion, *The Independent*, 10 February, 14.

Schratz, M. and Walker, R. (1995) *Research as Social Change: New Opportunities for Qualitative Research.* London: Routledge.

Scollon, R. (1998) *Mediated Discourse as Social Interaction: A Study of News Discourse.* Harlow: Addison Wesley Longman.

Scott, Jay (1984) *Midnight Matinees.* Toronto: Oxford University Press.

Scott, Jay (1994) *Great Scott! The Best of Jay Scott's Movie Reviews.* Toronto: McClelland & Stewart.

Seaton, James and Pimlott, B. (1987) *The Media in British Politics*. Aldershot: Dartmouth Publishing.

Shah, Idries (2000) *The Englishman's Handbook*. London: Octagon Press.

Shah, Saira (2001) 'Inside Afghanistan: behind the veil', *BBC*, 27 June.

Shaw, Colin (1999) *Deciding What We Watch: Taste, Decency and Media Ethics in the UK and the US*. Oxford: Clarendon.

Shawcross, William (1992) *Rupert Murdoch: Ringmaster of the Information Circus*. London: Chatto & Windus.

Short, J. F., Jr (ed.) (1971) *The Social Fabric of the Metropolis: Contributions of the Chicago School of Urban Sociology*. Chicago: University of Chicago Press.

Sinclair, Upton (1920) *The Brass Check*. Pasadena, CA: Published by the author.

Ó Siochrú, Seán and Girard, Bruce with Mahan, Amy (2002) *Global Media Governance*. New York/Oxford: Rowman & Littlefield.

Sjöden, Gudrun (2003) *Spring 2003: The Four Elements, Part One*. Stockholm: Gudrun Sjöden.

Snyder, L. L. and Morris, R. B. (1962) *A Treasury of Great Reporting*. New York: Simon & Schuster.

Society of Professional Journalists (1992) Code of Ethics. Available at: http://nww.spj.org/ethics_code.asp.

Solomon, Arthur (1991) *Songs for the People: Teachings on the Natural Way*, ed. Michael Posluns. Toronto: New Canada Publications.

Solomon, Norman (1999) *The Habits of Highly Deceptive Media: Decoding Spin and Lies in Mainstream News*. Monroe, ME: Common Courage Press.

Somerville, Frances (1991) 'A reader's thoughts', *Saturday Night*, May, 9.

Sontag, Susan (1977) *On Photography*. London: Anchor Doubleday.

Sorel, N. C. (1999) *The Women Who Wrote the War*. New York: Arcade Publishing.

Spender, Dale (1995) *Nattering on the Net: Women, Power and Cyberspace*. Toronto: Garamond.

Spradley, James R. (1980) *Participant Observation*. New York: Holt, Rinehart & Winston.

Steffens, Lincoln (1904) *The Shame of the Cities*. New York: Sacamore; (1957) McClure, Phillips, Doubleday.

Steffens, Lincoln ([1909]/1968) *Upbuilders*. Seattle, WA and London: University of Washington Press.

Steffens, Lincoln (1931) *The Autobiography of Lincoln Steffens*. New York: Harcourt, Brace.

Steffens, Pete (2001) *Early History of the British Press*. Lecture, University of Sunderland, School of Arts, Design and Media, History of the Press module, October.

Stone, I. F. (1970) *Polemics and Prophecies 1967–1970: A Nonconformist History of Our Times*. London: Little, Brown.

Suzuki (2002) *Room for the Tribe* (advertisement published in UK magazines). Japan: Suzuki.

Talbot, Mary M. (1998) *Language and Gender: An Introduction*. Cambridge: Polity Press.

Taylor, Kate (1993a) 'Show breaks sex taboo, "Eli Langer, paintings and pencil drawings at the Mercer Union"', *The Globe and Mail*, 20 December, C5.

Taylor, Kate (1993b) 'Don't shoot the messenger ... or arrest the artist', *The Globe and Mail*, 24 December, C5.

Taylor, R. N. (1990) *In Defence of the Realm? The Case for Accountable Security Services*. London: Civil Liberties Trust.

Television Northern Canada (1993) Press kit. Yellowknife. TVNC.

The Guardian (2003) 'TV wars in Neverland: Michael Jackson fights back' (leader), 22 February, 21.

The Guardian Education Higher (2003) 'Higher browsing: Universe, Government own goal', *The Guardian Education, Higher*, 11 February, 11.

The Guardian, G2 (2003) 'A few stories you won't be reading about the tennis stars* at Wimbledon ...', 18 June, 1–3.

The Independent (2003) 'Asylum. The facts' (front page spread), 23 May, 1.

The Sun (2003) '1 in 4 asylum seekers ends up in Britain', 22 April, 1.

The Telegraph Magazine (1991) 'Dressed to kill: hunting with the Eskimos of Holman Island' [complete reference unavailable].

Thomas, Lorraine (1992) 'Communicating across the Arctic', *Canadian Association of Journalists Bulletin*, 14, Spring, 20.

Thompson, Francis (1992) 'British newspaper article deserve "harsh rebuttal" – Holman Mayor', News/North, 2 November, A3, A30.

Thornham, Sue (1997) *Passionate Detachments*. London: Arnold.

Toynbee, Polly (2003) 'What the papers won't say: crime is actually falling', *The Guardian*, 16 July, 20.

Tuchman, Gaye (1978) *Making News*. New York: The Free Press.

Tumber, Harold (1999) *News: A Reader*. Oxford: Oxford University Press.

Tunstall, Jeremy (1996) *Newspaper Power: The New National Press in Britain*. Oxford: Clarendon.

Tunstall, Jeremy and Machin, D. (1999) *The Anglo-American Media Connection*. Oxford: Oxford University Press.

Tunstall, J. and Palmer, M. (1991) *Media Moguls*. London: Routledge.

Valaskakis, Gail Guthrie (1995) 'Sacajawea and her sisters: images and indians', Burgess, M. and Valaskakis, G., *Indian Princesses and Cowgirls: Stereotypes from the Frontier*. Montreal: OBORO, 11–39.

Valaskakis, Gail Guthrie (1988) 'The Chippewa and the Other: living the heritage of Lac du Flambeau', *Cultural Studies*, vol. 2, no. 3, October.

Van Zoonen, Lisbet (1994) *Feminist Media Studies*. London: Sage.

Verkaik, Robert (2003) 'Employers who snoop on e-mails risk penalty', *The Independent*, 11 June, 9.

Viets, Elaine (1998) *Rubout*. New York: Bantam Doubleday.

Viets, Elaine (2000) *Doc in the Box*. New York: Random House.

Waite, Maurice (ed.) (1996) *The Oxford Colour Spelling Dictionary*. Oxford: Clarendon Press, 277.

Walker, J. A. and Chaplin, S. (1997) *Visual Culture: An Introduction*. Manchester: Manchester University Press.

Weinberg, Arthur and Weinberg, Lila (1961) *The Muckrakers.* New York: Capricorn.

Weller, Tom (1987) *Culture Made Stupid.* Boston: Houghton Mifflin.

Welsh, T. and Greenwood, W. (1998) *McNae's Essential Law for Journalists.* London: Butterworths.

Wheeler, Thomas H. (2002) *Phototruth or Photofiction? Ethics and Media Imagery in the Digital Age.* London: Lawrence Erlbaum Associates.

Williams, G. (1994) *Media Ownership and Democracy.* London: Campaign for Press and Broadcasting Freedom.

Winship, Janice (1987) *Inside Women's Magazines.* London: Pandora.

Woolmar, Christian (1993) *Censorship.* East Sussex: Wayland Publishing.

Yamada Language Center (2003) Available online at: http://babel.uoregon.edu/yamada/guides/Inuit.html. Eugene, OR: University of Oregon.

Young, Hugo (2003) 'What are we for?', *The Guardian,* 27 June, 6–7.

Younge, Gary (2003) 'The capped crusader', *The Guardian Weekend* magazine, 4 October, 16–21.

Index